# Justification Is for Preaching

# Justification Is for Preaching

*Essays by Oswald Bayer, Gerhard O. Forde, and Others*

EDITED BY

VIRGIL THOMPSON

PICKWICK *Publications* · Eugene, Oregon

JUSTIFICATION IS FOR PREACHING
Essays by Oswald Bayer, Gerhard O. Forde, and Others

Pickwick Publications
An Imprint of Wipf and Stock Publishers
199 W. 8th Ave., Suite 3
Eugene, OR 97401

www.wipfandstock.com

ISBN 13: 978-1-61097-409-7


*Cataloging-in-Publication data:*

    Justification is for preaching : essays by Oswald Bayer, Gerhard O. Forde, and others / edited by Virgil Thompson.

    xx + 262 p. ; 23 cm.—Includes bibliographical references.

    ISBN: 978-1-61097-409-7

    1. Preaching. 2. Lutheran Church—United States. 3. Lutheran Church—Doctrines. 4. Justification (Christian Theology). I. Thompson, Virgil. II. Bayer, Oswald. III. Forde, Gerhard O. IV. Title.

BX8065.3 J10 2012

Manufactured in the USA.

*To*

*Oliver K. Olson*
*founding editor, Lutheran Quarterly, new series,*
*editor from 1987 to 1996*
*President of the Board of Directors since 1984*

# Contents

## Part Two: PREACHING

# Foreword

*Oswald Bayer*

Lutheran Quarterly
Jubilee 2012

G ERHARD O. FORDE'S "RADICAL Lutheranism" (1987) is and remains the journal's charter. Undoubtedly, one of the main marks of this radical Lutheranism is reflected in the expression "Justification is for Preaching." That is the title of this jubilee volume and also Forde's thesis. It presents a decisive moment of Lutheran identity that has been a special highlight of *Lutheran Quarterly* over the past twenty-five years, and the articles that have been selected for this anniversary edition are no exception. They exhibit in a multifaceted way something that must not be concealed but taught publicly—within the walls of the church as well as outside, such as in a publication like *Lutheran Quarterly*. In its own way and for its part, this journal wants to carry out the enormously broad commission that our Lord gave his church (Mark 16:15) and to be accountable to everyone for what the church preaches, namely, justification by grace alone, by Christ alone, by faith alone, by the word alone. In what follows, I would like to emphasize the points that I consider especially important in view of the title and the thematic content of this volume.

Lutheran identity is bound up with an understanding of the righteousness of God, which can never be isolated from the manner in which it is preached. "God's righteousness" cannot be abstracted from the mode and medium of its self-communication in the reliable word that promises and gives salvation, the *promissio* that creates certainty, as distinct from the law. This promise does not refer primarily to the future but to the present; it is a legally valid promise with an immediate effect.

Salvation is not a basic anthropological structure that could only be expressed in the proclamation of the church and that could only be represented by it. The preaching of the church is no secondary information about previously given facts, nor is it an expression of an underlying religious vitality. It is promise and gift, pledge and presentation, encouragement and communication, bestowal and distribution. Luther makes an immensely helpful distinction between two related moments of salvation: The salvation "acquired" on the cross *sub Pontio Pilato* once and for all, and that "distributed" in the word of the cross from the beginning to the end of the world. Neither of these two moments is without the other. The christological and trinitarian competence is manifest in the sacramental performance of the preached word; without that competence, together with its historical moorings *sub Pontio Pilato*, this would become myth (*mythos*). The once-for-all death of Jesus Christ makes his eternally valid testament—the *new* testament—legally valid; by virtue of his resurrection, he opens it and distributes the inheritance himself. Thus Good Friday and Easter form a differentiated unity of death and life, God and man: "A testator is the same as a promiser who is going to die, while a promiser . . . is a testator who is going to live" (*testator idem est quod moriturus promissor, promissor autem victurus . . . testator* (WA 6:513.37—514.1 = LW 36:38 (alt.); cf. WA 2:521.35–7 = LW 27:268; on Gal 3:18). The one who is really present in baptism, absolution, and the Lord's Supper is not represented as absent but presents himself as present.

If justification needs to be preached, its forensic character must be taken seriously. That can only happen if the forensic aspect is not isolated or limited to a special world but is identified as a fundamental and all-embracing structure of reality, such as we have, for example, in Psalms 96 and 98. Therefore, the fundamental anthropological significance of "justification," as well as its ontological importance, must be highlighted. This means that the preaching of justification must always show an awareness of its link with the theology of creation. That finally is the only way to overcome the unfortunate polarization between the "forensic" and "effective" aspects of justification. For God's bodily promise and verdict of acquittal by means of an earthly human mouth *does* exactly what it says. Conversely, it is also true that he *says* and imputes exactly what he does in effecting the new creation through the forgiveness of sins. God's communication of his mercy and our participation in it, and thus in God's essence itself, does not happen anonymously or in a vague impersonal way. Christ rather is present in the special faith in the particular word of promise. The real union of the sinful human with the God who justifies is, according to Luther, "not to be thought of in terms of the category of substance but only in terms of the category of relation" (*WA* 40/II:354.3f.; on Ps 51:4; cf. *LW* 12:329; on Ps 51:2). Being and essence consist in right relations—just as, on the other hand, sin consists in the reversal of our original relation to God and to all our fellow creatures, where humans are now curved in on themselves in an empty and unproductive life of total self-reflection and self-referentiality.

The self-communication of Jesus Christ, and with him of the triune God, comes to me from outside in the promise and gift; faith is *fides adventitia* (Gal 3:23 and 25), adventitious faith., Christ encounters me in the external, bodily word and yet, even as a word that is given to me and received in faith, it remains the word of another and in this sense remains "alien"; *my* righteousness will always remain *his* righteousness: *iustitia aliena*.

Nevertheless, he who comes to me in the word of promise, the promise of salvation—*pro vobis*—comes to his own (John 1:11) and dwells in us (John 14:23). For the God who comes to me together with all creatures in the word is the same God who has always already come to me and to all creatures in the word, and is with us and in us, in fact is closer to us than we are to ourselves. Thus the "*pro nobis*" is never without the "*in nobis*," never without God's inhabitation in his creatures.

Just how critical the motto "Justification is for Preaching!" is can be seen from the theology and practice of the Lord's Supper. Is it, as a whole, a "Eucharist"? Are the words of institution to be subordinated to the prayer of thanksgiving by the congregation, so that the downwards character of these gift-giving words becomes unclear? Or do we follow Luther's theology, with its sharp distinction between "*sacramentum*" and "*sacrificium*" (De captivitate; *WA* 6:526.13–17 = *LW* 36:56), and see the high point and climax of the Lord's Supper in the double gift-giving word of the narrative of institution ("This is . . ."), perceived as the *promissio* to the assembled congregation? Here the word, in, with, and under the eating of the bread and the drinking of the wine, grants a share in the body and blood of Christ and thus a share in the new covenant, God's eternal kingdom. Here Christ's body and blood are taken and received with thanks, in the sacrifice of praise, so that the Eucharist answers to the gift and in that way—as an answer to the word—is indeed a principal moment of the Lord's Supper even though it does not constitute it as a whole?

The controversy over these alternatives is therefore of enormous importance because what is at stake here is the criteriological significance of the doctrine of justification. Is justification preached in a celebration of the Lord's Supper that is basically understood, upwards, as the church's act of thanksgiving? Again, if the high point of the Lord's Supper is the gracious action of God that precedes the human sacrifice of praise, is justification still preached if God's gift-giving word, taken up in the prayer, is thus no longer addressed to the congregation and so no longer really confronts it as the external word that first creates faith?

Constitutive for the preaching of justification is the distinction between law and gospel. It is not that the gospel can only be understood in the light of the experience of sinner with the law—hence *ex negativo*. The gospel has, positively, a surplus of that experience; otherwise it would be no more powerful than the law. Nevertheless, if the gospel is not understood as undeserved liberation from the accusing and condemning power of the law, if it is not understood as unconditional acquittal in spite of evident guilt, it loses its incredibly miraculous nature, and ends up being eviscerated and reduced to a self-evident truth that basically appeals to the free will of the listener to do good. The gospel, and therefore God's love, is trivialized whenever his judgment is silenced. The church's preaching is seriously flawed if it speaks of peace with God without making clear that this peace is preceded by enmity and strife (Rom 5:10). God's love is not something self-evident. For in his compassionate love, God speaks against himself: against the God who speaks completely *against* me in the law and in his judgment. In the gospel, however, God speaks completely *for* me. The gospel is based on a revolution in God himself, where God's own will is overturned in himself (Hos 11:8); the New Testament expresses this with the difference between Father and Son, between God's life and Jesus's death. Only if we perceive the radical distinction between law and gospel will we grasp the saving significance of the death of Jesus Christ; he redeemed us on the stake of the cross "from the curse of the law by becoming a curse for us" (Gal 3:13; see 2 Cor 5:21). With his Son, God himself pleads our cause, he sacrifices himself for us. Our freedom, "acquired" for us on the cross, is "distributed" in the proclamation—paradigmatically in the Lord's Supper: given for you. The basic gesture involved in preaching the gospel are the opened hands that give and bestow the gift of freedom on those who hear through the Holy Spirit in faith, so that they themselves are empowered to open up their own hands, otherwise tightly clenched in self-reference to thank God and give to the neighbor.

It is my hope that *Lutheran Quarterly* continues in the way it has been going, struggling for the sacramental word and the word-bound sacrament and that in this way it also serves in the future to promote the preaching of justification, the preaching of the *libertas Christiana*. For the charisma of Lutheranism—the gift entrusted to it historically—is clarity of doctrine with its focus on the God who justifies the sinner. As with every charisma, so this one too is not meant for grandstanding but for service. When this is grasped, the Lutheran Confession can never be an end in itself but must be seen as a service to the ecumene.

*Translated by Jeffrey Silcock*

# Acknowledgments

T HE ESSAYS THAT COMPRISE this volume, as indicated below, were first published by *Lutheran Quarterly*, either in the journal or in *Lutheran Quarterly* Books in partnership with Eerdmans Publishing Company. They are presented here according to our theme, justification is for preaching, and in observance of the twenty-fifth anniversary of *Lutheran Quarterly*, new series, which we celebrate in 2012. On the Internet find us at lutheranquarterly.com.

We gratefully acknowledge permission to reprint materials previously published as indicated below.

"Radical Lutheranism" by Gerhard O. Forde has served as the charter of the *Lutheran Quarterly* mission. It first appeared in *Lutheran Quarterly* 1/1 (1987) 5–18. In 2004 it reappeared in the *Lutheran Quarterly* Book, *A More Radical Gospel*, 3–17, jointly published with Eerdmans Publishing Company.

"Justification as the Basis and Boundary of Theology" by Oswald Bayer first appeared in German under the title, "Rechtfertigung: Grund und Grenze der Theologie" in *Leibliches Wort: Reformation und Neuzeit im Konflikt* (Tübingen: Mohr/Siebeck] 1992) 9–34. It was translated into English by Christine Helmer. In English it has previously appeared in *By Faith Alone: Essays on Justification in Honor of Gerhard O. Forde* (Grand Rapids: Eerdmans, 2004) 67–85, edited by Joseph A. Burgess and Marc Kolden. It also appeared in *Lutheran Quarterly* 15/3 (2001) 273–92.

"The History, Shape, and Significance of Justification for Preaching" by Mark Mattes appears in print for the first time in this volume.

"Forensic Justification and the Christian Life" by Gerhard Forde previously appeared in the *Lutheran Quarterly* Book, *A More Radical Gospel* (Grand Rapids: Eerdmans, 2004) 114–36.

"Living Out of Justification" by Wilfried Härle appeared in *Lutheran Quarterly* 18/4 (2004) 455–66. The essay was translated by Amy Marga and Mark Mattes from the conclusion of "Zur Gegenwartsbedeutung der 'Rechtfertigungs'–Lehre. Eine Problemskizze," in *Zeitschrift für Theologie und Kirche* 93/10 (1998) 131–39.

"Justification and Reality" by Klaus Schwarzwäller previously appeared in *Lutheran Quarterly* 24/3 (2010) 292–309.

"Categorical Preaching" by Steven Paulson appeared in *Lutheran Quarterly* 21/3 (2007) 268–93.

"Preaching the Sacraments" by Gerhard Forde has previously appeared in the *Lutheran Quarterly* Book, *The Preached God* (Grand Rapids: Eerdmans, 2007) 89–115. Prior to its publication there it had appeared in *Luther Seminary Bulletin* 64/4 (1984) 3–27.

"Absolution: Systematic Considerations" by Gerhard Forde previously appeared in the *Lutheran Quarterly* Book, *The Preached God* (2007) 152–64.

"The Word of the Cross" by Oswald Bayer first appeared in *Lutheran Quarterly* 9/1 (1995) 47–55. The essay was translated by John R. Betz from chapter 9, "Das Wort vom Kreuz," in *Autorität und Kritik: Zu Hermeneutik und Wissenschaftstheorie* (Tübingen: Mohr/Siebeck, 1991) 117–24.

"Preaching the Word" by Oswald Bayer appeared in *Lutheran Quarterly* 23/3 (2009) 249–69. The essay was translated by Jeffery Silcock from the original German, "Das Wort predigen. Eine kurze Grundlegung der Homiletik" in *Zugesagte Gegenwart* (Tübingen: Mohr/Siebeck, 2007) 386–403.

"Lutheran Assertions Regarding Scripture" by Steven Paulson first appeared in *Lutheran Quarterly* 17/4 (2003) 373–85.

"Preaching Repentance" by James Arne Nestingen appeared in *Lutheran Quarterly* 3/3 (1989) 249–65.

"Preaching the Justification of Zacchaeus" by Virgil Thompson appeared in *Lutheran Quarterly* 23/4 (2009) 465–79.

Special thanks also to Paul Rorem and Mark Mattes for their editorial support and wise counsel in the preparation of this volume and to Amy Whisenand who assisted editorially with the preparation of the notes, bibliography, and the list of abbreviated works.

# Contributors

**Oswald Bayer** is Professor Emeritus of Systematic Theology at the University of Tübingen, Germany. In this volume, he is the author of "Justification as the Basis and Boundary of Theology," "The Word of the Cross," and "Preaching the Word." *<bayer@unitybox.de>*

**Gerhard O. Forde** (d. August 9, 2005) was Professor of Systematic Theology, Luther Theological Seminary, St. Paul, Minnesota. Professor Forde was a founding director of *Lutheran Quarterly*, new series. In this volume he is the author of "Radical Lutheranism," "Forensic Justification and the Christian Life," "Preaching the Sacraments," and "Absolution: Systematic Considerations."

**Wilfried Härle** is Professor of Systematic Theology at the University of Heidelberg, Germany. In this volume he is the author of "Living Out of Justification." *<wilfried.haerle@wts.uni-heidelberg.de>*

**Mark Mattes** is Professor of Religion and Philosophy, Grand View University, Des Moines, Iowa. He also serves as an Associate Editor of *Lutheran Quarterly*. In this volume he is the author of "The History, Shape, and Significance of Justification for Preaching." *<mmattes@grandview.edu>*

**James Arne Nestingen** is Professor Emeritus, Luther Theological Seminary, St. Paul, Minnesota. In this volume he is the author of "Preaching Repentance." *<jnesting@luthersem.edu>*

**Steven Paulson** is Professor of Systematic Theology, Luther Theological Seminary, St. Paul, Minnesota. He also serves as an Associate Editor of *Lutheran Quarterly*. In this volume he is the author of "Categorical Preaching" and "Lutheran Assertions Regarding Scripture." *<spaulson@luthersem.edu>*

**Klaus Schwarzwäller** is Professor Emeritus of Systematic Theology, University of Göttingen, Germany. In this volume he is the author of "Justification and Reality." *<hweissenfeldt@gmx.de>*

**Virgil Thompson** is Senior Lecturer in New Testament at Gonzaga University, Spokane, Washington. He also serves as Managing Editor for *Lutheran Quarterly*. He is the editor of this volume and the author of "Preaching the Justification of Zacchaeus." *<thompsonv@gonzaga.edu>*

# Abbreviations

| | |
|---|---|
| *BC* | Robert Kolb and Timothy J. Wengert, editors. *The Book of Concord: The Confessions of the Evangelical Lutheran Church*. Minneapolis: Fortress, 2000. |
| *BC/T* | Theodore G. Tappert, editor. *The Book of Concord: The Confessions of the Evangelical Lutheran Church*. Philadelphia, Fortress, 1959. |
| *BSLK* | *Die Bekenntnisschriften der evangelisch–lutherischen Kirche*. 11th ed. Göttingen: Vandenhoeck & Ruprecht, 1992. |
| *CR* | C. G. Bretschneider and H. E. Bindseil, editors. *Corpus Reformatorum*. 101 vols. Halle: Schwetschke, 1834–60. |
| *EG* | *Evangelisches Gesangbuch* of the Evangelische Kirche Württemberg. Stuttgart: Gesangbuchverlag, 1999. |
| *LBW* | *Lutheran Book of Worship*. Minneapolis: Augsburg, 1978. |
| *LW* | Jaroslav Pelikan and Helmut Lehman, editors. *Luther's Works*. 55 vols. St. Louis: Concordia; Philadelphia: Fortress, 1955. |
| *WA* | J. F. K. Knaake et al., editors. *Luthers Werke, Kritische Gesamtausgabe*. 57 vols. Weimar: Böhlau, 1883ff. |
| *WA DB* | Knaake, J. F. K. et al., editors. *Luthers Werke, Kritische Gesamtausgabe* (*Die Deutsche Bibel*). Weimar: Böhlau, 1883ff. |
| *WA TR* | Knaake, J. F. K. et al., editors. *Luthers Werke, Kritische Gesamtausgabe* (*Tischreden*). Weimar: Böhlau, 1883ff. |
| WUNT | Wissenschaftliche Untersuchungen zum Neuen Testament |

# Editor's Introduction

*Virgil Thompson*

THE PROPER SUBJECT OF theology, Martin Luther contended, is the human being condemned of sin and God the justifier and savior of the sinner.[1] This volume features the work of contemporary theologians who share Luther's theological orientation, principally Oswald Bayer and Gerhard O. Forde, along with contributions by other theologians from the United States and Germany. From the pages of *Lutheran Quarterly* over the past twenty-five years, these essays set forth in historical and theological perspective the doctrine of justification for contemporary preaching. Thus, for example, they challenge the modern gospel of the autonomous self, stuck in the *cul de sac* of postmodernity. Humanity, that is, appears inescapably bound to the worship of the autonomous self while, at the same time, seeking to escape the particularity and finitude of the parochial self. These essays expose the deadly bondage of the modern self[2] and direct preachers to the Word that alone raises up a new humanity, free of its self-imposed bondage.

This theme is developed against programmatic theologies that locate the promise of salvation in one aspect or another of the human condition, as though the experience of economic or political or sexual oppression provides the hermeneutical key to human justification. Whatever critical value such hermeneutics may provide, from the vantage point of justification, they fail, finally, to get to the heart of the human *incurvatus in se*. The deeper question is this: *why* do we humans exploit and oppress others, along with all the rest of creation, in service of the self? The answer runs

---

1. *LW* 12:311.
2. For a discussion of the modern self see Taylor, *Sources of the Self.*

1

through the volume as its unifying theme. When we lose our faith in the justifying Word of God then we are bound to justify ourselves over against our neighbors and over against God. Thus, yet another round of strife is provoked, human against human against God. Our differences—sexual, political, and economic—become the occasion and the means by which we seek to determine who will justifiably lord it over whom. Into the conflicted human story of the "justification wars," Jesus introduces a new dynamic; he alone brings forth the "peaceable kingdom," the kingdom of everlasting innocence, blessedness, and righteousness. In this kingdom humanity is given to live, on the one hand, as a "perfectly dutiful servant of all, subject to all."[3] "For the Son of Man came not to be served but to serve, and to give his life a ransom for many" (Mark 10:44–45). And on the other hand, to live "perfectly free lord of all, subject to none,"[4] for "all things are yours . . . all belong to you, and you belong to Christ, and Christ belongs to God" (1 Cor 3:21b–23). Salvation from the compulsive anxiety to be recognized, respected, honored, and justified comes not from elevating some aspect or another of human experience as the redeeming dynamic. Salvation is from God who comes down in Jesus of Nazareth to restore us to loving service one of the other.

God is determined to keep this saving promise, "I am the Lord your God, you shall have no others." The promise of God in Christ grants freedom from the bondage of our divine ambition to be as gods, so that we may live here and now as a human creature of God, destined to live as "helpmate" of the neighbor and caretaker of creation. As Leander Keck has pointed out in a study of Paul's theology, what is at stake in the doctrine of God's justification of the ungodly is whether humanity will have the true God or an ideological no-god: "God is never more authentically and characteristically God than when he 'rectifies the ungodly.'"[5] What is at stake in the doctrine of justification then is "the independence of God from all human domestication, the radical otherness of God from all human effort to make god in our image, and the freedom of God to rectify precisely the relation to a wrongly imaged God. A God who cannot do this is really an ideological no-god, a tribal deity of class, race, sex, or power block."[6]

3. *LW* 31:344.

4. Ibid.

5. Keck, *Paul and His Letters*, 122.

6. Ibid., 123.

Making known this promise of God for the sake of faith constitutes *the* ministry of the church. The doctrine by which the church's ministry of God's promise rises or falls is the doctrine of justification by faith. In fact it is not only the church that rises and falls with the proclamation of the promise but also the fortunes of all creation. As Luther explains in the Small Catechism, the whole creation has its life out of God's "pure, fatherly, and divine goodness and mercy, without any merit or worthiness of ours at all!"[7] Luther's inclusion of justification in the article on creation acknowledges the cosmic scope of the doctrine. Justification articulates the truth of God's creative and saving activity with respect to all that has been, is, and will be. The truth is that the creation itself owes its existence to God's fatherly graciousness. God is not in the business of rewarding humanity for good behavior. Rather, humanity's life in the entirety of its particularity—from birth, all along every breath of its present existence—is unmerited and freely given. Where the promise of God's gracious justification is heard in faith the human is set free from sin. That is, the believer is set free from the compulsion to use this life as a means to the end of justifying the self in order to earn heaven or a respectable self-image or a clear conscience or the advantage over the other or the right to establish one parochial vision or another as the kingdom to come. The sermon that grants God's justifying action liberates the sinner to live in service of our God-given vocation (Genesis 2). This is the promise which itself shapes both theological method and theologians, so that theology and theologians may in turn serve the proclamation of the promise, God's justification of the ungodly. This is the story of the Christian faith as confessed in the catechetical symbols of the faith—the Ten Commandments, Creed, and Lord's Prayer—and as enacted toward the sinner in the Word and sacrament ministry of the church. It is in this sense that Oswald Bayer, especially, characterizes theology as "catechetical systematics."

This is the story at the heart of all Christian theology and for which that theology labors in service of the gospel's proclamation. From Genesis to Revelation the biblical story tells of the human desire "to be as gods," a tempting aspiration which humans find irresistible. The aspiration, however, has not worked out so well. Instead of being gods, autonomous and in control of our destiny, we now find ourselves, as to God and to one another, trapped in suspicion, denial, and fear: "I heard the sound of you in the garden, and I was afraid, because I was naked; and I hid myself"

---

7. BC 354.

(Gen 3:10). That verse tells the human story, beginning, middle, and end, leaving nothing else to tell but the consequences. Human life would be finished before it began, except that human sin is not the end of the story. God is unwilling to give up on his creation. "See, I am making all things new . . . these words are trustworthy and true . . . I will be their God and they will be my children" (Rev 21:5, 7b). The ministry of the church at its heart means enacting this decision of God toward sinners.

The theme of the volume, justification is for preaching, provides the ordering schema for the collection of essays. The first section sets forth the doctrine of justification in clear and compelling terms. The second section lays out how justification shapes and informs the public sermon of the church.

## JUSTIFICATION

The lead essay of the volume, "Radical Lutheranism" by Gerhard O. Forde, was first published in the inaugural issue of *Lutheran Quarterly*, new series, and has served as the journal's charter. In the midst of the merger negotiations, which led to the formation of the Evangelical Lutheran Church in America (1987), the essay addresses the question of Lutheran identity. For Forde and for the journal, Lutheran identity is not so much a decision to be made—What shall we be? Rather, having heard the "for you" promise of Jesus, Lutheran identity is determined, informed, and shaped by the gospel of God's justification of the ungodly. As Forde puts it, "Let us be radicals, . . . radical preachers and practitioners of the gospel of justification by faith without the deeds of the law. We should pursue it to the radical depths already plumbed by St. Paul, especially in Romans and Galatians."[8]

As the essays in this volume show, *Lutheran Quarterly*, in this new series, has been dedicated for a quarter century to the history and theology of this evangelical tradition. Our purpose has been not merely to remember its history, as though it were a bygone tradition, but also to recall what it means to give voice to the explosive promise of Christ for sinners. Especially in the context of modernity and postmodernity, we have sought to publish that which is consequential for the continuing proclamation of the radical gospel of God's final judgment toward hu-

---

8. See p. 19 in this volume.

manity and the creation, executed in the death and resurrection of Jesus Christ.

We know that these labors to set forth the gospel of God's justification by faith apart from works of the law appear to some to be a vain labor. There are those within and without the Christian community who claim that understanding the gospel in terms of justification by faith is reductionist, dangerous, quietistic, and/or irrelevant. Others argue that even if the formulation of the gospel as God's justification of the ungodly may have been appropriate during the era of the Reformation, nonetheless, today it is "much ado about nothing" in an empty theater. Contemporary humanity, so the argument goes, no longer troubles itself about the judgment of God in particular or its own justification in general.

In the second essay, Oswald Bayer addresses this criticism in its starkest terms. At the outset, Bayer recalls Swedenborg's sarcastic criticism that the Lutheran preoccupation with justification is like a person "locked up in a darkened room his entire life. Pacing back and forth in the room, unable to see anything, he searches for light by repeating only one sentence to himself: 'I am justified by faith alone; I am justified by faith alone; I am justified by faith alone!'"[9] Against the criticism that Lutheran preoccupation with justification is egotistically centered on personal salvation, Bayer draws on Luther's Catechisms and hymns to show that the Reformer understood justification in its social and cosmic breadth as well as in existential depth. The justifying Word of God recreates not only the human relationship to God, but at the same time the individual's relationship with all creatures. The gospel grants to the believer a "new perception of space and time" in relationship to God and to the world.[10] For Bayer the new justified existence may today be appreciated in strongest relief by contrasting it with the "modern will to create and constitute oneself" through our work (Marx) or through our actions (Fichte). The prospects of generating life from within the self have not materialized exactly as promised. Confidence in the human capacity to self-generate its life has vacillated between presumption and despair. As Jean-Paul Sartre put it, human beings are what they make of themselves, no more, no less. They are what they do in the freedom to which they are condemned. When human freedom is received under the obligation to make something of

9. Ibid., 31.
10. Ibid., 32.

oneself at long last, it makes of life an unbearable, Sisyphean burden. Even the most pedestrian judgments of our temporal works and actions tend to be heard as "the final judgment," against which we are forever seeking to defend and justify ourselves. What is more, the neighbor and all creation become a means to the end of finally making something of oneself. The promise of *God's* justification, however, liberates the believer from receiving life as a project in self-justification to live in service and enjoyment of creation. In the certainty of God's unconditional care and promise of justification the believer receives, graciously and mercifully, a certain distance from the self. This distance frees one from pronouncing final judgment on the self and on others. It frees the believer from what others say; what they say is not the final judgment, but is always provisional. I am not forced to balance my books once and for all. I am free to let everything be provisional and to live with what is incomplete. Far from creating a ghetto-like existence in a darkened room, *incurvatus in se*, the gospel of justification turns the believer outward by trust in God and his saving judgment and by love for the neighbor and care for the well being of creation.[11]

Mark Mattes then traces the formation and history of the doctrine of justification. He argues that while the doctrine emerges from Scripture it was developed polemically against late medieval views of salvation. What stands out when viewing Luther's formulation of justification against the Nominalist formulation is "decisively *forensic*, a decree of acquittal, as opposed to something God does in order to initiate a process on the ladder of ontological, moral, and mystical fulfillment. Likewise, faith is not to be understood as a 'theological virtue,' but as a state of being grasped by God's unconditional claim and promise. Grace is not the power behind the scenes initiating our process in mimetic growth in holiness but the very pronouncement of forgiveness itself. Therefore, it is faith, not love, that saves."[12] The sticking point between Luther and his Nominalist contemporaries remains the sticking point in the theological context of the early twenty-first century. In Luther's formulation of the doctrine, the evidence of one's justification before God lies in the spoken external word of God's promise as it is received in faith. Formulations of the doctrine which seek verification of justification in the believer's works of love or

---

11. Ibid., 31–50.
12. Ibid., 56.

moral improvement result once again in curving human existence in upon self-justification.

Mattes's essay concludes by considering past and current misperceptions of justification among Luther's theological heirs, particularly as these misconceptions impact preaching. An examination of nineteenth-century theologians—Albrecht Ritschl, Theodosius Harnack, and Karl Holl—shows the tendency to "revamp Luther's view of justification in terms of Kantian approaches to ethics, accentuating human autonomy, the separation of metaphysics from ethics, and the quest for a 'kingdom of ends,' in which agents honor the autonomy of their peers."[13] More recently the Finnish scholar Tuomo Mannermaa, along with theologians under his influence, has sought to present Luther's view of justification in terms of the believer's deification through the indwelling of Christ. Against the understanding of Mannermaa, theologians like Timo Laato and Mattes himself argue that for Luther, "salvation is based not on the indwelling Christ who deifies, but forensically on Christ who died for us."[14] The implication for preaching justification is clear. "Just as God's word originally spoke and speaks creation into being so God's word of promise granted in Jesus Christ bespeaks a new creation out of nothingness of sin and death. We have an alien righteousness and live as new beings out of the life of another: Jesus Christ, crucified and risen."[15] The task of preaching accordingly is to speak the good news in such a way that forgiveness, life and salvation of Christ are granted in the speaking.

In the next essay, "Forensic Justification and the Christian Life," Gerhard Forde answers recent "Lutheran" attacks on forensic justification. In so doing, he draws out the implication of Luther's understanding of justification for the whole of the Christian life. By and large the anxiety that the Lutheran tradition has suffered with respect to forensic justification has resulted from the failure to observe the radical reorientation to the Christian life that the doctrine implied for Luther. Historically, the problem of justification stems from being misconceived as a movement from sin to righteousness. The problem, simply put: "If justification comes at the beginning of the 'movement' . . . it is a logical fiction. If, however, it comes at the end of the movement, it is superfluous. If one

13. Ibid., 64.
14. Ibid., 65.
15. Ibid., 66.

has already made the 'movement,' one is just and need not be pronounced so."[16] Luther's understanding of justification represents a complete break with the medieval understanding. For Luther, God's justification of sinners does not entail the movement of a continuously existing self from sin to righteousness. Rather, justification is understood in terms of death and resurrection. The Word of God's justification puts to death old self-justifying sinners and brings forth by faith believers who trust the justifying Word. As Forde puts it,

> The imputation of righteousness by God for the sake of Christ as a totality unmasks its opposite, namely, all the schemes and pretensions of human righteousness, sin as a totality, and in that very fact attacks it. Sin as a total state can only be fought by faith in the total imputed righteousness. Anything other than that would lead only to hypocrisy or despair . . . The "conscience" is ruled and captivated by the gospel, the imputed righteousness breaking in from God's eschatological judgment. The "flesh," the empirical life I live in this age, remains however, *in lege* [under the law]. And that in a double sense. Both in the sense that the law attacks "the flesh" as inimical to the will of God, and also in the sense that under the impulse of the spontaneity and joy fostered by the gospel in the conscience, the empirical life I live in this age is to become the actual "incarnation," the fulfillment of the will of God.[17]

In his contribution to the volume, "Living Out of Justification," Wilfried Härle further develops the understanding of the Christian life as it arises out of the preached promise of God's justifying Word. According to Härle, the Word of God's justifying judgment reorients the believer in three ways: to the self, to the neighbor, and to God. "'Justification' has to do less with righteousness as a quality, and more with right relationships, less with being righteous and more with bring right with God and neighbor."[18] As Luther's treatment of the Apostles' Creed in the Small Catechism emphasizes, the central themes of God's creative, redemptive and sanctifying activity—creation out of nothing, the gracious justification of sinners, and the resurrection of the dead—constitute the proclamation of the good news. Where the good news of the freely giving and saving God awakens faith, the believer arises as a new being in relation

16. Ibid., 73.

17. Ibid., 75.

18. Ibid., 92.

to self, neighbor, society, and God. Confident in the gracious activity of God, believers are free from using life as a project in self-justification. They are free to enjoy and care for the creation. As Härle concludes, the preaching of God's justification of the ungodly leads to a sober perception of oneself and others, and at the same time creates and sustains faith, love, and hope. Believers are destined to live together with the Lord of faith in the everlasting kingdom of God's righteousness, blessedness, and innocence.

The final essay in part one makes the transition to the heart of the volume: justification is for preaching. In "Justification and Reality," Klaus Schwarzwäller comes quickly to the heart of the matter with a thesis from Luther's *Disputation on Man*: "We hold that the human is justified by faith apart from works." The article briefly sums up the definition of the human, saying, "the human is justified by faith." In other words, as Schwarzwäller goes on to explain,

> What is asserted here is that God, and only God, defines us: who we are, who we will be, what is due to us, and what our life weighs. It is God's definition of us that counts, . . . Thus, neither we our- selves nor anyone else is allowed or has the power to define our lives and their value. Human definitions are only temporary at best, if at all, for we belong not to ourselves but to God.
>
> Since God is always in action, his definition is never static but dynamic throughout. It marks our place within the time granted to us and, thus, within the framework of God's acting, preserving, changing, and shaping our reality.[19]

In this light the obvious and critical question focuses on the occasion and the means by which God shapes the existence of his creatures into true humanity. The answer is that God acts through the merciful dynamic of his twofold Word—Law and Gospel—to execute sinners, "pretentious but unhappy gods," and to raise up the new humanity in the image of the true human, Jesus Christ. This then informs the purpose of Christian witness and preaching. The purpose of the sermon is not to talk *about* justifica- tion but rather actually to speak the justifying word of God to the hearer. The aim is to turn the hearer away from self-justifying schemes, to live by faith in the justifying word of God and by love for the neighbor.

19. Ibid., 104.

## PREACHING

The inference to be drawn from the understanding of justification as it has been articulated by the essays in the first section of the volume is precisely what Paul says in his letter to the Romans: "Faith comes from what is heard, and what is heard comes through the word of Christ . . . How are they to hear without someone to proclaim him? And how are they to proclaim him unless they are sent? As it is written, 'How beautiful are the feet of those who bring good news'" (Rom 10:17; 14–15). Thus, the second group of essays is devoted to explicating what it means to preach the justifying Word of God. They make the argument explicit: the primary purpose of Christian preaching is to speak the justifying Word of God so that believers may arise to new life by faith in the promise of God. In that sense, proclamation of God's justification of the ungodly is the beginning and the end of theology. Preachers seek to do again to and for others what has been done to themselves by the Word of God. Theology is what goes on between the hearing and the doing again.

In the first essay of the section, "Categorical Preaching," Steven Paulson steams straight down the scandalous path of the Pauline argument: "When Paul said, 'Faith comes by hearing' (Romans 10), he answered the question of how one gets a gracious God."[20] That answer however has been the source of endless scandal. The scandal may be summed up in one single objection, "If preaching [alone!] gives faith, it does so far too selectively to be trusted," as the old Adam is compelled to reason. Nonetheless—folly to Greeks, scandal to Jews—Paulson follows the Pauline argument out to the logical conclusion. Yes! "Preaching is by nature historical, specific, here and now, personal, direct, and either occurs in time and space or does not occur at all."[21] But just there—in the scandalous reality of God's way of coming down to speak his saving Word—lies the good news. "By its nature, preaching denies pure subjectivity. It is a real, objective phenomenon, like a car accident that happens without one's intention, desire or will. It is also external like a criminal sentence from a court judge, and even more life changing to my subjectivity because of its objectivity."[22] Preaching justification involves not merely talking *about* justification of the ungodly as though it were something

20. Ibid., 123.
21. Ibid., 124.
22. Ibid., 125.

that happens somewhere else at some other time. Rather, preaching is actually speaking the promise of the justifying Word of God so that it may work to create faith in the hearer where and when it pleases God.

As Gerhard Forde argues in his two contributions to this section ("Preaching the Sacraments" and "Absolution"), preaching functions like the sacraments. In the sacraments God acts through the ministrations of the preacher to claim the baptismal candidate as God's own, destined to live and die and live again in the freedom of God's decision for us and not against us. Likewise in the Lord's Supper God in Christ gives himself through the means of the bread and the wine in the promise of forgiveness for our refusal to allow God to be God for us. As Forde puts it, "In the sacraments . . . we do not just *explain* Christ or the gospel, or *describe* faith, or give instructions about how to get salvation, or whatever (though we may well do all of that), we just give it, do it, flat out, unconditionally."[23] It was precisely for this reason that Luther was initially inclined to regard the act of absolution as the third sacrament. In the act of absolution the preacher announces, over and again, the final verdict of God toward sinners who confess their "unbelief along with other great and shameful sins." In the absolution the preacher does not merely talk about the eventual prospect of forgiveness. Rather the preacher unconditionally declares it by the authority of Christ: "On the basis of your confession and in obedience to our Lord's command I declare to you the entire forgiveness of all your sin." In like manner the Christian sermon aims to deliver the redeeming Word of the Cross. That is, the sermon aims, mercifully, to crucify sinners who are curved in upon the compulsive determination to be their own god. In the same breath the preacher gives voice to the Word that alone brings forth the new creation. The new creation in Christ has no choice but to live by trust in the life-giving Word of God's promised forgiveness. The new creation either lives by faith in the promise of Christ or it has not yet come forth. The aim of the sermon is thus twofold: to pull down the curtain on the old life in which humans live as "pretentious but unhappy gods" and to raise the curtain on new life in which humans are happy to care for the good earthly creation of God. In that sense the Word of the sermon is the Word of the cross; the Word of the cross is the Word of the sermon.

23. Ibid., 147.

This connection between the cross and sermon is the subject of Oswald Bayer's contributions to this section of the volume. To the sinful self, anxious to preserve its existence at all costs, the "Word of the Cross is no more convincing than it is self-evident."[24] The problem, however, lies not in the Word, as though it were unintelligible in its self-expression. In fact, the Word of the cross is its own power to convince. The problem of unintelligibility, as the case of Nicodemus in John 3 illustrates, lies in the hearer. Jesus's assertion that "no one can see the kingdom of God without being born from above" (v. 3), utterly confounds the old sinner, Nicodemus. He can only stand there in the face of Jesus, stuttering, "How can such things be? Can one enter a second time into the mother's womb and be born?" (vv. 9, 4b). Old beings, like Nicodemus bound to life as a project in self-justification, have no ears for it. A "word can only convince when the speaker and the hearer have a common relation to truth. But if the one spoken to turns away and departs from the truth . . . then truth can be imparted only in a rebirth through the death of the "old man" (John 3; cf. 1:13)—through baptism (Rom 6) and a "journey through the hell of self-knowledge."[25] How then is one to go about preaching sermons that aim to crucify and raise up new beings? While such preaching cannot be reduced to a formula, the final essays of the volume explore some specifics.

The power of the sermon to convict, shock, make new, lies singularly in the authority of God to accuse and forgive. God, however, does not speak except through means. Just as God works through means to create and sustain the earthly life of his creatures, so in the same way, in speaking the Word of his redemption to sinners God speaks through the means of flesh and blood preachers. Of course, if the efficacy of the sermon depended upon the dignity and purity of the preacher, then sinners would remain in their sin and those dead to God would remain in their tombs. The efficacy of God's Word in the sermon does not depend upon human authenticity and credibility. In fact, as Oswald Bayer points out, there is no way around the scandalous reality that the one who "administers" the sermon of God's promise does so as sinner, "living in contradiction to God . . . 'false witness, betrayer, and liar.'"[26] In other words, preachers preach the saving word of God in solidarity with the sinners to whom

24. Ibid., 186.
25. Ibid., 188.
26. Ibid., 207.

*[handwritten margin notes: confront / challenge — comfort } sinner / saint]*

they preach—forgiven sinners preaching God's forgiveness to sinners in need of forgiveness.

The key to preaching in this way lies, as Luther never tired of repeating, in the right distinction between law and gospel. Steven Paulson, in his essay, "Lutheran Assertions Regarding Scripture," develops the point with respect to the way preachers regard the Bible, the source book of Christian preaching. Like a blast of fresh air into the present-day smoggy preoccupation with method, Paulson argues that "law and gospel is . . . not a *method* of preaching or interpretation, but the way that God authors you as unmistakable sinner in yourself; then outside yourself, in Christ, God authors you as pure saint. [Thus t]he preacher must learn the proper application of the pronoun: 'you are the one' (as Nathan said to David) and "given for you for the forgiveness of sins" (as Jesus said to his betrayers).[27]

Developing the art of speaking the Word of God in its two forms of address, law and gospel, is the subject of James Nestingen's essay, "Preaching Repentance." As Nathan might have attested, preaching law and gospel is fraught with dangers, both theological and pastoral, to say nothing of the preacher's survival. Appealing to the Lutheran confessional tradition for insight, Nestingen argues that in preaching law and gospel there is a certain overlap. Both words aim to liberate sinners from the project of self-justification for the life of faith in Christ as the promise of God "for you." The effect of preaching law and gospel is to say, "Only sinners are forgiven. If you are forgiven you must be the one," as Nathan announced to David. Apart from the gospel the accusing voice of the law merely drives sinners into the swamp of despondency. It is the overlap of the gospel, the spoken promise of God's affection for the ungodly, that apprehends and turns sinners back to the promise of God for you, as the Word of Jesus for Zacchaeus brought to an end the old life and granted new life. The story of Zacchaeus from Luke 19 provides then in the final essay of the volume a case study for how justification provides the hermeneutical key to proclaiming the biblical story in such a way as to enact toward sinners the justifying promise of God "for you." As "The Hound of Heaven," the poem of Francis Thompson (1859–1907) has it,

> Now of that long pursuit
> Comes on at hand the bruit;
> That Voice is round me like a bursting sea

27. Ibid., 226.

. . .
Lo, all things fly thee, for thou fliest Me!
All which I took from thee I did but take,
Not for thy harms
But just that thou might'st seek it in My arms.
Halts by me that footfall:
Is my gloom, after all,
Shade of His hand, outstretched caressingly?
"Ah fondest, blindest, weakest,
I am He Whom thou seekest!"

## BIBLIOGRAPHY

Keck, Leander E. *Paul and His Letters*. Proclamation Commentaries. Philadelphia: Fortress, 1979.

Kolb, Robert, and Timothy J. Wengert, editors. *The Book of Concord: The Confessions of the Evangelical Lutheran Church*. Minneapolis: Fortress, 2000.

Pelikan, Jaroslav, and Helmut Lehman, editors. *Luther's Works*. 55 vols. St. Louis: Concordia, 1955.

Taylor, Charles. *Sources of the Self: The Making of the Modern Identity*. Cambridge: Harvard University Press, 1989.

# 1

# Radical Lutheranism

## Gerhard O. Forde

FOR SOME TIME NOW, Lutherans both here and abroad have been suffering from what contemporary jargon calls an identity crisis. Lutherans do not seem to know anymore what they ought to be or to do. On the international scene this is demonstrated by persistent studies sponsored by The Lutheran World Federation/Lutheran World Ministries going back some twenty years or so. John Reumann chronicles and sums up this study under the rubric, "The Identity of the Church and its Service to the Whole Human Being." The big question precipitating the crisis is indicated by the title. It becomes most evident, no doubt, in connection with the mission of the church, particularly in the "third world." Is the church to be concerned now with proclamation or development? Individual salvation or social justice? Peace with God or peace among humans?[1] Lutherans seem to have a difficult time deciding which way to go.

The crisis in identity is in many ways intensified on the national scene.[2] For the most part Lutherans in America are just lately emerg-

1. Reumann, "Introduction," 1–31. The entire book is an interesting testimony to the agonies of Lutheran identity today.

2. The prevalence of that word in the debates and documents of the newly forming Evangelical Lutheran Church in America is noteworthy. "Crisis" and "identity" appear quite often in current Lutheran self-scrutiny, both at home and abroad. Robert H. Fischer, professor at the Lutheran School of Theology at Chicago, observes that "for many reasons North American Lutheranism is confronted by an identity crisis. In its larger dimensions this is a crisis in understanding, both our churchly mission in the world and our

ing from geographic, ethnic, and synodical isolation onto the broader American scene with ambitions towards "inclusivity." We used to be predominantly Germans, Swedes, Danes, Norwegians, Finns, and a smattering of other northern European and Nordic folk, and it was probably more our geographic isolation and ethnicity that kept us together and determined our identity than our Lutheranism. Now that we are apparently about to launch out more into the mainstreams of American Christianity, the identity question is posed with heightened urgency. Who or what in this opulent religious cafeteria shall we be? Shall we be conservative, liberal, confessional, orthodox, charismatic, neo-Pentecostal, fundamentalist, or "evangelical" (perhaps "fundagelical," as someone recently put it)? Shall we be sectarian or ecumenical; protestant or catholic; high, low, or in the middle? Lutherans are pulled in all these directions today. They seem to be looking for someone to sell out to.

*Is* "Lutheran" anything to be in America today? Chances are Americans don't even know how to spell it. It usually comes out "Lutheran" or something like that. In the "homeland" established Lutheranism was predominantly a folk religion, a quasi-political and ethnic reality, closely identified with national and social life. Take all that away and what is left? What is Lutheranism at rock bottom? Some of my colleagues like to say—and I have echoed the thought myself—that Lutheranism is a confessional movement within the church catholic, or that its primary reason for being is that it has a dogmatic proposal to make to the church catholic,[3] or, as Tillich used to say, it advocates the "Protestant Principle" vis-à-vis a catholic substance.[4] But what then is the core, the substance of Lutheranism? Can a "movement" or a "proposal" or a "principle" give identity to the long haul, not to say serve the human soul for daily bread? Other Christian denominations are recognizable at least by distinctive forms of polity or perhaps even what is today called types of spirituality. Lutherans dabble pragmatically in whatever forms and types seem to work best in a given context, but canonize none of them.

Who then are we? The new church proposes to call itself "The Evangelical Lutheran Church in America." But what would that mean? "Evangelical," "Lutheran," "in America"? The debates and suggestions

---

Lutheran identity within the Christian ecumenical scene" (Reumann, *Church Emerging*, 6). See also Marty, "Scenarios," 6–10.

3. Gritsch and Jenson, *Lutheranism*, 2ff.

4. See the essays in Tillich, *The Protestant Era*, especially 161.

floated in the Commission for a New Lutheran Church are themselves indicative of the identity crisis. Several people thought we should at last drop the adjective "Lutheran" and call ourselves "Evangelical Catholics." Others thought we should probably drop both "Lutheran" and "Catholic" and just call ourselves "The Evangelical Community in Christ" or some other generic title. Some thought we should drop the adjective "Evangelical," since it is misleading today and already redundant when put together with "Lutheran." How can a Lutheran not be evangelical? But in the end we decided we are still Lutherans after all and Evangelical to boot! But what that means still seems to be a matter for debate. Is retention of the name anything more than romantic nostalgia? Even the protracted and hesitant debate over a headquarters' site indicates something of our uncertainty about who we think we are, or hope to become. We feared being identified with parochial interests and looked for a "world-class city." But what business do we have to do there? The arguments seemed to assume that it would be good for us to be *affected by* such an environment; the question of whether we have anything to *effect* there was largely unanswered.

The most persistent and serious identity crisis is manifest at the grass-roots level. These Lutherans seem somewhat at a loss as to what to make of the American religious scene. For the most part they do have a sense of the importance of the *evangel* and seem more ready to support the outreach mission of the church than anything else. Perhaps basically conservative, they are often puzzled and confused by clergy and leadership that seem to be leading elsewhere—just where is not very clear. The incessant drive for "inclusivity" can give the impression that they have been abandoned, perhaps, for a more desirable clientele. Emerging from their ethnic past, they can be impressed by and drawn to those who can dress a cause or a human longing in appealingly religious trappings. They remember there was something vital they were supposed to be for, and thus they are tempted by those whose piety seems impressive and/or offers more solace. They are attracted by "American" religion: "fundagelicals," charismatics, the Hal Lindseys, Falwells, Robert Schullers, and so on, sometimes even by high-liturgical Anglo-Catholicism. Is "Lutheran" any recognizable thing to be any more? Garrison Keillor says he can always get a laugh when he mentions Lutherans. Why? Is it something to be apologetic about?

In an article on Lutheran identity written some ten years ago, Martin Marty saw Lutheranism standing between two forces, "both of them attractive and capable of overwhelming Lutheranism, permitting it to remain as a shell or husk or form, but not as a confessional witness or a promise."[5] Reformed neo-evangelicalism is one force, Marty wrote, and the most likely winner, because America is "genetically programmed to tilt toward" it, and Lutheran conservatives and even some moderates are attracted by it. The other force, in Marty's view, is a "more natural kin," but less likely to prevail: it is "a kind of evangelical Catholicity."[6] Today it seems obvious that both of these forces are powerfully at work dividing the Lutheran house.[7] Marty's analysis still leaves us with the question, however: is one or the other overwhelming Lutheranism?

Without wishing unduly to complicate matters, I want to mention at least one more force today. One might call it decadent pietism. Lutherans who came to this country were for the most part pietists of one stamp or another. Under the pressure of American Arminianism, Personalism, psychologism, individualism, human potential movements, and what not, pietism simply becomes decadent. The old pietism thought it vital first of all "to get right with God" through the experience of grace in conversion. But now, since God is, in general, love and no longer wrathful with anyone, God more or less drops out of the picture as a serious factor with which to be contended. In decadent pietism, since God is "affirming" in general, the task is to "get right with oneself." The old pietism contended that conversion was to be manifest in a morally upright life of service. Decadent pietism seems to hold that the way of the Christian is to become "affirming" of others in their chosen life styles. Along with this there is very often a rather sanctimonious "third use of the law" piety centered mostly around current social causes and problems. No longer concerned with one's own sins, and certainly not the sins of those one is supposed to affirm, one shifts attention to the sins of those other entities (more or less anonymous) which inhibit the realization of our affirmed and affirming human potential. Generally, these are summed up under

5. Marty, "Scenarios," 8–9.

6. Ibid., 9.

7. Marty remarks: "I think that the typical conservative Lutheran congregation today has not the faintest idea of how to sort out Francis Schaeffer or Anita Bryant, Billy Graham or Johnny Cash, Robert Schuller or Hal Lindsay from their own tradition. And some Lutheran moderates fall under the same sway" (ibid., 9). No doubt Marty is right. But one should also add that the typical "Evangelical Catholic" congregation or theologian today likewise has not the faintest idea of how to sort out the work of a Gregory Dix, Odo Casel, J. A. T. Robinson, Schillebeeckx, or an Aidan Kavanagh, from their tradition.

the rubric of "the establishment" or perhaps personified by those who happen to be in power.

Is it fair to call this a pietism? We need not quibble about the nomenclature. In any case one has only to visit contemporary churches and note the religious fervor and piety with which the view is promoted (especially among contemporary clergy, I fear) to get a sense of its power as a contending force in the battle for identity. Among Lutherans, the gospel is equated mostly with this general drive toward being permissive, affirmed, and affirming. Ministers must become therapists, church gatherings must be therapeutic and supportive if they are to meet people's needs, and ministry must be "prophetic" and have a social payoff if it is to be at all relevant.

## THEOLOGICAL IDENTITY: RADICAL LUTHERANISM

One could continue discussing the problem of identity endlessly, since there are so many dimensions and aspects to interpret and haggle about. My purpose here, however, is not to belabor the problem but rather to propose a way towards a solution, to suggest a course for the future which is helpful, promising, and faithful to the tradition. My thesis is that Lutherans, to be true to their identity, yes, even to reclaim their identity, or rather be reclaimed by it, should become even more radical proponents of the tradition that gave them birth and has brought them thus far. The crisis in identity indicates the necessity for staking out some turf on the ecclesiastical map. What shall we be? Let us be radicals: not conservatives or liberals, fundagelicals or charismatics (or whatever other brand of something-less-than gospel entices), but radicals: radical preachers and practitioners of the gospel by justification by faith without the deeds of the law. We should pursue it to the radical depths already plumbed by St. Paul, especially in Romans and Galatians, when he saw that justification by faith without the deeds of the law really involves and announces the death of the old being and the calling forth of the new in hope. We stand at a crossroads. Either we must become more radical about the gospel, or we would be better off to forget it altogether.

We should realize first of all that what is at stake on the current scene is certainly not Lutheranism as such. Lutheranism has no particular claim or right to existence. Rather, what is at stake is the radical gospel, radical grace, the eschatological nature of the gospel of Jesus Christ crucified and risen as put in its most uncompromising and unconditional form by St. Paul. What is at stake is a mode of doing theology and a practice in church and society derived from that radical statement of the gospel. We need to take stock of the fact that while such radical Paulinism is in itself open to both church and world (because it announces a Christ who is the end of the law, the end of all earthly particularities and hegemonies), it is, no doubt for that very reason, always homeless in this age, always suspect, always under attack, always pressured to compromise and sell its birthright for a mess of worldly pottage.

Lutheranism, we have said in the past, is not so much a denomination as a confessional movement with perhaps a proposal of dogma to make to the church catholic, a critical principle to apply over against a catholic substance. I wonder more and more of late whether such at once overmodest and pretentious estimates of self-identity will serve the radical nature of the gospel as Paul, for instance, saw it. Would Paul have been satisfied with such a description of his own mission? What is the catholic substance, after all? What if it turns out to be a fantastic universal synthesis between this age and the next which quietly ignores or disarms New Testament eschatology and absorbs it in its universal ecclesiology? What if all critical principles and proposals of dogma are benignly ordered somewhere in the hierarchy of truths and filed away in a Denzinger? Can there really be such a thing as a *catholic* church? Should not someone be asking whether it is not likely that the radical eschatology proclaimed especially by Paul will have to be pursued to the end of the age? Is what Lutherans have stood for a passing fancy?

I don't know that I am prepared to give full answers to all such questions yet, but I do want to pursue the proposition that Lutheranism *especially* in America might find its identity not by compromising with American religion but by becoming more radical about the gospel it has received. That is to say, Lutherans should become radicals, preachers of a gospel so radical that it puts the old to death and calls forth the new, and practitioners of the life that entails "for the time being."

We must realize there is not just external reason for our identity crisis but deep theological and, for want of a better word, existential reason. It lies simply in Lutheranism's fateful attachment to the Pauline gospel in a world whose entire reason for being is opposed to it. All who adopt such a stance will find themselves constantly on the defensive not only before the world but especially before the religious enterprises, not to say the churches, of the world. Witness already Paul's own anguished and repeated defenses of his own apostolate against "those reputed to be something."

If we are to probe to the root, the *radix,* of our identity crisis, however, we must dig beneath even the world's general disapproval. Theological anthropology, the understanding of human existence itself before God, is perhaps the place where the crisis becomes most apparent. The fact is that the radical Pauline gospel of justification by faith without the deeds of the law calls for a fundamentally different anthropology and with it a different theological "system" (if there be such!) from that to which the world is *necessarily* committed. The radical gospel of justification by faith alone simply does not fit, cannot be accepted by, and will not work with an anthropology which sees the human being as a continuously existing subject possessing "free choice of will" over against God and/or other religious goals. The radical gospel is the *end* of that being and the beginning of a new being in faith and hope.✓

This is readily apparent in virtually all of Paul's writings (especially in Romans and Galatians) when he pursues the logic of justification by faith alone to its end. The law does not end sin, does not make new beings, it only makes matters worse. Where the old continuity is maintained, sin does not end. No matter how much religious pressure is applied, sin only grows. But, Paul has the audacity to say where sin abounded, grace abounded all the more. But this is disaster for the old and its thinking. For then, it seems, the floodgates of iniquity are opened! Shall we not sin the more that grace may abound? Here we arrive at the crucial point. Here the pious old Adam can only recoil in horror from the thought of unconditional grace and try to protect the continuity of the old self by making compromises: some fateful mixture of grace and law, a little bit of human cooperation, perhaps the addition of a third use of the law, some heavy breathing about sanctification, and so on.

But the radical gospel will have none of that. Shall we sin the more that grace may abound? By no means! Why? *For you have died* and how can you who have died to sin still live in it? The reason why abounding grace does not lead to sin lies in the fact that in its radicality it puts an end to the old, not in some species of compromise with the old. Furthermore, we miss the radicality of that if we do not see that this death is announced as *accomplished* fact: you *have* died. The death is not something yet to be done, one last act of spiritual suicide for "free choice." If Jesus died for all, then all have died (2 Cor 5:14). The being of the hearer is simply stamped with the *theologia crucis,* the death and resurrection of Jesus is done to us by the proclamation of the accomplished fact. There is no justification except by faith alone. The radical forgiveness itself puts the old to death and calls forth the new. It is simply not possible to work with an anthropology which assumes a continuity that survives the cross, and turns it into an object for free choice to dally with.

The continuing crisis for anyone who is grasped by that radical gospel comes both from the fact that the world and its church cannot do other than resist and attack that gospel (as a matter of self-defense), and from the fact that they cannot escape the constant temptation to make compromises which disguise or blunt the sharp edges of its radicality. Lutheranism in particular, and perhaps especially now in this country where it is losing its more "worldly" folk-trappings, finds itself in this crucible. Lutheranism was born because Martin Luther was grasped by the radical gospel. Doctrinally he prosecuted his case predominantly as an attack on the anthropology derived from and dependent on the belief in free choice of the will. An even cursory study of the genesis of his theology demonstrates this, from the very first disputations *(Against Scholastic Theology,* the *Heidelberg Disputation),* on through the radical attack on emerging humanistic anthropology in *On the Bondage of the Will,* to the final massive *Commentary on Genesis.* In basic anthropological presupposition there is no difference between scholasticism and modern humanism or, for that matter, various other brands of contemporary Christianity, be they catholic, evangelical, charismatic, or even Mormon.[8] The differences among them on this score are more or less in-house disputes about how what is left of the continuously existing free choice can be cajoled, enticed, controlled, frightened, persuaded, impressed, and so forth, into making "the right choice." But in a pluralized society, the will is unable to make such a choice and can only lapse into a skepticism which has to settle for relativism. Whatever is right for you is the right choice.

In his debate with Erasmus, Luther saw that the attempt to combine the radical Pauline gospel with even the slightest hint of free choice could only lead to thoroughgoing skepticism, a permanent "identity crisis."[9]

---

8. Cf. Luther, *Lectures on Galatians* (1535), 295–96: "Whoever falls from the doctrine of justification is ignorant of God and is an idolater. Therefore it is all the same whether he then returns to the Law or to the worship of idols; it is all the same whether he is called a monk or a Turk or a Jew or an Anabaptist."

9. Luther, *BW,* 140.

Hans-Joachim Iwand, a theologian little known in America because most of his work was published posthumously and remains untranslated, demonstrates this most clearly and consistently.[10] The positing of free choice means that the subject stands over against the gospel as an object, a theory which is to be accepted on grounds dictated by the subject. But what could such grounds be? Can the subject will its own death? Willy-nilly, the subject, claiming to be free, constructs a defense mechanism against the gospel, and permanent skepticism is the outcome. One can avoid it, perhaps, only by submitting to the authority of an institution like that of the Roman church. Freedom is given with one hand only to be taken back by the other! From this point of view the Enlightenment is simply a kind of institutionalization of skepticism over against ecclesiastical authoritarianism.

The tragedy of post-Reformation Lutheranism, along with the theological root of its identity crisis, is to be found in the persistent attempt to combine the radical gospel of justification by faith alone with an anthropology which cannot tolerate it. Thus, as Iwand maintains, Lutheranism has for the most part been a house divided against itself. "The doctrine of justification was retained, but it was combined with an anthropology which had its entire pathos in a faith in the freedom of the will." Thus, the radicality of the gospel was blunted and frittered away. The anthropology was borrowed largely from humanism. "Humanism from Melanchthon to Ritschl indeed permits justification to occur even *sola fide,* but nevertheless breaks off the spearhead by which it would itself be mortally wounded, the bondage of the will."[11] The attempt to combine two diametrically opposed theological positions can only issue in a fundamental skepticism in thought and hesitancy in practice.[12]

This is the source of what we might call the inner and outer aspects of Lutheranism's crisis. The attempt to combine two incompatible views means that internally it has always had to battle its fundamental skepticism, its uncertainty about the basis for its faith. So in its practice it has resorted mostly to a dogmatic absolutism largely dependent on a view of scriptural inerrancy, which usually brought with it disguised moral absolutisms of various sorts as well. A will which supposedly begins in a state

10. See, for example, the collection of essays titled *Um den rechten Glauben.*

11. Ibid., 17.

12. Ibid., 9.

of freedom ends in captivity. The message becomes a perverted mirror image of itself: "Yes, you are free, but you jolly well had better choose to believe in justification by faith alone or you will go to hell. The Bible says so! And then you had better show your thanks by your sanctification."

The outer side of the crisis comes from the fact that justification by faith alone without the deeds of the law can only appear dangerous, if not somewhat ridiculous, to the outside world premised on free choice of the will. Thus, Lutheranism easily becomes the target of religious disapproval, not to say ridicule. The litany of complaint is a familiar one: "How can there be serious evangelism if there is no free choice?" "Lutherans don't believe in good works." I have a Baptist friend who likes to say that the trouble with Lutherans is that they never get any better! "Lutherans preach cheap grace; Lutherans are quietists; Lutherans don't have any social ethics; Lutherans are too passive; and so on." Many Lutherans themselves seem to take masochistic delight in rehearsing this litany. No doubt it is a way of getting back at justification by faith turned into dogmatic absolutism.

The division of the house against itself is thus quite evident. Lutheran theological ranks, especially in America, seem filled by practitioners who on the one hand are spooked by the ghosts of past absolutisms, dogmatic and moral, and on the other are somewhat embarrassed by Lutheranism's fateful attachment to the gospel of justification by faith alone and, of course, frightened to death of exaggerated assertions about the bondage of the will and such unpleasantries. So where then does one end? Somewhere in the middle, no doubt, in a theological no-man's land where one will be shot at from all sides. "Yes, justification is nice, but it's not the *only* choice in the biblical cafeteria." A little criticism and relativism to counter the absolutism, a dash of "free grace" to relax the moralism (but not to be overdone), a little resorting to the Lutheran Confessions when in a tight spot (but not to be exaggerated), and a general tailoring of the message to "meet one's needs." The result is a loss of recognizable identity, a tendency to fade into the woodwork of generic religion, and an almost complete failure of nerve.

## PROCLAIMING THE RADICAL GOSPEL

What is to be done? Whither Lutheranism? The analysis leads to a crossroads. The radical gospel of justification by faith alone does not allow for a middle-of-the-road position. Either one must proclaim it as unconditionally as possible, or forget it. We must somehow muster up the nerve to preach the gospel in such fashion as to put the old to death and call forth the new. In one sense, of course, the litany of complaint against Lutheranism is all too true. Preaching the gospel of justification by faith alone *to* old beings in such fashion as to leave them old can only be a disaster. The proclamation either makes the old beings worse, or it puts an end to them to make them new. If Lutheranism is to recover a sense of its identity and mission today, it must begin to consider what it means to preach the gospel in radical fashion.

A short paper such as this is not the place to attempt laying out such a program. But in the space remaining I will venture some observations about the dimensions of the task. First of all, we do not adequately gauge the depth of the problem unless we see that is ultimately a problem for the *proclamation* (Word and sacrament) of the church. Of course, theological reflection is vital. But one does not preach justification by faith alone or the bondage of the will and such doctrines. They are presuppositions for preaching. It is the *proclamation* that makes new beings, not theology, or even ethics. If we begin with the presupposition of bondage, it is obvious that the difficulty we face, as Iwand likes to insist, is not merely a logical or even a historical mistake.[13] If it were so, it could simply be corrected theologically. The fact, as we have maintained all along, that justification was combined with the wrong anthropology could be fixed simply by getting a new and improved dogmatic anthropology. But if the will is in fact bound, we must deal with what, for want of a better term, is an existential matter. To persist in the wrong anthropology is not just an exegetical or dogmatic mistake but a *temptation* about which the old being *per se* can do nothing, precisely because it wills to do nothing. And it wills to do nothing because it has no hope and no vision of the new. There is no freedom here; everyone theologizes as they must.[14] Whatever talk there might be about a new anthropology based on death and resurrection, for instance, would only be turned into metaphor for moral improvement. The old remains bound.

What does this mean for theology? Is this a new and more vicious form of absolutism? The ramifications for theology and its task are indeed many, and we cannot tackle them here. The point, however, is not

13. Ibid., 17–18.
14. Ibid., 19.

*Where and when it pleases God —*

that a new absolutism is proposed, but that theology comes to realize precisely its limit and must give way to the sheer proclamation of grace. Theology does not make new beings. It is precisely the business of a theology which knows about bondage to see this, and thus to drive toward a proclamation in Word and sacrament which by the power of the Spirit *ubi et quando visum est deo* will do it. When theology learns its task it will be relieved of its endless theoretical skepticism and can proceed with regained confidence. Such theology is neither absolutist nor relativist, conservative nor liberal. Theology drives to proclamation. Its thinking is dedicated to making that proclamation hearable in a given context as a radical gospel which sets free from bondage and makes all things new. Whither Lutheranism? Here we might find a way into the future worthy of the tradition which gave us birth.

Second, it follows from all we have said that the proclamation, to be radical, must be uncompromising, *sola gratia, sola fide.* The most common failing, the most persistent temptation, is a failure of nerve. A pastor said to me the other day after a lecture on absolution, "I think we know we are supposed to do the unconditional absolution, but I suspect we just don't dare!" Who has not experienced the fear of perhaps having gone too far this time in preaching the gospel, and perhaps has been afraid of having wrecked the whole program of the church, so carefully built up! After all, for the time being we do stand in the old age; we see through a glass darkly. We walk, and talk, and prophesy by faith, by hope. But there is no middle ground in this matter. Certainly that was the burden of Luther's argument against Erasmus. If there is to be any point to the continued existence of Lutheranism (not to mention Protestantism in general), we must simply be ready to prosecute the case for this radicality.

Virtually all the failures and shortcomings of Lutheranism can be seen in the hesitancy to proclaim the gospel in uncompromising, unconditional fashion, to proclaim as though we were about the business of summoning the dead to life, calling new beings into existence. Most generally, it seems, the gospel is preached as though it were a repair job on old beings, a "new patch on an old garment." It is preached *to* old beings instead of *for* new beings. When that is the case, the litany of complaint turns out to be mostly true. Its understanding and proclamation of the gospel undercuts and enervates the moral projects of old beings and seems only to invite license. When the gospel is not "anti-old Adam/Eve" it just becomes antinomian. The only way one can rescue it from absolute disaster then is to make compromises with the projects of old beings. But that is the end of the gospel. Either the gospel must be preached in radical fashion, or it is best left alone altogether.[15]

A radical Lutheranism would be one which regains the courage and the nerve to preach the gospel unconditionally; simply let the bird of the Spirit fly! There is too much timidity, too much worry that the gospel is going to harm someone, too much of a tendency to buffer the message to bring it under control. It is essential to see that everything hangs in the balance here. Faith comes by hearing. Will the old persist? Will we understand ourselves to be continuously existing subjects called upon to exercise our evanescent modicum of free choice to carve out some sort of eternal destiny for ourselves? That depends. It depends on whether someone has the courage to announce to us, "You have died and your life is hid with Christ in God!" "Awake you who sleep, and arise from the dead!" It could be that we will be only continuously existing subjects doomed to our own choices. Is the law eternal? It could be and will be if Christ is not preached so as to end it for us. We tremble on the brink of freedom. Is this all, this old age, this confusing mixture of *regnum mundi* and *regnum diaboli?* It could be. That is the terror of it. And it will be for us unless someone sounds the trumpet of the *regnum dei* with an absolutely uncompromising clarity. How shall they hear without a preacher? We have a hard time realizing that everything hangs here on the unconditional announcement, the absolutely new start of God in the resurrection of Jesus. The vision, the hope, yes, even the ecstasy or the "rapture," as even Luther could say,[16] hang on the radical unconditionality of the proclamation.

*[handwritten marginalia: Kingdom of world of the devil]*

Finally, it is only out of this radical unconditionality that an appropriate understanding of the life of the Christian for the time being can arise. We simply do not understand the pathos of the Reformer's utterances about faith doing the good spontaneously and naturally unless we see this. Precisely because the declaration is unconditional we are turned around to go into the world of the neighbor to carry out our calling as Christians. The works of the Christian are to be done in the world, but not as conditions for salvation. The persistent and nagging debate about the two kingdoms among Lutherans arises mostly out of reluctance to be radical enough. Precisely because the gospel gives the kingdom of God

15. Luther maintained that semi-Pelagianism was much worse than outright Pelagianism! See Luther, BW, 292.

16. Ibid., 311.

unconditionally to faith, this world opens up and is given back as the place to serve the other. Will it be so given? That depends, of course. It is not a static affair. To the degree that one is grasped and set free by the unconditional gospel, to that degree one can be turned from the sort of life created by the self (and its supposed free but actually bound will) to the world of the neighbor. To the degree that the theological use of the law comes to an end in Christ, to that degree a political use of the law for others becomes a possibility. If somehow this could be grasped, perhaps we could cease the silly debates about whether the church's mission is proclamation *or* development, personal salvation *or* social justice, and so on, and get on with the business of taking care of this world and the neighbor as lovingly, wisely, and pragmatically as our gifts enable.

Radical Lutheranism? Is there, and can there be such? That depends, of course. It depends, for our part, at least, on whether or not we are "encouraged" enough to preach that radical and unconditional gospel. Beyond that, of course, it depends on the Spirit. But after all, in spite of our reluctance and timidity, it isn't some herculean task we are being asked to do. It has all been done. All we have to do is say it; just let the bird fly!

## BIBLIOGRAPHY

Gritsch, Eric W., and Robert W. Jenson. *Lutheranism: The Theological Movement and Its Confessional Writings*. Philadelphia: Fortress, 1976.

Iwand, Hans J. *Um den Rechten Glauben; Gesammelte Aufsatze*. Edited by Karl Gerhard Steck. Theologische Bücherei 9. Munich: Kaiser, 1959.

Luther, Martin. *On the Bondage of the Will*. Translated by J. I. Packer and O. J. Johnston. Westwood, NJ: Revell, 1957.

———. *Luther's Works*. Vol. 26, *Lectures on Galatians*, 295–96. Edited by Jaroslav Pelikan and Helmut Lehman. St. Louis: Concordia, 1955.

Marty, Martin E. "Scenarios for a Lutheran Future: A Case Study of Identity." *Lutheran Forum* 9 (May 1975) 6–10.

Reumann, John, editor. *Church Emerging: A U.S. Lutheran Case Study*. Philadelphia: Fortress, 1977.

———. "Introduction." In *Church Emerging: A U.S. Lutheran Case Study*, edited by John Reumann, 1–31. Philadelphia: Fortress, 1977.

Tillich, Paul. *The Protestant Era*. Translated, with a concluding essay by James Luther Adams. Chicago: University of Chicago Press, 1948.

# Part One

## JUSTIFICATION

# 2

# Justification as the Basis and Boundary of Theology

*Oswald Bayer*

## MONOTONY OR CONCENTRATION?

LUTHER'S DOCTRINE OF JUSTIFICATION has frequently been attacked for being monotonous, empty, and even obsessive. Swedenborg illustrates his attack in a particularly sarcastic way.[1] According to him, the Lutheran is locked up in a darkened room his entire life. Pacing back and forth in the room, unable to see anything, he searches for light by repeating only one sentence to himself: "I am justified by faith alone; I am justified by faith alone; I am justified by faith alone!"

This sarcastic illustration is directed against Luther's actual focus in his theology of the justifying God and the human being as sinner, believing in the justifying God. The focus is emphasized by Luther himself, who insists that the *only* proper subject matter of theology is "man guilty of

---

1. Peterson recalls "a vision of Swedenborg . . . the other great critic of Scandinavian Protestantism besides Kierkegaard. In a room without doors and without windows, the Lutheran preacher paces back and forth, ceaselessly repeating the words: *'sola fide.'* This vision [captures] in an extraordinary way the . . . monotony of Protestant rhetoric." Peterson does not cite any sources for this vision. Peterson, "Kierkegaard und der Protestantismus," 17–27. A possible source, although the echoes are faint, would be Swedenborg's vision of Melanchthon. See Swedenborg, *True Christian*, 2:356–59, § 797.

31

sin and condemned, and God the Justifier and Savior of man the sinner."[2]
Theology would not only be deluding itself but would fall into total error
if, departing from this focus, it would concern itself with other questions:
for example, medical, legal, or political matters.[3] Thus it appears that the
boundary of theology is quickly reached with the theme of justification.
If the justification of the sinful human being is the sole basis and subject matter of theology, then the arena of theological study appears to be
reduced to a small field. The theological situation would then be none
other than the grotesque condition described by Swedenborg, of a person
pacing back and forth in a darkened room.

But Swedenborg's sarcastic attack misses the point defined by
Luther's theology. The sarcasm, rather, lifts up onto the theological stage
an old and deep-seated prejudice often and unfortunately fed by theology
and the church. According to this prejudice justification by faith implies
a denial of all this-worldly relationships; it is without a world, complete
unworldliness. Linked to this prejudice is the suspicion that the Lutheran
understanding of the event of justification is individualistic, even egoisti-
cally centered on salvation.

Against this prejudice I would like to underscore that Martin Luther
understood the event of justification in its social and cosmic breadth just
as profoundly as he perceived it in its existential depth. To him as biblical interpreter, particularly as the Old Testament scholar he primarily
was, it was precisely the social and cosmic breadth of justification that
was disclosed to him by its existential depth. Not only our relationship to
God and ourselves is made new through justification by faith but at the
same time our relationships with "all creatures" are renewed. Even a new
perception of space and time is included in our new relationship to God
and the world.

Justification understood by Luther in its depth and breadth stands
in opposition to the sarcastic remarks above. In the remaining sections of
this essay, I propose to develop an understanding of justification summarized in the following thesis: *Justification is not a separate topic apart from
which still other topics could be discussed. Justification is the starting point
for all theology and it affects every other topic.* Not only concerned with me

---

2. Luther, *Commentary on Psalm 51*, WA 40/2:328; *LW* 12:311.

3. "Whatever is asked or discussed in theology outside this subject, is error and poison" (ibid.). Medical, legal, and political matters become a subject for *theology* only in the
context of determining the *subiectum theologiae* as cited in the text.

individually and my own life-story, it is also concerned with world history and natural history. Justification is concerned with everything.

## THE ONTOLOGICAL SIGNIFICANCE OF JUSTIFICATION

Because justification has ontological significance, it is misleading and inadequate to speak about the article of justification as the *articulus stands et cadentis ecclesiae,* the article by which the church stands and falls.[4] When Luther writes about justification in the Smalcald Articles, he makes use of a different context: the context of the doctrine of creation: "Nothing in this article can be conceded or given up, even if heaven and earth . . . passed away."[5]

The Small Catechism, like the Smalcald Articles, shows how justification is part of the broad context of the theology of creation. Not fulfilling usual expectations, which associate the particular terminology of justification with the explanations to the second or the third article of the creed, the article of justification appears conspicuously in the explanation to the first article, the article of creation: "I believe that God has created me together with all creatures. God has given me and still preserves my body and soul: eyes, ears, and all limbs and senses; reason and all mental faculties. In addition, God daily and abundantly provides shoes and clothing, food and drink, house and farm, spouse and children, fields, livestock, and all property—along with all the necessitates and nourishment for this body and life. God protects me against all danger, and shields and preserves me from all evil. All this is done out of pure, fatherly, and divine goodness and mercy, without any merit or worthiness of mine at all!"[6]

As Luther was writing his Small Catechism, the word "merit" stood out in controversy over the doctrine of justification; the word "worthy" was significant in the controversy over the Sacrament. It is decisive for

4. The formulation first appears in Löscher, *Vollständiger Timotheus Vennus,* 1:342–43. Cf. Loofs, "Der articulus stantis," 323–420. In his commentary on Psalm 130:4, Luther already refers the article as: "Stante enim hac doctrina stat Ecclesia, rúente autem ruit ipsa quoque." WA 40/3:352. Cf. also the detailed passages quoted by Loofs, "Der articulus stantis," 324–33.

5. "On this article stands all that we teach and practice against the pope, the devil, and the world. Therefore we must be quite certain and have no doubt about it. Otherwise everything is lost, and the pope and the devil and whatever opposes us will gain victory and be proved right." (Luther, "The Smalcald Articles," 415; BC 301; BC/T 292. Also cf. BSLK 416; BC 301; BC/T 292.

6. Luther, "Small Catechism," 510–11; BC 354; BC/T, 345.

understanding justification that the language of justification is shifted into the arena of the article on creation. Conversely, it is decisive for understanding creation that the development of the doctrine of creation explicitly makes use of the language of justification.

By making this theological decision, Luther shows that the first article is, for him, not to be mistaken for an "exterior courtyard" of the Gentiles.[7] The first article cannot be understood apart from faith in the triune God for it articulates the entire trinitarian faith. Luther's explanation points out with respect to what is most elementary in our lives what it means to be justified by faith alone in God's Word. Faith is not something attached to the human person. My very being is faith, that is, my trusting that life and what is necessary for life is given to me. Waiting for the gift and reaching out toward it is faith. Faith, that is, my being, is nothing else than what is granted out of pure goodness and, in the face of life-threatening dangers, granted out of pure mercy.

In the Western Christian tradition the question of "merit" was associated with the language of justification. Such language was oriented toward the future, toward balance sheets and rewards, toward achievement and the completion of one's individual history and of world history. The future is seen in light of what we as individuals, communities, and society in general will have earned and merited through every deed we commit or omit. What is implied by including the concept and fact of justification in the article on creation is that God as judge not only does not owe me a reward. Rather, my very beginning, my birth, and now my present existence are unmerited and freely given.

In his last will and testament Paul Gerhardt reminds his only son, still living after all his other children had died: "Do good to people, even if they cannot pay you back because . . ." The reader expects that the sentence will continue with: "God *will*[8] repay you." However, Paul Gerhardt frustrates this expectation by continuing: ". . . because for what human beings cannot repay, the Creator of heaven and earth *has* already repaid long ago when he created you, when he gave you his only Son, and when he accepted and received you in holy baptism as his child and heir."[9]

7. Cf. "It is not just a vestibule in which natural theology might find a place." Barth, *Dogmatics*, 52. "Sie ist nicht etwa ein Vorhof, in dem die natürliche Theologie Raum fände." Cf. Barth, *Dogmatik*, 59–60.

8. Italics original.

9. "Tue Leuten Gutes, ob sie dir es gleich nicht zu vergelten haben, denn was Menschen mcht vergelten können, das hat der Schopfer Himmels und der Erden langst

Our self-evident expectation that God repays according to the proverb, "*Do, ut des*" (As I give to you, so you give to me), is fundamentally
frustrated. God does not repay in the sense of a fair exchange. Our expectation of future repayment is turned upside down. Paul Gerhardt's last
will and testament to his son testifies to faith in a repayment that has
already been paid. Already paid, the payment cannot be understood any
more in the sense of a repayment. It is a *gift* that is unearned and solely
granted—a categorical gift.

> To speed his recovery, Luther once drove to Jessen [a small town
> near Wittenberg] with Dr. Jonas, Viet Dietrich, and other table
> companions. In Jessen Luther gave alms to the poor in spite of the
> fact that his financial situation was not rosy. Dr. Jonas followed his
> example and explained: "Who knows when God will return me
> the favor!" Luther responded to Jonas' statement, laughing: "As if
> your God had not already given to you!"[10]

"As if your God had not already given to you!" Luther's response
to his friend captures in understandable, everyday idiom what technical
theological language in a quite misleading way terms *creatio ex nihilo*,
creation out of nothing. Romans 11 raises the question of repayment in
the context of doxology, concluding with praise of the Creator and Judge
in verse 35. Paul (citing a version of Job 41:3) writes: "Or who has given a
gift to him, that he might be repaid?" (RSV).

The world was not called into being because of any this-worldly necessity, but out of pure freedom and goodness. Creation out of nothing
means that all that is exists out of pure goodness; it is unmerited: "All this
is done out of pure, fatherly, and divine goodness and mercy, without any
merit or worthiness of mine at all!"[11]

---

vergolten, da er dich erschaffen hat, da er dir seinen lieben Sohn geschenket hat, und da
er dich in der heiligen Taufe zu seinem Kinde und Erben auf- und angenommen hat"
(Gerhardt, "Testament, 1676," 493).

10. "Als Luther einmal mit Dr. Jonas, Veit Dietrich und anderen Tischgenossen zu
seiner Erholung nach Jessen fuhr, gab er daselbst, obgleich seine Verhaltnisse keine glan-
zenden waren, den Armen Almosen Dr. Jonas folgte seinem Beispiel mit der Erklärung:
Wer weiß, wo mirs Gott wieder bescheret' Darauf erwiderte Luther lachend: Gleich als
hatte es Euer Gott nicht zuvor gegeben; frei einfaltig soll man geben, aus lauter Liebe
willig" (Roßling and Ambros, *Reisen zu Luther*, 190).

11. Luther, "Small Catechism," 511; *BC* 354; *BC/T* 345.

## AGAINST THE MODERN WILL TO SELF CONSTITUTION

The justifying divine and creative word, considered in its cosmological and ontological breadth and depth, sharply contradicts the modern will to create and constitute oneself. However, not all modern thought on autonomy must globally be suspected to aim at self-empowerment. From Descartes to Kant the concepts of autonomy and freedom were based on self-ascertainment and do not claim to legitimize or ground the self. Since Fichte, Marx, and Sartre, however, what is human has been understood in a more radical light than what was thought to be human nature in the Middle Ages, with which Luther was concerned. The modern human being thinks of himself, from beginning to end, as a doer and maker. In the terms of Karl Marx, a human being produces him- or herself through work. "Self-production" by "work"![12]

The human being who tries to create himself and his world by work alone fails to understand what the Sabbath and Sunday are for. The distinction between Sunday and every day is a remarkable expression of what justification by faith alone is all about. But the self-actualizing human being has lost this distinction. For the philosopher Johann Gottlieb Fichte man is defined by his activity: "You are here for action; your action, and your action alone, determines your worth."[13] That man is defined by his activity is also affirmed by Jean-Paul Sartre in his thesis that existence does not arise from essence, but, conversely, the essence of man comes from his existence. The human being is precisely what he makes of himself, no more and no less; he is what he does in the freedom to which he is condemned.[14] "I become for myself," says Fichte, "the sole source of my own being . . . , and, henceforth, unconditioned by anything without me, I have life in myself."[15] In this sense for Fichte the act stands

---

12. Marx is concerned with understanding the "true, because actual, man as the product of his own work" (Marx, "Nationalökonomie," 269).

13. "zum Handeln bist du da; dem Handeln und allein dein Handeln bestimmen deinen Werth" (Fichte, *The Vocation of Man*, 84). Cf. Fichte, "Bestimmung," 1:253.

14. See Sartre, *Existentialism*, 28: "Existence precedes essence"; "man is nothing else but that which he makes of himself." Sartre, *L'Existencialisme*, 21, 22: "l'existence précède l'essence"; "l'homme n'est rien d'autre que ce qu'il se fait"; "l'homme est condamné à être libre" (37); "il est responsable de tout ce qu'il fait" (37).

15. "Ich werde mir selbst zur em[z]igen Quelle alles meines Seyns und meiner Erscheinungen; und habe von nun an, unbedingt durch etwas außer mir, das Leben in mir selbst" (Fichte, *The Vocation of Man*, 125; Fichte, "Die Bestimmung." 285).

at the beginning. The first sentence of John's Gospel should be rewritten to read: "In the beginning was the act," my act!

It is not surprising that for Fichte the "presupposition of creation . . . is the absolutely fundamental error of every false metaphysics and religious teaching." "Properly speaking, it is impossible even to think creation."[16] Fichte's statement means nothing else than that justification by faith alone is simply absurd, pure nonsense.

One of the first to see and grasp the signs of his time was the poet Jean Paul. While in the depths of dismay, he composed his "Speech by the dead Christ, looking down from heaven, that 'there is no God.'"[17] The historical context in which Jean Paul wrote this piece provides a key for interpreting his speech. At the end of the eighteenth century a strong wave of nihilism swept through Europe and became for the first time in history a major topic of discussion.[18] In his speech describing the nihilistic and atheistic spirit of the times, Jean Paul invokes the goodness of God the Creator, of the merciful Father. As he writes his vision, Jean Paul is terrified by an "I" who is alone, all by himself in the void.[19] He concocts the vision in order to rejoice all the more in his merciful Creator. A comment attached to the title of the speech clearly reveals that he intends to reassure himself through his poem of the Creator's mercy: "If the situation would arise in which my heart would be so unhappy and so empty as though dead, that in it all feelings affirming the existence of God were destroyed, then I would shock myself with this my speech. It would heal me and it would

16. "Die "Annahme einer Schöpfung [. . .] der absolute Grundirrthum aller falschen Metaphysik und Religionslehre"; "eine Schöpfung laßt sich gar nicht ordentlich denken" (Fichte, "Anweisung zum seligen," 5:479). It was Jacobi who, in his Spinoza tractate, communicated Lessing's conviction that the *creatio ex nihilo* was inconceivable. Jacobi, "Über die Lehre des Spinoza," 52–190. See especially, 67–68, 123. For a study on Jacobi as well as the reception of Fichte's work by the young Hegel, Hölderlin, and Schelling, see Henrich, "Philosophisch-theologische," 60–92. On the question of the *creatio ex nihilo*, see 85–86.

17. Paul, "Tod und Hochzeit," 1:247–52; Casey, *Jean Paul. A Reader*, 179–83. Cf. Rehm, "Experimentum medietatis," 7–95. On the circulation of the "Rede des toten Christus" —"Le songe"—above all in French Romanticism, see Hommel, *Sebasmata*, 1:3–43, esp. 26 n. 154. On the context of Jean Paul's work see Benz, *Jean Paul*.

18. Muller-Lauter, *Historisches Wörterbuch der Philosophie*, 846.

19. Cf. "Da sah ich mich selbst mit mir allein im Nichts . . . ." Klingemann, *Nachtwachen*, 168. Cf. "Wo komm ich her? . . . Aus nichts . . . Wo geh ich hm? . . . Ins Nichts . . . Wo bin ich' . . . Hart zwischen Nichts und Nichts'" (Kleist, *Die Hermannschlacht ein Drama*, 4).

restore my feelings to me."[20] Jean Paul develops, in an unforgettable way, the desperate defiance lying at the heart of the will to self-constitution; he displays that deadly, razor-sharp logic which makes it understandable why suicide, along with murder as in the Gulag archipelago, has become for many the only really serious philosophical problem in our time.[21] "Oh, if every "I" were his own Father and Creator, why could this "I" not be his own killer?"[22]

The modern will to constitute and actualize the self is seen most clearly in Fichte's philosophy. But the disintegration and fragmentation of the self in our postmodern context is radically different from Fichte's modern understanding of the self. The individual agent acting responsibly is dismissed as an obsolete fiction. The elements founded on human subjectivity and individuality, united in the identity of self-consciousness, have been broken down into roles, functions, and processes of adaptation. Such fragments of the self can be described according to evolutionary, cybernetic, and systems-theory models, but they can according to postmodern thought no longer be held together by or integrated into an individual self-consciousness. Whether it is legitimate to use the concept of "self-consciousness" at all or even whether to use the word is disputed. If it means anything, self-consciousness refers to an anonymous system of relationships. The term "autopoiesis,"[23] meaning self-effectiveness, the capacity to organize oneself, is then applied to the self. Even though it

20. "Wenn einmal mein Herz so unglücklich und ausgestorben ware, dass in ihm alle Gefühle, die das Dasein Gottes bejahen, zerstört waren: so wurd' ich mich mit diesem meinem Aufsatz erschüttern und er wurde mich heilen und mir meine Gefühle wieder geben" (Paul, *Blumen-, Frucht- und Dornenstucke*, 247; Casey, *Jean Paul: A Reader*, 179.

21. "There is but one truly serious philosophical problem, and that is suicide" (Camus, *Myth of Sisyphus*, 3); "Il n'y a qu'un problème philosophique vraiment sérieux, c'est le suicide." (Camus, *Mythe de Sisyphus*, 16). The main focus of *L'Homme révolté* is on the revolutionary who forcefully strives to attain the Absolute by political means and to set it completely in motion. In his efforts he helps himself with the use of terror and murder. On the correlation between the murder of God and the murder of human beings, see especially: "In principle, the rebel only wanted to conquer his own existence and to maintain it in the face of God. But he forgets his origins and, by the law of spiritual imperialism, he sets out in search of world conquest by way of an infinitely multiplied series of murders" (Camus, *The Rebel*, 103; see also 55–61). In German: Camus, *Der Mensch in der Revolte*, 47–52, 86.

22. "Ach wenn jedes Ich sein eigener Vater und Schopfer ist, warum kann es nicht auch sein eigener Würgengel sein?" (Paul, *Blumen-, Frucht- und Dornenstucke*, 251; Casey, *Jean Paul: A Reader*, 183.

23. Cf. Luhmann, "Autopoiesis," 402–46; Buhl, "Grenzen der Autopoiesis," 25–54.

may be possible, when formulating theories in natural science, to speak of a "self-organization" of the universe,[24] the applied meaning of this term, used as an incantation conjuring up a religious world-view, states the contrary of *creatio ex nihilo* and, with it, of justification by faith alone.

Without doubt, the postmodern incantation "autopoiesis" and Fichte's "I" are worlds apart. The Titanism of Fichte's and Sartre's philosophy is oriented towards the "I" who despairingly wills to be him- or herself.[25] In the meanderings of postmodernism, the "I" wills despairingly *not* to be him- or herself.[26] The difference between the two cannot be ignored. Nevertheless, commonality exists. In both, the concept of "creation out of nothing," and thus an existence that is unearned and radically unmerited, appears to be totally meaningless, even nonsensical, absurd. In the framework of such philosophical orientation, or rather, disorientation, it is no wonder that harsh, apocalyptic fears of the future exist along with euphoric hope in further cosmic evolution and new cosmic possibilities. Dramas and films, as, for example, "The Day After," try to whip us into action or else—and this is merely the flipside—cripple any needed or possible action.

In spite of all this, the situation today is not so new after all. The ancient simultaneity and complementarity of despair and presumption, of *desperatio* and *praesumptio,* come once again to the fore. Modernity and postmodernity, each presuming their situation to be entirely new, are merely recycling the basic situation of the human being who, oscillating between defiance and despondency, *superbia* and *desperatio,* cannot ultimately know himself.[27] Such inability to fathom the defiant and despondent heart corresponds to his inability to see the surrounding world in any other light than that of his own defiance and despondency. (What the heart produces also determines the structures of life!)[28] The human being audits and judges the world from this perspective—even until he becomes his own killer and the killer of his fellow creatures.

24. Cf. Jantsch, *Self-Organizing Universe.*

25. See Kierkegaard, *Sickness,* 107–17.

26. Ibid., 78–96.

27. "The heart is deceitful above all things, and desperately corrupt; who can understand it?" Jer 17:9 (RSV). Luther translates: "Es is das Herz ein trotzig und verzagt Ding" ("The heart is a defiant and despondent thing").

28. Bayer, *Schöpfung,* 70.

## LIBERATION FROM THE LAW, SIN, DEATH

To be freed from judging or justifying oneself is the meaning of being justified by faith alone. And this means nothing less than being removed from the situation in which "every 'I' tries to be his own Father and Creator," in which one may—or even must—be also "one's own killer." The "I" is freed, like Israel liberated out of Egyptian captivity.

In our contemporary ecclesial and theological situation, we are tempted to rush too quickly into speaking about the gospel as the divine power of liberation. But Luther prevents us from doing this. With his understanding of the captivity from which the divine power frees us, he points the way. He had experienced the power of liberation in an unprecedented and radical fashion. Therefore he stressed that the captivity from which the gospel frees us is not a captivity for which others can be held primarily responsible. The kind of captivity from which God liberates is completely and utterly one's own fault.

The fact that this captivity is one's own fault leads Luther to discuss the condemning law that also kills. The law forces me to confront myself so that I am unable to move; it ties me down so that I cannot escape myself, being the one who has tied myself down by my own actions. Luther thanks God for the freedom from captivity that has occurred through Jesus Christ, using biblical terms such as freedom from slavery under the law, under sin, and under eternal death, the wages of sin.

> Fast bound in Satan's chains I lay,
> death brooded darkly o'er me,
> sin was my torment night and day;
> in sin my mother bore me.
> But daily deeper still I fell;
> my life became a living hell,
> so firmly sin possessed me.
> My own good works all came to naught,
> no grace or merit gaining;
> free will against God's judgment fought,
> dead to all good remaining.
> My fears increased till sheer despair
> left only death to be my share;
> the pangs of hell I suffered.[29]

---

29. Luther, "Nun freut euch lieben Christen g'mein," *LBW* hymn 299, verses 2–3. See *WA* 35:133–35. See also *EG*, hymn 34. See also *WA* 35:423–24.

Is this a descent into the hell of self-knowledge? Or is it an experience of conscience that could possibly be interpreted existentially? Whatever validity there might be in posing such questions, we must not simply turn Luther into one of our contemporaries. The perspective he shared with his contemporaries differs from our modern perspective. It is undeniable that our contemporaries experience many fears. For the most part, however, there is no fear of the judge of the world, a fear Luther encountered every time he entered the city church in Wittenberg. On a stone relief above the entrance to the cemetery surrounding the church, Luther saw Christ seated on the rainbow as judge of the world, so angry the veins stand out, menacing and swollen, on his forehead. A lily emerging from the right side of his mouth and a sword from the left symbolize Christ judging both the spiritual and the worldly realms, thus judging everywhere: Nobody and nothing escapes his judgment.[30]

The image of Christ as judge of the world defines an entire epoch. God is seen face to face in this Christ,[31] who is the embodiment of the power that punishes sin. This power applies the juridical righteousness that is reckoned to all according to their works and merit. Our existence unto death is lived in light of God's judgment on sin, a goal and destination with no exit.

> In the very midst of life death has us surrounded . . .
> In the midst of bitter death, sharp the hell-drawn harrow . . .
> Through the midst of hells of fear our transgressions drive us . . .[32]

Death and the devil, sin and hell: these fears connected with each other were the fears of an entire epoch. Albrecht Dürer, himself facing great anxieties, depicted them in his cycle of paintings on the book of Revelation.

> When shall we a helper find . . . ?
> Who will break its teeth and save . . . ?
> Who will help us to escape . . . ?[33]

---

30. Cf. Junghans, *Wittenberg,* picture 12. For this picture of Christ see WA 8:677 (*LW* 45:59); WA 39/1:574; 41:198, 268; 45:261; 47:275, 310; *WA Tr* 6:87 (No. 6628). For the wider context see Schwarz, "Die spatmittelalterhiche," 526–53.

31. Cf. "the image of the invisible God" (Col 1:15).

32. The first line of each of the three verses in Luther's hymn "Mitten wir im Leben sind," hymn 265. *EG,* hymn 51; WA 35:453.

33. The second line of each of the three verses of "Mitten wir im Leben sind" (Ibid.).

The captivity from which Luther had been freed consisted in the fact that the distinction between law and gospel had been closed to him. "But when I discovered the proper distinction—namely, that the law is one thing and the gospel is another," he says in his Table-Talk, looking back to his early years, "I broke through."[34]

Prior to his breakthrough, Luther had understood the gospel as law. He thought the righteousness of God, which according to Rom 1:17 is revealed in the gospel, is the righteousness "with which God is righteous and punishes the unrighteous sinner."[35]

> Though I lived as a monk without reproach, I felt that I was a sinner before God with an extremely disturbed conscience. I could not believe that he was placated by my satisfaction. I did not love, yes, I hated the righteous God who punishes sinners, and secretly, if not blasphemously, certainly murmuring greatly, I was angry with God, and said, "As if, indeed, it is not enough, that miserable sinners, eternally lost through original sin, are crushed by every kind of calamity by the law of the Decalogue, without having God add pain to pain by the gospel and also by the gospel threatening us with his righteousness and wrath! Thus I raged with a fierce and troubled conscience."[36]

This is the experience Luther tells of in the Preface (1545) to the first volume of his Latin works. His report corresponds exactly to what we have already heard in his hymn of freedom, "Dear Christians, One and All": "My fears increased till sheer despair / Left only death to be my share; / The pangs of hell I suffered."[37]

Will this descent into hell be reversed? Must I remain in hell? Or will I be led out of it? The reversal occurs because of God's mercy. It is grounded in God's creative power, saving us from all evil, sin, death, and hell. Our complaining questioning and our cry for deliverance are answered from eternity. They are answered in such a way, however, that the answer and our salvation occur as an historical event: in the cross and resurrection

---

34. *WA Tr* 5:210 (No. 5518); *LW* 54:443. This table-talk shows that Luther's discovery of the *Iustitia dei passiva* coincides with his discovery of the distinction between law and gospel. "I lacked nothing before this except that I made no distinction between the law and the gospel" (*WA Tr* 5:210; *LW* 54:442).

35. "Preface to the Complete Edition of Luther's Latin Writings," *WA* 54:185; *LW* 34:336.

36. *WA* 54:185–86; *LW* 34:336.

37. The last three lines of *LBW* hymn 299, verse 3; *EG* hymn 34; *WA* 35:424.

of Jesus Christ. We participate in this event—likewise historically taking place in the present—by the fact that the resurrected-crucified One is communicated to us visibly in the word of baptism and the Lord's Supper.

This communication of the liberation is what Luther calls in his treatise On the Freedom of the Christian:

> the joyful exchange. . . . Because Christ is at once God and human (who has never sinned), and his righteousness is invincible, eternal, and almighty, he makes the sin of the believer's soul his own. He acts in no other way than if he himself had done it, by virtue of the soul's wedding ring, which is faith. So in him the sins must be swallowed and drowned, for his invincible righteousness is too powerful for any sin. By virtue of her dowry, the soul is cleansed from all her sins, that is, free and exempt through faith, presented with the eternal righteousness of her bridegroom, Christ. Is that not a happy transaction, where the rich, noble, righteous bridegroom Christ marries the poor, despised, wicked little whore and frees her from all evil, adorns her with all goods? So it is impossible that the sins condemn her; for now they lay on Christ and are devoured with him. Now she has got such a rich righteousness from her bridegroom, that she again can stand against all sins. . . . Of this Paul says in 1 Cor 15:57: "Praise and thanks be to God, who has given us such an overcoming in Christ," in whom death together with sin is devoured.[38]

38. "A most pleasing vision not only of communion but of a blessed struggle and victory and salvation and redemption. Christ is God and man in one person. He has neither sinned nor died . . . his righteousness, life, and salvation are unconquerable, eternal, omnipotent. By the wedding ring of faith he shares in the sins, death, and pains of hell which are his bride's. As a matter of fact, he makes them his own and acts as if they were his own and as if he himself had sinned . . . [Death and hell] were necessarily swallowed up by him in a mighty duel; for his righteousness is greater than all the sins of men, his life stronger than death, his salvation more invincible than hell. Thus the believing soul by means of the pledge of its faith is free in Christ, its bridegroom, free from all sins . . . endowed with the eternal righteousness, life, and salvation of Christ its bridegroom. . . . Who then can appreciate what this royal marriage means? Who can understand the riches of the glory of this grace? Here this rich and divine bridegroom Christ marries the poor, wicked harlot, redeems her from all her evil, and adorns her with all his goodness. Her sins cannot now destroy her, since confidently display alongside her sins in the face of death and hell and say, 'If I have sinned, yet my Christ, in whom I believe, has not sinned, and all his is mine and all mine is his,' as the bride in the Song of Solomon says, 'My beloved is mine and I am his.' This is what Paul means when he says in I Cor 15, 'Thanks be to God, who gives us the victory through our Lord Jesus Christ,' that is, the victory over sin and death" (Luther, "The Freedom of a Christian," *WA* 7:25–26; *LW* 31:351–52, author's translation from the German).

Luther continued to describe this one liberating event in ever new ways. According to his hymn, "Dear Christians, One and All," the exchange between the righteousness of God communicated in Jesus Christ and my sin takes place as a change of location and existence by means of God's promise: "Stay close to me, / I am your rock and castle. / Your ransom I myself will be; / For you I strive and wrestle."[39]

Through such a promise and such a gift, Luther experienced God's saving righteousness. The self-giving of Jesus Christ occurring in the joyful exchange establishes the freedom of a Christian. On the basis of experiencing God's saving righteousness in this exchange,[40] Luther, in the Preface (1545) to his Latin works, tells of the radical Reformation shift in his life and theology: "There I began to understand that the righteousness of God is that by which the righteous lives by a gift of God, namely by faith. And this is the meaning: the righteousness of God is revealed by the gospel, namely, the passive righteousness with which merciful God justifies us by faith, as it is written, 'The righteous shall live by faith.'"[41]

## FAITH: THE WORK OF GOD

The story I have outlined above is marked by a dramatic reversal. This shift in existence from sin to liberation is the story of the life and theology of Martin Luther. But it is not his story alone. Many of Luther's contemporaries joined in the chorus and saw reflected in the reversal in Luther's life the change in their own lives. Albrecht Dürer, for instance, testifies that Luther helped free him from "great fears."[42] Such anxieties were the fears of an entire epoch. So it is understandable that the liberation experienced by one individual affected the entire epoch as well. An individual in the depths of fear, facing God's judgment and doubting God's grace,

---

39. *LBW* hymn 299, verse 7; *EG* hymn 34; *WA* 35:424.

40. The Reformation understanding of *promissio* was, from the beginning with the *Resolutio* to theses 37 and 38 on indulgences, associated with a substitutionary Christology. See Bayer, *Promissio,* 180–82. Cf. "Sermo de duplici iustitia" (*WA* 2:143). "Two Kinds of Righteousness," *LW* 31:297–306.

41. *WA* 54:186; *LW* 34:337.

42. Dürer in the letter to Spalatin in early 1520. See Dürer, *Schriftlicher,* letter no. 32, 1:86–87. Cf. Dürer's lament concerning Luther in his diary noting the travel in the Netherlands from May 17, 1521, in ibid., 170–72, 196–99 nn. as well as the index written in 1520–1521 of the sixteen works of Luther from the years 1518 to 1520 that he possessed. In ibid., 221, 222 n. 2.

was given an answer. The answer for one individual became for others the basis of their faith and confession.

But the claim of Luther's reversal and discovery goes even further—reaching beyond his own epoch: The "I" that says "the pangs of hell I suffered,"[43] to whom Christ answers "stay close to me"[44] claims nothing less than to be stating what is true for every individual "I." Such universality, to be sure, cannot be demonstrated abstractly, nor is it possible to determine or guarantee such generalizing beforehand.

At this point we face the main difficulty in taking up Reformation thought. The difficulty affects both sides, the side of the law as well as the side of the gospel, and therefore the difficulty concerns Luther's entire understanding of justification by faith alone.

A gulf separates us from Luther's understanding of justification, a gulf greater than we can imagine. Our contemporaries do not experience the *law*[45] any more as the law of God. Rather, the law is experienced as anonymous, or, in the best case scenario, as the "categorical imperative." A sense of inescapable duty weighing heavily on every human heart is revealed to us by this anonymous law. Duty becomes deadly when the law coincides with the gospel, when they are not distinguished from each other.

In light of our duty toward peace and justice, the unavoidable question is: Are we then condemned to bring about this-worldly peace through activity carefully planned by us humans in the arena of this-worldly politics? Can humanity survive in any other way than by such an extreme, final, moral, and last ditch effort?[46]

This inescapable question places an enormous burden on us. It is the law under which we live. This law forces us to be Atlas, the figure in Greek myth who has to carry the entire burden of the world on his shoulders.

43. "Dear Christians, One and All," *LBW* hymn 299, verse 3, line 7; *EG* hymn 34; *WA* 35:424.

44. Ibid., verse 7, line 1.

45. Italics original.

46. Cf. Weizsäcker, *Bedingungen des Friedens*, 18, including the *laudatio* of Georg Picht on the occasion of receiving the peace prize of the German book trade. Von Weizsäcker also empathizes, "The path towards this is prepared, at the most, through political ordering and moral conduct; it actually leads through suffering and grace." The German text reads, "Der Weg dahin wird durch politische Ordnungen und moralisches Verhalten allenfalls vorbereitet; tatsächlich fuhrt er durch Leiden und Gnade" (Weizsäcker, *Die Zeit drangt*, 45).

Jean-Paul Sartre says of this burden that we are "condemned to be free."[47] Condemned to be free, we are forced to be like Atlas. The burden cannot be shrugged off. Is it not inevitable that we will be crushed to death under its weight? Is it at all possible for us, under this burden, to separate ourselves from our acts? Or are we to remain forever and inexorably chained to our own works and their consequences?

In our current situation characterized by justification through our works, what does justification by faith alone mean? What is the righteousness of God as the righteousness of faith?

At this point Luther is far more provocative to us here than in his understanding of the law, sin, death, and hell. The righteousness of the law is at work pinning down the self and the acts of the self.

Even those who have only a small sense for historical continuity can recognize that this kind of righteousness belongs to all time. However, the righteousness of faith is something different, totally different from the righteousness of the law. We usually suppose we know what faith is: human decision, the act of interpretation, making sense of the world, or acting in correspondence to God's acts. By comparison, Luther's understanding of faith as the sole work of God seems strange. Luther himself had experienced the strangeness of righteousness by faith in a radical way—by this, without doubt, in the footsteps of the Apostle Paul and John the Evangelist. Luther understood the righteousness of faith to be the righteousness of God, "that we let God alone work in us and that in all our powers we do nothing of our own."[48] This kind of righteousness, which Luther calls "passive" righteousness, happens to us;[49] we can only wait for it.

Faith—that is, the righteousness of God—is not a human ability[50] or act, not to mention the "human notion and dream that some people call faith."[51] To the contrary, the righteousness of God or faith is what Luther describes in the Preface to Romans in his September Testament (1522). In terms similar to the sermon, Luther writes in the Treatise on Good Works (quoted above) that the righteousness of God is "a divine work in us which changes us and makes us to be born anew of God [John 1:13].

---

47. Sartre, *Being and Nothingness*. (See also n. 14, above.)

48. *WA* 54:186; *LW* 34:337. See also *WA* 40/1:41; *LW* 26:5.

49. Ibid.

50. Faith is not a *virtus*. Cf. "The Freedom of a Christian," *WA* 7:49; *LW* 31:343.

51. Luther, "Preface to the Epistle of St. Paul to the Romans," *WA DB* 7:9; *LW* 35:370.

It kills the old Adam and makes us altogether different men, in heart and spirit and mind and powers."[52]

The word of faith as the work of God frees from the righteousness of the law. The kind of freedom Luther speaks about is understandable against the background of the inescapable burden the self experiences under the law and the righteousness demanded by the law. God alone is responsible for faith, that is, for me. In being freed from this burden, I am given the liberty to see myself in a healthy distance to myself. I am freed to come out of my own shell, to be open toward God, toward others, and toward all creatures.

The context of daily justification continues to be a process of evaluating myself and being evaluated, of being judged by others. I have to be able to work with the image I have of myself, of my capabilities and weaknesses; I have to consider how others see and judge me. My daily audit of my own self-evaluation and how I am evaluated by others has to be continued until death. Nevertheless, this balance sheet does not have the first and the last say about my existence. What is decisive is faith, freeing us from being determined now and finally by such an audit. We are not condemned but freed to live with the balance sheet permeated and enveloped by God's justifying word. In an unsurpassable way, Dietrich Bonhoeffer has written about such freedom in his poem, "Who am I?"[53] Am I what I know myself to be? Or am I who others determine me to be? These questions do not disappear from our lives. Nevertheless, Bonhoeffer concludes the poem with the affirmation, "Whoever I am,"[54]—this question can be left open—"thou knowest me, O God. I am thine."[55]

The question, Who am I? is not answered by prayer. Rather, the question is offered to God. It is received in good hands in the certainty that I am taken care of from eternity to eternity. Thus, in the certainty of eternal care, I have been given a certain distance from myself, removed from myself in a gracious and merciful way. This distance frees me from pronouncing final judgment on myself and on others. It frees me from what others say about me; what they say is not the final judgment, but is always provisional. I am not forced to balance my books once and for all. I am free to let everything be provisional and to live with what is incomplete.

52. Ibid. Cf. Deut 6:5; *WA* 7:10; *LW* 35:370.
53. Bonhoeffer, "Who Am I?," 197–98; German version in *Widerstand*, 179.
54. Ibid., 198.
55. Ibid.

## THE CREATION: THEOLOGICAL BREADTH AND THE EXISTENTIAL DEPTH OF JUSTIFICATION

In quite a provisional fashion, I have attempted to clarify both the fact that and the sense in which justification by faith alone is the basis, boundary, and the subject matter of theology. The event of justification is to be discovered as much in the social and cosmic breadth as in the existential depth. This would not promote a ghetto-like spirit but would enable theology to formulate more precisely the universality of the one subject matter with which theology is concerned, for it would bring out the theme that definitely does not confine theology to a darkroom: the theme of justification by faith alone.

---

## BIBLIOGRAPHY

Barth, Karl. *Dogmatik im Grundriß*. 3rd ed. Zürich: EVZ., 1947. Translated by G. T. Thompson as *Dogmatics in Outline*. New York: Philosophical Library, 1949.

Bayer, Oswald. *Promisso: Geschichte der reformatorischen Wende in Luthers Theologie*. Göttingen: Vandenhoeck & Ruprecht, 1989.

———. *Schöpfung als Anrede: Zu einer Hermeneutik der Schöpfung*. 2nd ed. Tübingen: Mohr/Siebeck, 1990.

Benz, R. "Introduction." In *Träume und Visionen*, by Jean Paul. Munich: Piper, 1954.

Bonhoeffer, Dietrich. "Who Am I?" In *Letters and Papers from Prison*, edited by Eberhard Bethge. Translated by Reginald Fuller. 3rd ed. London: SCM, 1967.

———. *Widerstand und Ergebung*. 13th ed. Gütersloh: Gütersloh/Mohn, 1985.

Buhl, W. L. "Grenzen der Autopoiesis." *Kölner Zeitschrift für Soziologie und Sozialpsychologie* 39 (1987) 25 – 54.

Camus, Albert. *Der Mensch in der Revolte: Essays*. Hamburg: Rowohlt, 1969. Translated by Anthony Bower as *The Rebel: An Essay on Man in Revolt*. New York: Random House, 1956.

———. *Le Mythe de Sisyphe Essai sur l'absurde*. Paris: Gallimard, 1942. Translated by J. O'Brien as *The Myth of Sisyphus, and Other Essays*. New York: Vintage, 1955.

Casey, Timothy J., editor. *Jean Paul: A Reader*. Translated by Erika Casey. Baltimore: Johns Hopkins University Press, 1992.

Dürer, Albrecht. *Schriftlicher Kachlass*. Edited by Hans Rupperich. Vol. 1. Berlin: Deutscher Verein fur Kunstwissenschaft, 1956.

Fichte, Johann Gottlieb. "Die Anweisung zum seligen Leben oder auch die Religionslehre, 1806." In *Sammtliche Werke 5*, Edited by I. H. Fichte. Berlin: n.p., 1845/46.

———. "Die Bestimmung des Menschen, 1800." In *Gesamtausgabe der Bayerischen Akademie der Wissenschaften*, *Werke 1799 –1800 1/6*. Edited by R. Lauth and H. Jacob. Stuttgart: Frommann/Holzboog, 1962.

———. *The Vocation of Man*. Edited with an introduction by Roderick M. Chisholm. New York: Liberal Arts Press, 1956.

Gerhardt, Paul. "Testament für seinen Sohn Paul Friedrich, 1676." In *Dichtungen und Scriften*, edited by Eberhard von Cranach-Sichart, 492–93. Munich: Mueller, 1957.

Henrich, D. "Philosophisch-theologische Problemlagen im Tübinger Stift zur Studienzeit Hegels, Hölderlins und Schellings." *Hölderlin-Jahrbuch* 25 (1986/87) 60–92.

Hommel, Hildebrecht. *Sebasmata: Studien zur antiken Religionsgeschichte und zum frühen Christentum*, 1:3–43. 2 vols. WUNT 31. Tübingen: Mohr/Siebeck, 1983.

Jacobi, Friedrich Heinrich. "Über die Lehre des Spinoza in Briefen an den Herrn Moses Mendelssohn. Neue vermehrte Ausgabe von 1789." In *Jacobis Spinoza Büchlein Nebst Replik und Duplik*, edited by Fritz Mauthner, 52–190. Munich: Mueller, 1912.

Jantsch, Eric. *The Self-Organizing Universe: Scientific and Human Implications of the Emerging Paradigm of Evolution*. Systems Science and World Order Library: Innovations in System Science. Pergammon International Library of Science, Technology, Engineering, and Social Studies. Oxford: Pergamon, 1980.

Junghans, Helmar. *Wittenberg als Lutherstadt*. 2nd ed. Göttingen: Vandenhoeck & Ruprecht, 1982.

Kierkegaard, Søren. *Sickness unto Death*. Translated by Walter Lowrie. Princeton: Princeton University Press, 1941. Originally published in 1849.

Klingemann, August. *Nachtwachen von Bonaventura*. Edited by Jost Schillemeit. Frankfurt: Insel, 1974.

Kleist, Heinrich von. *Die Hermannschlacht ein Drama in fünf Aufzügen*. Vol. 5. Vienna: Karl Graisere, 1885.

Knaake, J. F. K. et al., editors. *Luthers Werke, Kritische Gesamtausgabe*. Vol. 54. Weimar: Böhlau, 1883ff.

Loofs, F. "Der articulus stantis et cadenas ecclesiae." *Theologische Studien und Kritiken* 90 (1917) 323–420.

Löscher, V. E. *Vollständiger Timotheus Vennus*. 1:342–43. Wittenberg: Samuel Hannauem, 1718.

Luhmann, N. "Die Autopoiesis des Bewusstseins." *Soziale Welt* 36 (1985) 402–46.

Luther, Martin. "The Argument of St. Paul's Epistle to the Galatians." In *LW* 26.

———. "The Argument of St. Paul's Epistle to the Galatians." In *WA* 40.

———. "Commentary on Psalm 51." In *LW* 12.

———. "Commentary on Psalm 51." In *WA* 40.

———. "Dear Christians, One and All." In *EG*, hymn # 239

———. "Dear Christians, One and All." In *LBW*, hymn # 299.

———. "Dear Christians, One and All." In *WA* 35.

———. "The Freedom of a Christian." In *LW* 31.

———. "The Freedom of a Christian." In *WA* 7.

———. "Mitten wir im Leben sind [in the very midst of life]." In *EG*, hymn # 518.

———. "Mitten wir im Leben sind [in the very midst of life]." *Lutheran Worship*, hymn # 256. Translated by F. Samuel Janzow. St. Louis: Concordia, 1982.

———. "Mitten wyr im Leben sind [in the very midst of life]." In *WA* 35.

———. "Nun freut euch lieben Christen g'mein ["Dear Christians, One and All"]." In *EG*, hymn # 239

———. "Nun freut euch lieben Christen g'mein ["Dear Christians, One and All"]." In *LBW*, hymn # 299.

———. "Nun freut euch lieben Christen g'mein ["Dear Christians, One and All"]." In *WA* 35; *LW* 53.

———. "Preface to the Complete Edition of Luther's Latin Writings." In *LW* 34.

———. "Preface to the Complete Edition of Luther's Latin Writings." In *WA* 54.

———. "Preface to the Epistle of St. Paul to the Romans." In *LW* 35.

———. "Preface to the Epistle of St. Paul to the Romans." In *WA* 7.

———. "Sermo de duplici iustitia." In *WA* 2.

———. "Smalcald Articles." In *BC*.

———. "Smalcald Articles." In *BC/T*.

———. "Smalcald Articles." In *BSLK*.

———. "Small Catechism." In *BC*.

———. "Small Catechism." In *BC/T*.

———. "Small Catechism." In *BSLK*.

———. "Two Kinds of Righteousness." In *LW* 31.

———. *The Lutheran Book of Worship*. Minneapolis: Augsburg, 1978.

Marx, Karl. "Nationalökonomie und Philosophie." In *Die Fuhrschriften*, edited by S. Landshut. Stuttgart: Kroner, 1968.

Müller-Lauter, W. Art. *Historisches Wörterbuch der Philosophie*. Vol. 1, *Nihilismus*. Basel: Schwabe, 1984.

Paul, Jean. *Blumen-, Frucht- und Dornenstucke, oder Ehestand, Tod und Hochzeit des Armenadvokaten F. St. Siebenkas im Reichsmarktflecken Kuhschnappel, Erstes Blumenstuck*, 1796. Jean Pauls Sämtliche Werke: Historisch-kritische Ausgabe 6.1, Zu Lebzeiten des Dichters erschienene Werke. Edited by K. Schreinert, 247–52. Weimar: Bohlaus Nachfolger, 1928

Pelikan, Jaroslav and Helmut Lehman, editors. *Luther's Works*. Vol. 34. St. Louis: Concordia, 1955.

Peterson, Erik. "Kierkegaard und der Protestantismus." In *Marginalien zur Theologie*, 17–27. Munich: Kösel, 1956.

Rehm, W. "Experimentum medietatis: Eine Studie zur dichterischen Gestaltung des Unglaubens bei Jean Paul und Dostojewski." *Experimentum medietatis: Studien zur Geistes- und Literaturgeschichte des 19. Jahrhunderts* (1947) 7–95.

Roßling, Udo, and Paul Ambros. *Reisen zu Luther Erinnerungsstätten in der DDR*. 2nd ed. Leipzig: Tourist Verlag Berlin, 1988.

Sartre, Jean Paul. *Being and Nothingness*. Translated by Hazel E. Brown. New York: Philosophical Library, 1956.

———. *L'Existenciahsme est un Humanisme*. Paris: Les Editions Nagel, 1946. Translated as *Existentialism and Humanism* by P. Mairet London: Methun., 1949.

Schwarz, Reinhard. "Die spatmittelalterhiche Vorstellung vom richtenden Christus—ein Ausdruck religiöser Mentalität." *Geschichte in Wissenschaft und Unterricht* 21 (1970) 526–53.

Swendenborg, Emmanuel. *The True Christian Religion*, 1771. Vol. 2. New York: Swendenborg Foundation, 1952.

Weizsäcker, Carl Friedrich von. *Bedingungen des Friedens*. Göttingen: Vandenhoeck & Ruprecht, 1964.

———. *Die Zeit drangt: Das Ende der Geduld. Aufruf und Diskussion*. Munich: Deutscher Taschenbuch, 1989.

# 3

# The History, Shape, and Significance of Justification for Preaching

## *Mark Mattes*

THE DOCTRINE OF JUSTIFICATION is intended to formulate an answer to the question: "What must I do to be saved?" Justification's answer, "nothing," is startling, and it reframes the question itself by asserting that God is not in the salvaging business. Instead, what God does in saving us is to recreate us, that is, to make us to be creatures who have faith at the core of their being, and humble and contrite hearts (Ps 51:10–12). God's salvation is a recommitment to his original and continuing work of creating out of nothing (*creatio ex nihilo*) (1 Cor 1:27–30; 2 Cor 5:17–18). God not only re-creates us out of the nothingness of sin and death, but also providentially sustains our lives, together with those of all creatures (*samt allen kreaturen*),[1] from moment to moment, out of nothingness.

Just as God creates and sustains the world out of nothingness through his address, *speaking* creation into being and maintaining it in being, God re-creates humanity out of the nothingness of sin and death which results from humanity's attempt to serve as its own god for itself (*ambitio divinitatis*).[2] For this very reason, there is no pure separation

1. Luther, "The Small Catechism," *BC/T* 354:2.
2. "Man is by nature unable to want God to be God. Indeed, he himself wants to be

51

between theology as systematic or academic and theology as pastoral or practical. Instead, theology is for *proclamation*.[3] God's voice of judgment and mercy is most clearly heard in preaching and the word of absolution. Such proclamation conveys God's own word to sinners through preachers who properly distinguish law—God's commands—from gospel—God's promise to forgive.

We quickly assume that if there are directives, such as found in God's law, then we must be able to fulfill these commands. The language game of command implies the ability to fulfill the request. Otherwise, why make the request? Why give a directive to someone who cannot do it? However, in light of the distinction between law and gospel, we learn that ultimately no sinner can keep God's law. Rather than being doable, God's law for sinners is accusing—even killing. In light of God's accusing law, sinners discover that free will is an illusion. They are *bound* to justify themselves before God and others. But such self-justification is nothing other than the opposite of faith. We have no ability to liberate ourselves from such self-justification—only God's external word of forgiveness in Jesus's name can do that.

Properly understood faith allows God to do his work in us, making us malleable like clay shaped by a fine potter. Jesus promises abundant life to his followers (John 10:10). But this abundant life is no escape from transactions in this world, whether joyful or brutal, but instead is granted right in the midst of such translations. In Jesus's gift of abundant life we are invited into the full gamut of life's experiences—sorrow and joy. God works upon us in all our experiences, disentangling us from any self-trust that we could serve as our own gods, which every sinner is bound to do. Instead, by letting go of such control, we trust God's promise that he will sustain us (Exod 20:1–3).

Indeed, sinners who tenaciously justify themselves in the public forum before God are annihilated, reduced to nothing, and are thereby in a position to receive God's justification. Justification is first and foremost about the one true God, specifically God's action to claim this world as his own, to get what belongs to him in contrast to all opposition (including

---

God, and does not want God to be God" (See "Disputation against Scholastic Theology [1517], thesis 17, *LW* 31:10).

3. No one emphasized this truth better than Gerhard O. Forde. See Forde, *Theology Is for Proclamation*.

that of God's own law) to sinners.[4] In a word, God forgives sinners in order to keep his promise to sustain them as his own. God claims sinful creatures and liberates them and the entire creation from bondage to sin and death (Rom 8:18–25). In faith, we acclaim God as right and true in his justifying of his sinful world in the death and resurrection of Jesus Christ. Likewise, in faith we justify God by confessing that he is right.

## LATE MEDIEVAL VIEWS OF NATURE AND GRACE

The Reformation teaching of the doctrine of justification emerges from Scripture: Jesus Christ was crucified for your trespasses, raised for your justification (Rom 4:25), but it was developed polemically against the views of salvation of late medieval theologians. It employs the vocabulary of the doctrine of justification as influenced by Augustine (354–430) and as it had subsequently developed in the Western church, but it does so by altering its grammar, syntax, and semantics. The most obvious difference between the Reformation teaching and that of medieval theology is the insistence that justification is the final, future decree of acquittal, the "last judgment," bestowed in the present on the basis of God's justification of Jesus Christ who as the "greatest sinner" (*maximus peccator*) has borne our sins and has favored sinners by exchanging their sin for his righteousness.[5] The axis of justification is not to be seen anthropologically as a progression from grace to virtue, a movement from a starting point, *a terminus a quo*, toward an ending point, *a terminus ad quem*. Instead, justification is properly and decisively "forensic,"[6] a decree that puts to death the old sinner and raises the new creature.

---

4. Iwand, *The Righteousness of Faith according to Luther*.

5. Luther, "Lectures on Galatians" (1535) in *LW* 26:277.

6. Luther notes, "I cannot change at all what I have consistently taught about this until now, namely, that 'through faith' (as St. Peter says) we receive a different, new, clean heart and that, for the sake of Christ our mediator, God will and does regard us as completely righteous and holy. Although sin in the flesh is still not completely gone or dead, God will nevertheless not count it or consider it." See "The Smalcald Articles," *BC* 325:1. In this definitive statement, the overall shape of Luther's own exposition of his view of the article of justification is "forensic." That is, God evaluates sinners by means of an alien, external righteousness—that of Christ's—which offers a change of status before God who "reckons" sinners not on the basis of their merit but instead on the righteousness of Christ, our "mediator."

In the medieval and Roman Catholic perspectives, the primary metaphor for a saving relationship with God is that of a ladder. If humans are to see God face to face in heaven, they need grace to heal them from the wound of sin and aid them as finite creatures in their elevation towards becoming more and more like God, that is, deification. In the Scholastic system, grace is similar to a jump start for a nearly dead battery. It is less God's attitude of *favor* toward sinners and more a *donum*, an infusion of grace that can help sinners fulfill their potential to become like God, which has been crippled by sin and hindered by finitude. Apart from the gift of grace and our loving devotion to God and Christ-like deeds of love to our neighbors, we would not be able to conform more and more to the truth, beauty, and goodness which constitute the Triune life. In contrast, for the reformers, the medieval supposition that we need to climb a ladder toward God as the itinerary of our salvation is wrong. The ladder, if it exists, goes in only one direction: down. *For us and for our salvation he came down* and was incarnate of the Virgin Mary. This event is our salvation. The ladder is meant for one direction only: to go down to those in need.

For Thomas Aquinas (1225–1274), the movement that constitutes justification is nontemporal and happens all at once. It is nonetheless a movement, initiating growth in holiness, such that the person makes progress in the "theological virtues" of faith, love, and hope. It is composed of four features: (1) an infusion of grace into the heart of the sinner, (2) a movement of free will toward God in faith, (3) a movement of free will in recoil from sin, and (4) the remission of guilt.[7] All four of these steps are "under the power of grace." Lutherans and Roman Catholics agree that we are saved by grace—indeed, grace alone. Where they disagree is that Lutherans believe that faith *alone* saves and not faith *plus* the works of love. For Luther, faith is not quietistic—instead it opens one to honor God for his own sake and serves neighbors and creation for their own sakes.

A variant on this theme of the Christian life as progress is to be found in late medieval Nominalists, such as Robert Holkot (d. 1349) and Gabriel Biel (1420/25–1495), who contended that if we do that which is within us (*facere quod in se est*), God has covenanted to give us grace (*gratia infusa*). Such grace aids our transformation and growth in holiness and virtue enabling us to earn condign merit (*de condigno*), that is, we can thereby merit eternal life by our own full merit. If faith is to be real and

---

7. *Summa Theologica*, 12ae, esp. Q 113, Art. 6.

take shape, have "color" on a wall, as medieval thinkers metaphorically expressed it, it must be formed by love (*fides charitate formata*). Grace is thus a power behind the scenes that enables people to fulfill their ultimate potential, the decisive desire of their hearts—to rest eternally in God. By grace, our temporal lives mimic eternal truth. Our being is altered through the infusion of grace, the superadded gift of the Holy Spirit, and enables us to participate analogously in the divine life by activating works of love analogously akin to the divine life. In the medieval perspective, we are both ontologically and ethically altered by grace, which heals the wound of sin and allows us to progress in greater stages of conformity to God's eternal being.

Both the Nominalist perspective of divine acceptation (based on God's agreement to give grace to those who do their very best) and the Realist view of divinization (picked up by a long heritage of Christian *charity* mysticism) assume an Augustinian stance on love as *caritas*, love as desire for God and mimetically enacted in deeds, which promote growth in our ability to conform to God's own being. Augustine's view was developed in opposition to the British preacher Pelagius (ca. 354—ca. 420/440) who distanced himself from the view that humans are sinful in thought, word, and deed. For Pelagius, every person is born with the ability not to sin; we only recapitulate Adam's fall through imitation.

Many currents in the ancient world led early Christians to emphasize the role of the human will in salvation. Chief amongst these was opposition to the fatalism entertained by Gnostics and Manicheans. Additionally, it was important for early Christians to offer an alternate ethics and lifestyle in contrast to the decadence of the ancient Roman world. Early Christians sold their message to their pagan contemporaries by offering an alternate morality, but this entailed that they assumed that they needed to emphasize the freedom of the human will with respect to our relationship with God. Late in his career, Augustine went against this trend when he emphasized that grace was not chosen but freely given, and unmerited. It is, however, a divine quality infused in the heart of believers which enable them to become more like God in all their dealings. Eastern Orthodoxy however never accepted Augustine's view of grace and its anthropological implications. Instead, they steadfastly upheld freedom of the will. From Luther's perspective, as we shall see, Augustine failed to go far enough. For Luther, the Christian life is not primarily a growth in holiness, even if it is initiated by grace, but a constant, continuous, and passive reception of God's favor, God's own legitimation of his sinful creatures for Jesus's sake, and so a new creation. Sanctification happens as we more and more get used to our justification.

## DEFINING THE PROTESTANT VIEW OF JUSTIFICATION

The Lutheran understanding of justification, developed in contrast with the late medieval theologians, is most concisely stated and summarized in Article Four of the Augsburg Confession (1530), written by Philipp Melanchthon (1497–1560) (with Luther's endorsement): "Furthermore, it is taught that we cannot obtain forgiveness of sin and righteousness before God through our merit, work, or satisfactions, but that we receive forgiveness of sin and become righteous before God out of grace for Christ's sake through faith when we believe that Christ has suffered for us and that for his sake our sin is forgiven and righteousness and eternal life are given to us. For God will regard and reckon this faith as righteousness in his sight, as St. Paul says in Romans 3[:21–26] and 4[:5]."[8] In distinct opposition to the perspectives of late antiquity and the middle ages what stands out in this statement is that justification is decisively *forensic*, a decree of acquittal, as opposed to something God does in order to initiate a process on the ladder of ontological, moral, and mystical fulfillment. Likewise, faith is not to be understood as a "theological virtue," but as a state of being grasped by God's unconditional claim and promise. Grace is not the power behind the scenes initiating our process in mimetic growth in holiness but the very pronouncement of forgiveness itself. Therefore, it is faith, not love that saves. The patriarch Abraham trusted God's promise, and it was reckoned to him as righteousness, since "the righteous shall live by faith" (Hab 2:4).

## CHRIST THE END OF THE LAW

Evangelical reformers and medieval thinkers both used the same terminology about justification, but the Lutheran perspective subverts the inner logic of the ladder. Hidden behind Article Four of the Augsburg Confession is much theological spade work done by Luther prior to his evangelical breakthrough. Robert Kolb describes Luther's view of justification as grounded in the etymology of the German word *rechtfertigen*:

8. *BC* 38:1—40:3.

"'Justify' or 'render righteous'—meant 'to do justice to': that is to inflict punishment, 'judicially' on the basis of a conviction, and thus to execute the law's demands,' or 'to conduct a legal process as an activity of a judge,' 'to execute, to kill'. From early on, Luther spoke of God's killing and making alive as he described justification, for he presumed that sinners must die (Rom 6:23a) and be resurrected to life in Christ."[9]

For lack of a better term, the "logic" behind Luther's perspective is decidedly "eschatological." What this means is that God's judgment on all humanity to be rendered on the Last Day has already been done in time, in a specific act, that of the death and resurrection of his Son, Jesus Christ, and is conveyed to the world through the words of a preacher (Rom 10:14–17). It is on the basis of God's own vindication of his Son, who was himself without sin, but became sin for us and so was in the end justly accused as a violator of the Torah—God's own law—that all sinners can have assurance of eternal life. In violating the law, Jesus Christ was faithful to his Father's mission to rescue the "lost sheep of the house of Israel" (Matt 10:6). In the ministry of Jesus Christ, God would embrace

9. Kolb, *Martin Luther: Confessor of the Faith*, 126. Kolb builds on the work of Werner Elert. Elert notes that "when an accused person—in today's sense—justified himself we read that he 'proves his innocence', or he 'exonerates himself', or 'he is able to prove himself innocent of the misdeed of which he is accused'. The word 'justification', on the other hand, which also occurred frequently, conveyed an entirely different meaning. It designated either the criminal law suit in which hide and hair or life and limb were at stake, or—and most frequently that—the execution of a sentence, especially a death sentence. For example, as late as the seventeenth century the Saxon penal code listed the hangman's fees and other expenses incidental to the execution of bodily punishment under the caption *'Unkosten der peinlichen Rechtfertigung'* (expenses incidental to penal justification). It speaks of the *'Körper der mit dem Schwert Gerechtfertigten'*(the body of the person justified by the sword). The same linguistic usage is found also in Hans Sachs. Thus it was not confined to the speech of jurists, which was foreign to the people in general . . . Justification does not imply that man exculpates himself, but it means that the executioner 'must mete out justice to the transgressor'. Thus Luther conceives of it as the secular execution of punishment" (Elert, *The Christian Faith: An Outline of Lutheran Dogmatics*, 299–300). Elert concludes: "Justification by faith is judgment on 'the old man'. Justice has been done him. He receives death. That is the mortification carried out in repentance. And that is not to be understood figuratively, but very realistically. The man of faith is an other than the man of sin. To be sure, a final identity of the I remains. But it is the identity of the stalk of wheat with the seed-grain, which first had to be buried (John 12:24). As the sinner becomes a believing sinner, the enemy of God which he was but no longer is as soon as he receives forgiveness, dies. As our Confessions teach, justification is forgiveness of sin. However, forgiveness is not an exoneration for the 'old' man. It is, rather, his end. The declaration of righteousness is his justification because he is receiving justice. It is death for the sinner and resurrection for the believing sinner" (ibid., 305).

all those excluded by the law (prostitutes, tax collectors, prodigals, and sinners). For that reason, God's own Son himself was excluded and violently killed. If the law, in the hands of those who are self-justifying, even with all its good intentions eclipses God's promise in Christ alone, it must have its limits, and even its end (as both *telos* and *finis*) (Rom 10:4). For Luther, Jesus Christ is the "greatest sinner" in that he bears the sins of us all. His death is the death of our sin. But his death is also the end of the law as accusation—Jesus's resurrection places us sinners on a path outside the accusations of the law so that we might live by faith before God and before the world.

The law is true and wise, until it shockingly reaches its end in Christ, specifically in the death of Christ upon the cross, since it is written, cursed be everyone who hangs on a tree (Deut 21:23). Christ did not become sin in his trial. He was innocent before his accusers. But at the cross the curse of the Lord came upon him and made him not a transgressor but the greatest of all sinners, David, Peter, Luther, and all. Indeed, not just the greatest of sinners but sin itself (2 Cor 5:21). The law is indeed is worthy—God's own truth—until the cross. This is the logic from the cross, and apart from that, in this old world, the law remains in its entirety, not just in part, preserving life to some extent and accusing unto death. There the law is good, the law is holy, the law remains forever! The fault is not the law, but it does not have anyone else to convict once the cross of Christ ends this old world.

The gospel is itself not a "new law," one which would be doable since we have the "superadded gift of the Holy Spirit" to empower us. The gospel as grammar is not a directive at all, nor is it information about reality as such, nor is it a description of the landscape of our inner lives or spirituality. The gospel's grammar is that of a promise (*promissio*), a commitment on the part of God to be for us (*pro nobis*). The gospel, then, is not merely a way of incorporating gentiles into the covenant which God has already established with the Jews, as the "New Perspective" on Paul would have it. But as a "stumbling block" to the Jews and "foolishness" to the Gentiles it is the power and wisdom of God for both Jews and Gentiles who are equally guilty under the law, whether revealed as the Torah or discerned in nature (1 Cor 1:18–25).

That justification is forensic, a decree of acquittal, is often thought to be problematic. If it is a purely objective pronouncement of God's favor to sinners for Jesus's sake, then how are our lives changed? How does justification actually make a difference for people's lives and in the world? Hence, how justification can somehow be "effective" is a matter quickly raised. In light of Luther's critique one might suspect that this question arises from a concern to keep the human will intact and preserve the continuous existence of the person. That God's forensic word is effective seems counterintuitive. That it is effective can be understood only when we realize that this word of promise delivers the goods of forgiveness of sin, life, and salvation despite the fact that when we look at ourselves we still see sin. In this light, no vocation or office is quite as important as that of preaching. This preached word is the very in-breaking of God's new era promised in the Scriptures. The efficacy of the forensic word is not found in what we do to change our lives, but instead in how God's word opens us up from the inside out so that we are not so concerned about ourselves, including our own salvation.[10] Faith depends upon hearing God's promise; it does not rest upon seeing its own improvement. Instead, free of such egoism, we can honor and love God for his own sake and work for the well-being of our neighbor and this good earth.

## THE INNER LOGIC OF IMPUTATION

In the resurrection of Christ, God imputes righteousness to the world for Jesus's sake. However, when God imputes righteousness to us, he makes us to be sinners at the same time. If we have been imputed to be righteous, it is only because we first have been condemned as sinners. In a sense, we are not only justified by faith—in trusting God's promise of mercy to sinners—but in faith we also confess our own sinfulness. For it is not our own self-evaluation by which we can understand the depths of our sin but instead God's own judgment of our lives. Justification is forensic, a decree, delivered as a message through a preacher: "You are found condemned and guilty before God's law. You are a sinner and you bear the mark of death. But, for Jesus's sake, you are forgiven and acquitted. He has borne your sin and death for you and has exchanged your loss with his own life." The Christian life is not primarily a growth in righteousness—getting better at our efforts to be godly. Instead, God accuses sinners as ungodly, including our very best, so that he might have mercy on all (Rom 11:32). Jesus's cross is a judgment on us—and it judges not only our worst,

---

10. See Bayer, *Martin Luther's Theology*, 108.

but, ironically, *our best*. It was our best that sent Jesus to the cross. Our condemnation of him was on the basis of our best virtues, aptitude, and potentiality. This means, that for Luther, as for Paul, we are completely dead in trespasses and sins, and left with no basis for any self-justification whatsoever. Just as Christ, who knew no sin, became sin for us, we too have become thorough sinners in justification.

The core Lutheran insight about human nature is that our sin is best disclosed in that whoever we are, we are inherently self-justifying. This is why, if we would understand human nature aright, we must look to the doctrine of justification by faith. It alone discloses *what it means to be human*—one who is from the first and at the core—lives by faith, is completely receptive, and dependent on God for life.[11] We are not primarily human in what we do or fail to do but to whom we are related and from whom we receive, God himself as the source of life. Our righteousness before God is a receptive life (*vita passiva*). Truly, to be truly human is to live in trust that God will provide for, forgive, and guide one. The doctrine of justification implies a specific outlook on anthropology. A practical consequence of this reasoning is that we must distinguish who a person is—as one fundamentally related to God—from what a person does.[12] In contrast to Athanasius (293–373), God became human not so that we might become divine, but so that we—through faith—might become human ourselves but with death behind us once and for all.

## THE RELATIONSHIP BETWEEN SIN, LAW, AND DEATH

Because of our sin, humans seek to be their own gods for themselves . . . trusting in their own ability to chart the course of their lives. Luther called this *ambitio divinitatis*. Even the spirituality of the old Adam is nothing other than the godlessness of self-idolization. Luther expresses sin not primarily as failures of omission or commission but instead as being "curved in on oneself" (*incurvatus in se*). God is in the business of opening up the incurvated and delivering them from the problem their own egos have become for them.

For that reason, as old beings, we encounter God in a struggle. We want to control both our destinies and the destinies of others. Thereby we

---

11. See thesis 32 in "The Disputation Concerning Man," *LW* 34:139.
12. See Jüngel, "On Becoming Truly Human," 236.

fight with God, just like the patriarch Jacob did at the ford of the Jabbok (Genesis 32). Apart from God's word of promise, we encounter God as "naked" (*deus nudus*), as Luther put it. And we object to this God. He has not offered us the courtesy of asking for our counsel and, at some point, we eventually will actually hate this God, whom we perceive as an enemy. By contrast, in light of the promise, faith can even be said to be the "creator of divinity" (*fides creatrix divinitatis*).[13] Faith looks not to the "naked God" with whom we (as naked sinners) struggle in a fierce battle of recognition.[14] Instead, it looks to the "preached God," a word of promise that actually imparts the reality of Christ and his grace. Words for Luther are not merely descriptors or directives and labels for feelings but can actually bring reality, a new reality, especially as the gospel word of promise which forgives, imputes, and frees.[15] For Luther, grace does not perfect nature, elevating the finite to the infinite, but instead liberates nature, sets us free from our drive to control others, our lives, even our own thoughts.[16]

The medieval system assumes that the law is doable, given for our salvation. All we need is grace to help us get on the way. Why would God give commandments that would only condemn us? Surely that does not make any sense. But for Luther, the law was never given by God for salvation. It is not a path by which the old being can attain God or eternal life. For Luther, faith, which is itself granted by God in the promise which delivers God's forgiveness unites us with Christ. We have been co-crucified with Christ. Commenting on Galatians 2:20, Luther writes:

> But Christ is the Lord of the Law, because He has been crucified and has died to the Law. Therefore I, too, am lord of the Law. For I, too, have been crucified and have died to the Law, since I have been crucified and have died with Christ." How? Through grace and faith. When by this faith I am crucified and die to the Law, then the Law loses all its jurisdiction over me, as it lost it over Christ. Thus, just as Christ Himself was crucified to the Law, sin,

13. "Lectures on Galatians" (1535) *LW* 26:227.

14. *WA* 40/2:330.

15. See Bayer, "Luther as an Interpreter of Holy Scripture," 75–77.

16. "Grace is rather the power of God revealed in Christ which destroys the *unnatural*, destroys man's refusal to be natural. Grace thus makes nature what it was intended to be. In that sense grace perfects nature—not because it adds what was lacking, but precisely because it makes nature to be nature once again." See Forde, *Where God Meets Man*, 56–57.

> death, and the devil, so that they have no further jurisdiction over Him, so through faith I, having been crucified with Christ in spirit, am crucified and die to the Law, sin, etc., so that they have no further jurisdiction over me but are now crucified and dead to me."[17]

The justifying word first reduces us to nothing—condemns us even at our best—so that God re-creates a new being, new person, in Christ. The core of this person is freed not only from the accusation of sin but also—at least as one is in Christ—from our incurvation and the law's accusation. We are "perfectly free lords of all subject to none" as Luther says in the *Freedom of a Christian* (1520). Paradoxically, we are simultaneously just and sinful (*simul iustus et peccator*). If there is any growth to be had in the Christian life—loving God and neighbor more—it will only be achieved when the person is liberated from his or her own incurvation. Only an external word (*verbum externum*) of promise from God can do that because there is nothing in the sinner, including one's spirituality, that is not already an expression of such incurvation.

Luther makes it very clear that our death and resurrection in Christ is not something that we can do.

> But here Paul is not speaking about being crucified with Christ by imitation or example—for imitating the example of Christ is also being crucified with Him—which is a crucifixion that pertains to the flesh. 1 Peter 2:21 deals with this: "Christ suffered for you, leaving you an example, that you should follow in His steps." But he is speaking here about that sublime crucifixion by which sin, the devil, and death are crucified in Christ, not in me. Here Christ does everything alone. But I, as a believer, am crucified with Christ through faith, so that all these things are dead and crucified to me as well.[18]

We are not left intact when we are in God's hands. Nor does Jesus's crucifixion do away with our own death. Instead, the death we die through faith in Jesus is *the* death. The death at the end of our lives, for Luther, is a slight matter compared to this.

---

17. "Lectures on Galatians" (1535), *LW* 26:165.
18. Ibid.

## TWO KINDS OF RIGHTEOUSNESS

Hence, for Luther, faith is a painful matter. All of humanity is judged as condemned when Jesus dies on the cross and all of humanity is objectively justified in his resurrection. In faith we experience our death as self-centered, controlling people and the rebirth of an entirely new person who passively experiences God's work in him, and gives God the glory which is due him in this very passivity.

As receivers of God's love, we are opened from the inside out. God's word comes into the core of the person and breaks down all defenses before God—especially in light of our mortality. The person of faith—no longer centered on himself but living for God and the neighbor—is opened up to the world. Christian righteousness is twofold: passive before God and active in love toward the neighbor and (we can infer) the whole creation. Our salvation is that we are being restored to creation.

> Faith . . . is a divine work in us which changes us and makes us to be born anew of God, John 1[:12–13]. It kills the old Adam and makes us altogether different men, in heart and spirit and mind and powers; and it brings with it the Holy Spirit. O it is a living, busy, active, mighty thing, this faith. It is impossible for it not to be doing good works incessantly. It does not ask whether good works are to be done, but before the question is asked, it has already done them, and is constantly doing them.[19]

Recognizing these two kinds of righteousness, the passive and the active, as the chief pastoral task, Luther called "our theology."[20]

## PAST AND CURRENT MISPERCEPTIONS

The impact of Luther's view of the article of justification for theology and wider culture did not have the theological impact one might have hoped. Instead, Luther's theological heirs tended to weld the doctrine of justification by faith alone onto an anthropology inspired by philosophical and humanistic concerns that affirmed the free choice of the will, a position antithetical to Luther's position on the human before God (*coram deo*).[21] In essence, the Lutheran movement failed to construct an anthropology

19. Luther, "Prefaces to the New Testament," *LW* 35:370.
20. "Lectures on Galatians" (1535) *LW* 26:7.
21. See Forde, "Lutheranism," 354–57.

compatible with Luther's view of justification—a sad state, given that Luther himself believed that justification by faith alone was definitive of humanity. Increasingly, Enlightenment figures defined freedom as autonomy, which Immanuel Kant saw as a rational exercise in choice when an agent implements the "categorical imperative"—acting on principles which have universal and necessary applicability.

It was Albrecht Ritschl (1822–1889) who sought to apply Luther's teachings to nineteenth-century theological concerns. Ritschl appropriated Luther's views of forgiveness within an ellipses bounded by the twin points of forgiveness and ethical responsibilities. Nevertheless, especially noticed by Theodosius Harnack (1817–1889), "Ritschl had abridged or completely overlooked basic elements of Luther's theology. Among these were the ideas of the wrath of God, judgment, the dialectical distinction between the law and the gospel, as well as Luther's more radical statements about sin and grace. Ritschl took concepts that were really theological concepts for Luther and redefined them in terms of inner freedom and of ethics."[22] In contrast, Theodosius Harnack revived the centrality of law accusation and gospel regeneration in Luther's interpretation.[23] Adolph von Harnack revived an ethicizing approach to Luther and claimed that for Luther justification is "being righteous and becoming righteous."[24] Similarly, Karl Holl (1866–1926) tended to situate Luther's work within an ethical framework. For Holl, Luther's is "a religion of conscience,"[25] one which "included the element of 'duty' (*Pflicht*)."[26] Holl tended to blur the distinction between Luther's earlier pre-Protestant views from his later, more mature views. "Thus, according to Holl, as with Ritschl and von Harnack, Luther made no sharp distinction between being made righteous and being declared righteous. That distinction belonged to orthodoxy."[27] Nineteenth- and early twentieth-century Luther studies tended to revamp Luther's view of justification in terms of Kantian approaches to ethics, accentuating human autonomy, the separation of metaphysics from ethics, and the quest for a "kingdom of ends," in which agents honor the autonomy of their peers.

22. Lohse, *Martin Luther*, 220.

23. Ibid., 221.

24. Harnack, *History of Dogma*, 7:208.

25. See Holl, *What Did Luther Understand by Religion?*, 48ff.

26. Lohse, *Martin Luther*, 225.

27. Clark, "*Iustitia Imputata Christi*," 278.

More recently, a school of Luther studies has developed around the thinking of Tuomo Mannermaa (b. 1937). Guided by concerns for ecumenical relations with Eastern Orthodox church bodies, Mannermaa has aimed to present Luther's view of justification as properly divinization or *theosis*. In this perspective, a purely forensic view of justification falls short of the meaning of salvation for Luther, which Mannermaa regards as participation in God's very nature itself.[28] For Mannermaa, when Luther speaks of grace as *favor*, Luther never disassociates or separates God's forgiveness from the gift of divine indwelling. Indeed, Mannermaa claims that both *favor* and *donum* form an inseparable unity in the person of Christ, who through faith is really, ontically present. Hence, in Mannermaa, the Lutheran confessional perspective of a forensic justification is fundamentally at odds with Luther himself. This school accentuates Luther's view of Christ as the "form" of faith in the *Galatians Commentary* (1531).[29] The difference between Luther and his Roman Catholic opponents is over whether or not it is love which establishes "formal righteousness" (the Roman Catholic position) or Christ himself united with the believer through faith (Luther).

This view has been criticized by a number of scholars.[30] In responding to Mannermaa, Timo Laato indicates that throughout Luther's writings, especially the *Galatians Commentary* (1535), Christ's atoning work in "salvation history" precedes faith. Indeed, because Christ is the object of faith (God's *favor*), he is present in faith as *donum*. Hence, for Luther, salvation is based not on the indwelling Christ who deifies, but forensically on Christ who died for us.[31] *gift*

Additionally, Mannermaa's view leads to an unnecessary dilemma: *favor* is construed as objective while *donum* is somehow subjective. The truth, instead, is that we are dealing with a twofold objectivity. A spoken, "external word," which is God's *favor* in the form of a *gift*, grounded *both* in the objectivity of the cross and the proclamation to sinners as a benefit that requires such distribution, imparts both death and life to its hearers. Just as God's will is an active word ordering creation in Genesis, God's *favor* here is not a possession or essence of God's own, but *is* precisely the *gift*, applied to the unrighteous while and as they are unrighteous. Only

28. Mannermaa, *Christ Present in Faith*, 22.

29. Ibid., 39.

30. See for instance Schumacher, *Who Do I Say That You Are?*

31. Laato, "Justification: the Stumbling Block of the Finnish Luther School," 338.

on account of this truly objective foundation of imputation as forgiveness for Jesus's sake is the gift (*donum*) of the present Christ preached and so given—not to the old creature as old, but to the new creature as the act of new creation itself. Undoubtedly, Luther affirmed that "faith brings the believer into union with Christ and through that union Christ communicates not just the benefit of justification but himself. Nevertheless, it is equally clear that for Luther the Christian is justified on the basis of nothing else but Christ's imputed righteousness. He made a logical distinction between these aspects of union with Christ while not divorcing them."[32]

## CONCLUSION

The most important theological task of the Christian is decidedly pastoral: discernment. Do others need to hear God's expectations, law, an afflicting word? Or, do they need to hear a word of comfort, consolation, forgiveness, and thus gospel. The proper distinction between law and gospel Luther calls an art. Our justification is accomplished in the speaking of it: it is something that must be declared or preached to the sinner. And the sharing of this good news actually delivers the goods of forgiveness, life, and salvation. Where there is forgiveness there is also life—because our lives are given the very shape or form (*forma*) of Christ himself. *God's favor is his gift*: God's external word imparts the reality of Christ into believers, allowing them to honor God for his own sake and loving neighbors for their own sake. For Luther, it is no longer a matter of love which needs to shape the matter of our faith or "color" it as scholastic theologians put it. Instead, Christ himself is imparted through the word to our being and he shapes our lives. Christ is not only the object of our faith, but also the subject. Christ Jesus is our Lord. In this light, justification by grace alone through faith alone is not to be understood as an "existential" relationship of the self, harmonizing itself to itself, but as a distinctively eschatological word with powerful ontological overtones.[33] Christ remains an *alien resident* within us, conveying an alien righteousness. Just as God's word originally spoke and speaks creation into being so God's word of promise granted in Jesus Christ bespeaks a new creation out of the nothingness of sin and death. We have an alien righteousness and live as new beings out of the life of another: Jesus Christ, crucified and risen.

32. Clark, "*Iustitia Imputata Christi*," 292; see *LW* 27:241.
33. See Kierkegaard, *The Sickness unto Death*, 13.

While Luther felt kinship with Augustine's affirmation of grace, he acknowledged an "imperfection" in Augustine's thinking.[34] Grace is not an infusion that jumpstarts our life of holiness. Instead, by means of God's accusing law, we die. God offers no salvaging or reclaiming the old being. Through the promise, we are reborn and live from a gifted but alien righteousness. Jesus Christ—greatest sinner—is the sinner who justifies all other sinners. To hold out hope for salvaging the old being is nothing other than to "bury Christ,"[35] to make him ineffective, and to deny the cross. In preaching that delivers the goods—that actually conveys God's embrace of the sinner directly "you belong to me for Jesus's sake"—the risen Christ is active to gather his people into Christian community, enliven them with gifts, nourish and sustain their new life, and send them forth to embody the golden rule in the world. Although Luther shared with late medieval theologians a vocabulary which had developed over time, the grammar and syntax are now different. It is grace *alone* and faith *alone* which are salvific. Likewise, the semantics of justification is different. The promise is itself a word that gives what it promises instead of directing or describing either internal experience or external reality. The word of promise alters us by opening a new being, one not curved in on the self; and thereby the world itself is altered. Now the matter becomes: share this word of promise, since it truly belongs to sinners.

34. Luther, "Preface to Latin Writings," *LW* 34:337–38. See Paulson, "The Augustinian Imperfection."

35. The Apology of the Augsburg Confession, *BC* 134:81.

---

## BIBLIOGRAPHY

"The Apology of the Augsburg Confession." In *BC*.

Aquinas, Thomas, Saint. *Summa Theologica*. Translated by the Fathers of the English Dominican Province. 3 vols. New York: Benziger, 1947.

Bayer, Oswald. "Luther as an Interpreter of Holy Scripture." In *The Cambridge Companion to Martin Luther*, edited by Donald K. McKim, 73–85. Translated by Mark Mattes. Cambridge Companions to Religion. Cambridge: Cambridge University Press.

———. *Martin Luther's Theology: A Contemporary Interpretation*. Translated by Thomas Trapp. Grand Rapids: Eerdmans, 2008.

Clark, R. Scott. "*Iustitia Imputata Christi*: Alien or Proper to Luther's Doctrine of Justification." *Concordia Theological Quarterly* 70 (2006) 269–310.

Elert, Werner. *The Christian Faith: An Outline of Lutheran Dogmatics*. Translated by Martin H. Bertram and Walter R. Bouman. Columbus, OH: Lutheran Theological Seminary, 1974.

Forde, Gerhard O. "Lutheranism." In *The Blackwell Encyclopedia of Modern Christian Thought*, edited by Alister E. McGrath, 354–57. Oxford: Blackwell, 1993.

———. *Theology Is for Proclamation*. Minneapolis, Fortress: 1990.

———. *Where God Meets Man: Luther's Down-to-Earth Approach to the Gospel*. Minneapolis: Augsburg, 1972.

Harnack, Adolph von. *History of Dogma*. Vol. 7. Translated by Neil Buchanan. Boston: Little, Brown, 1903.

Holl, Karl. *What Did Luther Understand by Religion?* Edited by James Luther Adams and Walter F. Bense. Translated by Fred W. Meuser and Walter R. Wietzke. Philadelphia: Fortress, 1977.

Iwand, Hans J. *The Righteousness of Faith according to Luther*. Edited by Virgil F. Thompson. Translated by Randi H. Lundell. Eugene, OR: Wipf & Stock, 2008.

Jüngel, Eberhard. "On Becoming Truly Human: The Significance of the Reformation Distinction between Person and Works for the Self-Understanding of Modern Humanity." In *Theological Essays* 2:216–40. Translated by John Webster. Edinburgh: T. & T. Clark, 1995.

Kierkegaard, Søren. *The Sickness unto Death: A Christian Psychological Exposition for Upbuilding and Awakening*. Edited and translated by Howard V. Hong and Edna H. Hong. Kierkegaard's Writings 19. Princeton: Princeton University Press, 1980

Knaake, J. F. K. et al., editors. *Luthers Werke, Kritische Gesamtausgabe*. Vol. 40. Weimar: Böhlau, 1883ff.

Kolb, Robert. *Martin Luther: Confessor of the Faith*. Christian Theology in Context. Oxford: Oxford University Press, 2009.

Laato, Timo. "Justification: The Stumbling Block of the Finnish Luther School." *Concordia Theological Quarterly* 72 (2008) 327–46.

Lohse, Bernhard. *Martin Luther: An Introduction to His Life and Work*. Translated by Robert C. Schulz. Philadelphia: Fortress, 1986.

Luther, Martin. "Disputation against Scholastic Theology, 1517." In *LW* 31.

———. "Disputation Concerning Man, 1536." In *LW* 34.

———. "Lectures on Galatians, 1535." In *LW* 26.

———. "Preface to Latin Writings." In *LW* 34.

———. "Prefaces to the New Testament." In *LW* 35.

———. "Smalcald Articles." In *The Book of Concord: The Confessions of the Evangelical Lutheran Church*, edited by Robert Kolb and Timothy J. Wengert. Minneapolis: Fortress, 2000.

———."Small Catechism." In *BC/T*.

Mannermaa, Tuomo. *Christ Present in Faith: Luther's View of Justification*. Edited and introduced by Kirsi Stjerna. Minneapolis: Fortress, 2005.

Melanchthon, Philipp. "Augsburg Confession, 1530." In *BC*. Minneapolis: Fortress, 2000.

Paulson, Steven. "The Augustinian Imperfection: Faith, Christ, and Imputation and Its Role in the Ecumenical Discussion of Justification." In *The Gospel of Justification in Christ: Where Does the Church Stand Today?*, edited by Wayne Stumme, 104–24. Grand Rapids: Eerdmans, 2006.

Schumacher, William. *Who Do I Say That You Are? Anthropology and the Theology of Theosis in the Finnish School of Tuomo Mannermaa*. Eugene, OR: Wipf & Stock, 2010.

# 4

# Forensic Justification and the Christian Life

## *Gerhard O. Forde*

FOR AT LEAST A hundred and fifty years the doctrine of justification has been under attack from "within." Of course, it has always been under a certain amount of attack "from without," either from the world of "cultured despisers" or from Christian communions that do not find it so central to their perception of the Christian message. But it is perhaps somewhat surprising to discover that attacks from within Protestant, even Lutheran theological ranks, are hardly a novelty. Usually we are led to believe that it is only *Der Mensch von heute* who has gotten up the gumption to ask such "radical" questions. Karl Holl dates the beginning of such polemic contemporaneously with the rise of the so-called *religionsgeschichtliche Schule*. Paul de Lagarde summed up the resistance in 1873 when in opposition to Ritschl's attempt to revive the doctrine he wrote: "The doctrine of justification is not the gospel, but a Pauline invention, born out of Paul's Jewish spirit. Even in Paul it is not the only or the most profound form of solving the question of a person's relationship to guilt. Nor is it the fundamental principle of the Reformation and today in the Protestant Churches is dead. And that with perfect right. Because the doctrines of justification and atonement are mythologoumena valid only for those who seriously acknowledge the ancient church's doctrine of the Trinity, which today is true of no one."[1]

1. Quoted in Holl, "Sammlung Gemeinverstandlicher," 1.

*the human of today*

The 1963 Declaration of the Fourth Assembly of the Lutheran World Federation in Helsinki hardly marked much of an advance over de Lagarde when it pronounced that "*Der mensch von heute* no longer asks: How do I find a gracious God? He inquires more radically, more elementarily, he inquires after God *schlechthin:* where are you God?"[2] As Ernst Wolf once remarked, that kind of thing had already been said around 1910 and 1920 when there was much less knowledge of what Luther was talking of than there is today and which Karl Barth had rightly characterized as "one of the most superficial phrases of our time." Nevertheless, Wolf continues, "it remains the expression of a profound ignorance of Luther in his radicality as well as a serious miscalculation of the 'radicality' of the man of today." For "man is at all times fated to inquire after God, but the question about a God gracious to me is the only legitimate form of this question. If one inquires about God apart from the question of grace then the question comes to naught. For if the word "God" is to be meaningful and not merely a cipher for a world view it must disclose my relationship to God; it must at the same time be able to declare to me how the human being as human being is established by God."[3]

But if the doctrine of justification as such has not fared well in recent years, the doctrine of *forensic* justification has fared even less well. Here the attacks are at least as old as the doctrine itself, beginning with Osiander and continuing in various ways until the present. The ambivalence within Lutheranism in the attitude towards forensic justification has meant that seldom have Lutherans come to a clear or unified understanding of it or its significance for the Christian life.

It is not within the scope of this paper to conduct an apology for justification in general nor for forensic justification in particular. Rather, my task is to explicate as clearly as possible what forensic justification means according to the Lutheran tradition and what role it plays—or should play—in the Christian life. In doing that I shall attempt to assess its origins in Luther and to explore some of the highways and byways leading from this seemingly troublesome doctrine. The thesis of the paper is that justification as it stems from Luther and as handed on in the tradition is "forensic" in character and must retain that character if one is to remain true to the tradition (though one might perhaps quibble with the term).

2. Wilkens, *Helsinki*, 456.

3. Wolf, "Luther—Mein Herr," 99–100

Furthermore, however—and this is also part of the thesis—such "forensic" justification as one finds in Luther proposes a radical reorientation in the understanding of the Christian life which has not been appreciated by the tradition. The difficulties within the tradition, it will be maintained, have arisen because of the attempt to retain the forensic justification without the radical reorientation. The result has been confusion, if not paralysis, in attempting to relate justification to life.

## DEFINITIONS

Forensic justification is here taken to mean that justification comes to the sinner from without by the judgment of God, by his "imputation," his "reckoning." It comes from the divine "forum," the divine "tribunal." As *actus forensis,* a purely "legal" judgment made solely on the part of God and his "reckoning" in the light of Christ, it is to be distinguished from an *actus physicus,* a judgment made on the basis of or entailing some physical, moral, ontological, psychological, or otherwise empirically verifiable endowment in the creature. To my knowledge, Luther himself never used the term "forensic" as such, but of course repeatedly speaks of "imputation" as the divine act through which righteousness comes to the sinner and does on occasion speak of the divine "tribunal."[4] It was Melanchthon, I believe, who first gave the term "official" currency when he spoke of "forensic usage" in the Apology: "to justify signifies, according to forensic usage, to acquit a guilty one and declare him righteous, but on account of the righteousness of another, namely, Christ, which righteousness of another is communicated to us by faith."[5] From these beginnings, the concept developed into the *actus forensis* of the later dogmaticians. Heinrich Schmid sums up the view of the orthodox fathers thus:

> The effect of faith is justification; [1] by which is to be understood that act of God by which He removes the sentence of condemnation, to which man is exposed in consequence of his sins, releases him from his guilt, and ascribes to him the merit of Christ. Br (574): "Justification denotes that act by which the sinner, who

---

4. Elert notes, "But before the tribunal of God *(Dei Tribunal),* where He Himself is the Judge, where no judge, executioner or jailer sits, it happens that He is merciful and compassionate to sinners. Before Him no saints carry weight, but only sinners" (*WA* 34/2:140. 6). See Elert, *Structure of Lutheranism,* 105.

5. Bente, *Concordia Triglotta,* 206–7.

is responsible for guilt and liable to punishment *(reus culpae et poenae),* but who believes in Christ, is pronounced just by God the judge." [2] This act occurs at the instant in which the merit of Christ is appropriated by faith, [3] and can properly be designated a forensic or judicial act, since God in it, as if in a civil court pronounces a judgment upon man, which assigns to him an entirely different position, and entirely different rights. [4] By justification we are, therefore, by no means to understand a moral condition existing in man, or a moral change which he has experienced, but only a judgment pronounced upon man, by which his relation to God is reversed, [5] and indeed in such a manner, that a man can now consider himself one whose sins are blotted out, who is no longer responsible for them before God, who, on the other hand, appears before God as accepted and righteous, in whom God finds nothing more to punish, with whom He has no longer any occasion to be displeased.

Through this act of justification emanating from God we receive, 1. Remission of sins . . . 2. The Imputation of the Righteousness of Christ.[6]

One can sense from Schmid's summation something of the beauty and precision of the father's views, but perhaps also something of the anxiety attendant on holding such views. The view is stated boldly, but they are anxious to protect such forensic justification from any "contamination" by a "moral condition" or a "moral change" in one so justified.

## THE SYSTEMATIC PROBLEM

Whence comes the anxiety in the orthodox view? No doubt because the very term justification implies a legal or moral process. It implies a standard, a law, according to which the justice in question is to be measured. Thus the term "justification" *(iustum facere)* in its common usage can only mean to "make just" according to such a standard. Justification would have to mean, therefore, some sort of movement from the state of being unjust to the state of being just, a movement from the state of sin or guilt to the state of righteousness. The misdeed or fault could not co-exist with the righteousness. The medieval tradition had, therefore, been more consistent when it described justification as a movement from a *terminus a quo* to a *terminus ad quem* comprising (a) the infusion of grace, (b) a

---

6. Schmid, *Doctrinal Theology,* 424–25.

movement of the free will toward God in faith, (c) a movement of the free will in recoil from sin, and (d) the remission of guilt. Such movement "could be called" justification or remission of sins because every movement takes its species from its end, the *terminus ad quem*. Even though the "movement" may be instantaneous temporally, it can be understood only as a movement, a change in the moral subject from sin to righteousness, effected by the infusion of grace.[7]

The inevitable result of such thinking in terms of movement, however, has meant that the dogmatic tradition has been plagued with a problem, especially when justification is identified with remission of sins. In its simplest form it may be put thus: If justification comes at the beginning of the "movement" or process, it is a legal fiction. If, however, it comes at the end of the movement, it is superfluous. If one has already made the "movement," one is just and need not be pronounced so. Thus, one finds oneself in a position where "forensic" justification seems to be at odds with the very scheme it presupposes, and this antinomy is raised to its zenith and betrays its anxiety when it feels called upon to insist that it cannot entail any "moral" change or progress. With this notation we move on to Luther.

## LUTHER ON JUSTIFICATION AND THE CHRISTIAN LIFE (*simul iustus et peceator*)

Luther's view of justification can be understood only as a complete break with the attempt to view it as a "movement" according to a given standard or law, either natural or revealed. For Luther the divine imputation meant a shattering of all such schemes. It does not come either at the beginning or end of a "movement." Rather, it establishes an entirely new situation. The fact that righteousness comes by imputation only, thus creating faith, means that it is absolutely not a movement on our part, either with or without the aid of grace. We can be candidates for such righteousness only if we are completely sinners. That means of necessity for Luther that in place of all schemes of movement from sin to righteousness, we must put the absolute simultaneity of sin and righteousness: imputed righteousness as a divine judgment brings with it the *simul iustus et peccator* as *total* states.

---

7. Aquinas, *Summa Theologica*, 12ae, esp. Q. 113, Art. 6, in *Nature and Grace*, 11:192–93.

Thus already in his *Lectures on Romans* Luther finds no other way to understand Paul or the scriptures than in terms of the *simul*. Commenting on Romans 4:1–7, he maintains that the imputation of righteousness to Abraham and its connection with the forgiveness of sins can be understood only by propounding two theses:

(1) The saints are intrinsically always sinners, therefore they are always extrinsically justified; but the hypocrites are intrinsically always righteous, therefore they are extrinsically always sinners.

(2) God is wonderful in his saints (Ps 68:35); to him they are at the same time righteous and unrighteous. And God is wonderful in the hypocrites; they are to him at the same time unrighteous and righteous.[8]

Luther leaves no doubt throughout the entire commentary that the most vital enemy of the righteousness of God is not so much the "godless sinner" as the "righteous" who thinks in terms of law and "intrinsic" moral progress. Such theologians think *ad modum Aristotelis* akin to Aristotle's *Ethics* where sinfulness and righteousness and the extent of their actualization are based on what a person does.[9] The gaining of righteousness can then only be real to the extent that sin is expelled. For such thinking, imputation could only be a legal fiction or "a manner of speaking" due to the incompleteness of the process or "in view of its end." Against such thinking, Luther proposes a thinking *ad modum scripticurae* in which the divine imputation is the creative reality which, by the fact of the imputation, unmasks the reality and totality of sin *at the same time*. It would make no sense for God to impute righteousness if we were already either partially or wholly righteous. It would make no sense for God to forgive sin if we were not actually sinners. Thus in order that "God may be justified when he speaks and true when he judges" the "human" way of speaking and judging *ad modum Aristotelis* must be rejected. Before the divine tribunal no saints but only sinners can stand![10] For Luther, "forensic" justification means a complete break with thinking in terms of schemes and processes—and necessarily so because the divine imputation is fully as opposed to human "righteousness" as it is to unrighteousness.

---

8. Luther, "Lectures on Romans," 124–25.

9. Ibid., 28.

10. For an excellent recent treatment of this, see Grane, *Modus Loquendi*.

So, for Luther, the divine imputation makes us sinners at the same time as it declares us righteous. And Luther was insistent that these be understood as total states. But this requires a radical reorientation in thinking about the Christian life. If one persists in thinking in terms of a process, the *simul iustus et peccator* will of course turn to poison, perhaps at best a false comfort for lazy sinners. It becomes merely the word that no matter how hard we try, we have to settle for the fact that we will never completely make it because we are, after all, *simul iustus et peccator*. It becomes a counsel of last resort. But that would be to treat the *simul* as merely a rescue for the legal scheme in the face of failure—the way it has all too often been treated. Luther's insistence that the *simul* means two totalities is designed precisely to combat such thinking. The imputation of righteousness by God for the sake of Christ as a totality unmasks its opposite, namely, all the schemes and pretensions of human righteousness, sin as a totality, and in that very fact attacks it. Sin as a total state can only be fought by faith in the total imputed righteousness. Anything other than that would lead only to hypocrisy or despair:

> The *simul* is not the equilibrium of two mutually limiting partial aspects but the battleground of two mutually exclusive totalities. It is not the case that a no-longer-entire sinner and a not-yet completely righteous one can be pasted together in a psychologically conceivable mixture; it is rather that real and complete righteousness stands over against real and total sin . . . The Christian is not half-free and half-bound, but slave and free at once, not half-saint, but sinner and saint at once, not half alive, but dead and alive at once, not mixture but gaping opposition of antitheses . . .
>
> Luther goes even further: that realm of judgment in which the situation of our being as sinner is so totally depotentiated, is nothing other than the Kingdom of the last things. In the final analysis it is this and the coming Aeon that stand opposed to each other in the *simul iustus ac peccator*. The person in Christ is the person of the new age. The judgment of God which proclaims this person as established over against the opposing earthly situation, is likewise the anticipatory proclamation of the new world. The faith which receives and grasps that new status in Christ is an eschatological event; it is ever and anew the step out of this world of the visible, tangible, given reality, the world in which the *totus peccator* is the reality, into the eschaton.[11]

---

11. Joest, *Gesetz and Freiheit*, 58–59. In my opinion Joest's book is the best Luther study on this issue.

It is precisely the divine imputation as total state that reveals the totality of sin, and it is only in the faith that accepts both that the true battle of the Christian life is joined. For the battle is not merely against sin as "moral" fault, but also against sin as "spiritual" fault, as "intrinsic" righteousness and hypocrisy. Only faith in the imputed righteousness of God is truly equipped to do battle here. Thus the understanding of the Christian life undergoes radical transformation.

## LUTHER AND THE QUESTION OF "PROGRESS" IN SANCTIFICATION

What then becomes of sanctification? The *simul iustus ac peccator*, as total states, would seem to militate against any talk of "progress" in sanctification. And as Joest points out, there are indeed many utterances of Luther that would substantiate just that.[12] Sanctification is simply included in justification since it is a total state. Sanctification is simply to believe the divine imputation and with it the *totus peccator*. For where can there be more sanctification than where God is revered as the only Holy One? But God can be revered as the Holy One only where the sinner, the real sinner, stands still at the place where God enters the scene. That is the place where the sinner must realize that his or her own way is at an end. Only those who stand still, who know that they are sinners and that Christ is for them, only they give God the glory. Only they are "sanctified."

From this viewpoint, the way of the sinner in sanctification, if it is a "movement" at all, a *transitus*, is a *transitus* from nothing to all, from that which one has and is in oneself to that which one has and is in Christ. Such *transitus* can never be a completed fact this side of the grave. Nor is it a continuous line that admits of degrees of approximation toward a goal. Rather, each moment can only be at once beginning and end, start and finish. In this regard, the Christian can never presume to have reached a certain "stage" in sanctification, supposedly surpassed or left behind for good, which then forms the basis for the next "stage." The Christian who believes the divine *imputatio* is always at a new beginning. "*Proficere, hoc est semper a novo incipere.*"[13]

*This is ever to begin to make progress from the new —*

12. Ibid., 60.

13. *WA* 56:486.7ff. Quoted in Joest, *Gesetz und Freiheit*, 62.

By the same token, however, this means that the Christian never has an endless process of "sanctification" ahead that must be traversed to arrive. Whoever has the imputed righteousness may know that he or she has arrived. But such a one would know also, of course, that this is not a goal he or she has attained, but ever one that is granted anew for the sake of Christ. In such a view, the life of the Christian in *transitus* is not, as Joest says, a continuous or steady progress, but rather an "oscillation" in which beginning and end are always equally near. In attempting to "diagram" it Joest presents it thus:[14]

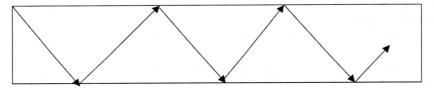

The bottom line represents the person *quoad in se* (*totus peccator*). The top line represents the person *quoad in Christo* (*totus iustus*). The zigzag line represents the *transitus*.

But this is apparently only one aspect of the picture. In many instances Luther does speak of a kind of progress, indeed, even of the Christian as one who is *partim iustus, partim peccator*.[15] He speaks of faith as beginning, but not yet the whole. Faith is not a perfect fulfillment of the law, but only the beginning of fulfillment. Indeed, what is still lacking will not be imputed for Christ's sake. Thus here the imperfection of our actual fulfillment of the law stands under the protective mantle of nonimputation. In such instances Luther speaks of faith in the imputed righteousness as the first fruits of the Spirit (*primitias spiritus*) which is not yet the whole. Such faith is the beginning because it is the beginning of the actual hatred of sin and its expulsion and the doing of good works. In faith, the law is fulfilled imputatively but thereafter is to be fulfilled expurgatively, for when the Spirit is given one begins *ex animo*, from the heart to hate all those things that offend the Spirit. Indeed, one begins to hate not only the things, but also to hate one's very self as sinner (*odium sui*) and to hope and long for the day when such will no longer be the case. Indeed, Luther

14. Ibid.

15. "Lex pro, miscue docenda est tam piis, quam impiis, quia pii partim iusti sunt, partim paccatores" (*WA* 39/1:542.5ff. Quoted in Joest, *Gesetz und Freiheit*, 65).

can say that we are to do good works in order finally to become externally righteous and that it is not enough to have sins remitted by grace but that they are to be totally abolished eventually.[16]

What have we here? Has Luther contradicted himself? Has he gone back on everything said about the imputed righteousness as necessarily bringing with it the *simul* as total states? Some would say that in the heat of later battles with antinomianism and in disappointment with the moral laziness of the Reformation movement Luther, like Melanchthon, changed his tune somewhat. But the puzzling thing is that statements of this sort are present from the very beginning precisely in those passages where Luther has just propounded the *simul*! So others, looking at passages of that sort in the *Lectures on Romans*, opine that they are instances where he has not yet rid himself of remnants of medieval Augustinian *humilitas* piety! Without entering into the complexities of the debate spawned by such opinions, it would seem safer to assume that because such material appears both early and late it belongs to the abiding substance of Luther's theology.

But how is one to interpret it? Does it mean that a notion of progress actually displaces all that has been said about "forensic" or imputed righteousness, the *simul*, and the *semper incipere*? This question is of course vital, so perhaps we should look more closely at a passage where such talk occurs precisely in the context of talk about the *simul*. Here we can do no better than to return to the *Lectures ore Romans* itself and the discussion on Romans 4:1–7 where the *simul* was set forth. After setting forth the theses on the *simul* referred to above, Luther moves immediately to a discussion about concupiscence. He castigates the scholastic theologians for thinking *ad modem Aristotelis* that concupiscence is actually removed by something they call "grace." He says that he was entirely led astray by this "because I did not know that though forgiveness is indeed real, sin is not taken away except in hope, i.e., that it is in the process of being taken away by the gift of grace which starts this removal, so that it is only not reckoned as sin." And he goes on to say a bit later:

> Yet this concupiscence is always in us; therefore, the love of God is never in us, except in so far as grace has given us a beginning of it. We have the love of God only in so far as the rest of concupiscence,

16. "Deinde operam dare debemus, ut etiam externe iusti sumus . . . Peccatum per graham remissum non sans est . . . Uellemus igitur non soium peccatum remitti, sed totem aboleri" (*WA* 40/2:351.27ff. Quoted in Joest, *Gesetz und Freiheit*, 69).

which still must be cured and by virtue of which we do not yet "love God with our whole heart" (Luke 10:27), is by mercy not reckoned as sin. We shall love God only at the end, when it will all be taken away and the perfect love of God will be given to those who believe and who with perseverance always yearn for it and seek it.[17]

What Luther seems to be saying is that thinking *ad modem Aristotelis* leads to an entirely false notion of human sanctification and progress. Then the notion of progress that it presupposes always remains intact. The only argument consequently can be about what one can accomplish according to such a scheme either with or without something called "infused grace." When, in order to exalt the supposed power of such "grace," it is asserted that concupiscence is actually taken away, it only succeeds in reaching the height of abstraction and nonsense. "Grace" is more or less a theological abstraction added to make the scheme "Christian." "Grace" becomes what Robert Jenson at one time aptly dubbed "the anti-Pelagian codicil" to the already existing scheme of what human powers are in fact supposed to accomplish.[18] But that is all the pious sublimation of natural desire, the "sanctified" self-centeredness that Luther knew all too well did not lead to actual love of God with the whole heart, but only to focus on the self and its concerns. It leads only to hypocrisy or despair. Faith born of the imputation of total righteousness, however, will see the truth of the human condition, the reality and totality of human sin; it will see that concupiscence indeed remains and that it is sin, but that God nevertheless does business with sinners. Such faith will see the fantastic magnitude of the divine act and actually begin, at least, to love God from the heart, to hate sin, and to hope for that righteousness which it knows full well it can never attain by any human powers either with or without what the Scholastics called "grace." Such faith makes a "beginning" precisely by believing the imputation of God which goes so contrary to all empirical evidence, and will cry to God "out of the depths," "wretched man that I am, who will deliver me," and actually "hunger and thirst after righteousness."

One must note carefully that when Luther speaks in this vein he is talking about actual affections: love, hope, and hatred of sin and "the body of death," not about theological abstractions. The radical nature of the divine imputation which sets the *totus iustus* against the *totus peccator*

17. Luther, *Lectures on Romans,* 128–29.
18. Gritsch and Jenson, *Lutheranism,* 39ff.

kindles the first beginnings of actual hope and love for God and his righteousness whereas before there had been only hypocrisy or despair. There is, I think, for Luther no contradiction between the *simul* and the *partim* once the divine imputation has blasted all thinking *ad modem Aristotelis* "out of the saddle."

But what sort of "progress" is here envisaged? Could it mean, perhaps, that the *transitus* in the life of the Christian is no longer simply a repeated "oscillation" between two extremes, and that under the impulse of the imputed righteousness one actually does begin to "improve" so that "nonimputation" covers what one has yet to accomplish? Could it mean perhaps that one does not have constantly to return to "point zero," and the *semper incipere*? Could the admonition, "become what you already are," find here its rightful home? Could one say that there is a certain "growth" of the sort where one would have a set of accomplishments behind one that provide a basis for the next step? Does one attain to a certain approximation of the goal?

Much as such a scheme might suggest itself by the language Luther uses, it does not apparently do justice to the full complexity of his thought. For such a scheme would suggest that progressive sanctification would mean progressive emancipation from the divine imputation. The more one progresses, the less grace one would need. *Iustitia imputativa* would be merely the starting point that one leaves progressively behind until it recedes into the background as an abstraction, perhaps even as a "legal fiction" compared to the "real" progress according to the scheme.

This, of course, cannot be. It would be a serious mistaking of Luther's intention that would be in danger of losing the whole thing. For Luther, the *iustitia imputativa* is not a mere beginning point that can be allowed to recede into the background. It is the perpetual fountain, the constant power of whatever *iustitia formalis* we may acquire. To look upon it as a stage that could be left behind or as something that we gradually would need less would be to deny it altogether. What this entails is that we cannot understand what Luther means by progress in "sanctification" unless all ordinary human perceptions of progress are completely reversed, stood on their head so to speak. The progress Luther has in mind is not our movement towards the goal, but the goal's movement in upon us. This has already been indicated in the idea that imputed righteousness is eschatological in character, and that a battle is joined in which the *totus iustus* moves against the *totus peccator*. The "progress" is therefore the coming of the kingdom of God among us. That is why for Luther "complete" sanctification is not the goal, but the *source* of all good works. *The way is not from the partial to the whole, but always from the whole to the partial.* "Good works do not make a man good, but a good man does good works." The *iustitia imputativa* is thus not a "legal fiction" without real dynamic, but a power, indeed, the "power of God unto salvation" that attacks sin as a total state and will eventually reduce it to nothing. It is always as a whole that it attacks its opposite in the form of both despair and hypocrisy. Good works are not "building blocks" in the "progress" of the Christian, they are fruits of the whole, the "good tree."

The "expulsion" of sin for Luther is thus quite the opposite of a morally conceivable process of sanctification. In such a "process" the person remains more or less constant and only the "properties" are changed. One supposedly "puts off sin" as Luther sarcastically remarks as though one were peeling paint from a wall or taking heat from water.[19] The sanctification that comes from and is identical with the *iustitia imputativa* does not offer a new "paint job." It does not, as Luther put it, merely "take sin away" and leave the "moral" person intact. Rather, it takes the person, that is, the heart, mind, soul, affections, away from sin. There is a death and a new life involved that proceeds according to no moral scheme. "Human righteousness . . . seeks first of all to remove and to change the sins and to keep man intact; this is why it is not righteousness but hypocrisy. Hence as long as there is life in man and as long as he is not taken by renewing grace to be changed, no efforts of his can prevent him from being subject to sin and the law."[20]

Any view of sanctification as a progress in "partialities," a changing of "properties," a mere "removing of sins," would be nothing but hypocrisy. Sanctification comes always from the whole, the penetration of the divine imputation into time, and thus involves the death of the old. The "beginning" is the "first fruits" of the resurrection.[21]

> Where he [Luther] is concerned to describe sanctification, he very often grasps at formulations that stand the natural-rational picture exactly on its head. For our question the following is the result: the progress of the sanctified Christian life for Luther is unconditionally a procedure sui generis. It can be compared with no immanent

19. Luther, *Lectures on Romans*, 194.
20. Ibid.
21. Cf. Joest, *Gesetz und Freiheit*, 95.

moral movement, with no continuous psychological development in the realm of the identity of the ethical subject with itself.
Furthermore: wherever that progress takes place—whether in the
beginning or farther on—it always happens as a whole. If it takes
place extensively only in little steps, or in isolated actions against
particular sins, intensively the whole is always there, the total crisis, the entire transformation of the person, death and becoming
new is wholly present . . . The expulsion of sin—which is really an
expulsion of the person from sin—is therefore not a series of partial moments which follow upon and expand the decisive turning
or even prepare for it, but is the full turning itself which is always
to be actualized anew.[22]

So, for Luther, the idea of progress must be stood on its head. The
movement Luther speaks of is always a reversal of this-worldly conceptions. Sanctification comes from the whole and is always grasped as such.
It comes from the *imputatio* which is the breaking in of the eschaton in
our time. "Just as the resurrection of Christ and with it the coming of
the last things is not to be empirically measured, so also the progress in
the life of the Christian cannot be psychologically measured. But just
as certainly as the resurrection of Jesus Christ has really happened, and
with it the coming of the Kingdom of God is real, so also is the progress
a real one."[23]

Joest suggests that if one were to attempt to diagram such "progress" (which he realizes is difficult and questionable) it would have to
look like this:[24]

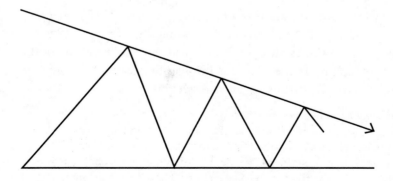

22. Ibid., 93.
23. Ibid., 98.
24. Ibid.

The way does not lead from below, the *totus peccator* line, upwards. Rather, the upper line symbolizing the totality of the righteousness imputed to faith descends toward the lower reality. The difference and opposition between the *totus peccator* and the *totus iustus* is not increasingly overcome from below, but rather from above, from the totality of grace. But the "movement" does lead and strive towards fulfillment when by the power of the coming reality the *totus peccator* shall finally die and by grace alone be turned completely to love the God who gave it. Then we shall love as we are loved.

## SOME REFLECTIONS ON THE SUBSEQUENT FATE OF LUTHER'S VIEWS

It seems virtually indisputable now that Luther's radical reversal was either not very well understood or else largely rejected by subsequent generations. The imputed righteousness indeed was accepted and became the talisman of the movement bearing his name in the form of "forensic" justification, but the radical reversal was not. We need not tarry here to ask where or why. Were his views too impractical for the young movement? Too subtle? Too radical to be grasped and made workable? Perhaps. At any rate, it seems that what happened largely was that Luther's followers for the most part did what he said could not be done: they attempted to mix the *iustitia imputativa* with thinking *ad modem Aristotelis*. What resulted, as Hans J. Iwand points out, was a theology that always carries within itself a profound inner contradiction.[25] Such a situation cannot, of course, produce very salutary results. Either the one or the other— the *iustitia imputativa* or the thinking *ad modum Aristotelis* will have to give way. History has, of course, largely relieved us of the necessity of speculation as to which.

It seems quite consequent, therefore, that virtually the first serious internal dispute should be about the place of law in the "system." Agricola, rightly sensing the impossibility of combining Luther's views with the place accorded to law by Melanchthon, tried to solve the problem by positing a temporal end to law. But this was a failure to grasp the eschatological nature of the *imputatio* and thus he also earned Luther's wrath. But the general result of such battles seems only to have been the

25. Iwand, "Um den Rechten Glauben," 17ff.

solidification of the conception of human progress according to law as the "systematic" backbone of the "orthodox" scheme.

Once that occurs, however, the *iustitia imputativa* must be antiseptically removed from all contamination by the "progress" in sanctification. It must become absolutely "forensic." Justification and sanctification must be stringently separated while at the same time one tries to insist that the latter must (may? will?) necessarily follow the former. But it becomes difficult to say exactly why. One lands willy-nilly back in the same systematic problem noted at the outset. Either the forensic justification makes the process unnecessary, or the process makes the justification a "legal fiction," a mere "anti-Pelagian codicil." So it is not strange that dispute should break out over whether "good works" were "necessary" or even "injurious" to salvation. When the eschatological reversal in Luther's views is forestalled by thinking in terms of immanent moral progress, justification threatens to become mere justification of the status quo so one must come down hard on the "necessity" of good works. But then the dynamic is lost. The "spontaneity," the *hilaritas* of faith, is nipped in the bud.

One lonely soul, Osiander, tried to remedy matters by attacking forensic justification itself. But the only tools he could come up with to do that were apparently carry-overs from mysticism: the indwelling of the divinity of Christ in the soul. He too failed to locate the neuralgic point and threatened only to make matters worse. Thus forensic justification became entrenched as the "objective" basis for faith, *because of* the merits of Christ, to be "*subjectively*" *appropriated*.

The increasing isolation of forensic justification as an "objective" fact could only mean that Lutheran divines were faced with the question of mediation all over again. Some way would have to be found to make the subjective appropriation of the objective fact conceivable as an *ordo*. One would have to provide, so to speak, a theological "shuttle service" between the objective and the subjective. The propter *Christum et per fidem* became a succession, a *reihenfolge* with the *propter Christum* the objective fact and the *per fidem* the subjective appropriation. As Wilhelm Dantine put it,

> the merit of Christ waits before the closed door of the heart like an immovable object, even though it carries in it the entire salvation of mankind. Only some action from within the heart can open the door and permit the salvation treasure to enter the existence of man. Even if one seriously takes into account the fact that

faith was correctly evaluated as a gift of the Holy Spirit, did it not nevertheless lead to an understanding of faith as an independent means, and, finally, as the merit of pious inwardness? . . . One can also diminish the merit of Christ by appealing to the Holy Spirit, especially if one reduces this merit to a dead, heavenly "thing" no longer capable of action as Lutheran Orthodoxy has already done . . . This so-called objective fact of salvation thus really forms only something like a common foundation. It represents a basis on which the so-called subjective fact is only then able to begin the really decisive action. It almost seems as if Cod had to be reconciled anew through faith.[26]

The split between the subjective and the objective could only mean that the theologians would have to busy themselves with the question of "order," issuing finally in the so-called *ordo salutis*. The first steps were taken already by Melanchthon with the *notitia, assensus, fiducia* scheme where one moves from knowledge of the objective fact, through assent and finally to trust.[27] But such beginnings seem virtually to demand further refinement. How does "assent" and "trust" come about? How is it conceivable as an *ordo*? Apparently under the impulse of such questions the later dogmaticians (Calovius and following) developed the idea of the *ordo salutis* involving such things as the call (*vocatio*), illumination, conversion and regeneration, mystical union and renovation. In doing this, according to Schmid, they "seek to collect under one general topic, all that is to be said concerning what God or more accurately the Holy Ghost, does, in order to induce fallen man to accept of salvation through Christ, and what takes place in order to bring about the designed change in man."[28]

Even Schmid, whose love for the orthodox fathers is evident, is constrained to remark that "the introduction of an independent development of these conceptions led to an arrangement of the entire doctrine which we cannot call a happy one."[29] Among other things, it led to the fact that a fundamental distinction was made in Dogmatics between "the means of salvation on the part of God" (Word and sacraments) and "the means of salvation on the part of man" (faith and good works), which means, again

---

26. Dantine, *Justification of the Ungodly*, 32–33.

27. Pelikan, "Origins," 94–104.

28. Schmid, *Doctrinal Theology*, 407.

29. Ibid., 408.

in Schmid's words, that "we meet with especially this difficulty, that the full discussion is delayed so long."[30]

The attempt analytically to describe an *ordo salutis* was, of course, a tricky task, and the dogmaticians could not at all agree on the proper "order." But the net result of the endeavor seems only to have been that forensic justification eventually tended to get lost in the dogmatic woods. As Dantine puts it:

> its limitation to the territory of applied grace took increasing effect . . . and perhaps one will even have to conclude that here the old truth has again proved itself, according to which the greatest radiance is always followed by the deepest misery . . .
>
> A contributing factor to this decline was, without a doubt, the particular development of the *ordo salutis* . . . into the scheme of which justification was squeezed as into a bed of Procrustes, there to lose its essential center and strength . . . The Spirit, in Himself free and sovereign, was transformed into a front rank man at attention, as it were, and the only consolation about this iron chain of interlinked divine operations was now that almost every dogmatician had a different notion of which order or march the living God should follow. At least a little freedom was left for the Holy Ghost, albeit only through the disunity of the dogmaticians! Later, a more and more penetrating interest in the proceedings and occurrences in the human realm was all that was needed to make a chain of religious occurrences in the human soul out of acts of a Spirit squeezed into a human scheme. Finally the whole order of salvation was transformed into a human process of development.[31]

For the orthodox fathers the problem of discerning the *ordo* was of course a purely analytic task, and such *ordo* was to be conceived as "instantaneous" and not as a temporal succession. But after all, Aquinas had said the same about his doctrine of justification, so one is once again back at the starting point. Once the move was made the way was open to the temporalization and indeed psychologization of the *ordo*. And it is difficult to escape the judgment that this is what indeed happened in at least some forms of Pietism. A "dead" orthodoxy could be vitalized only in the same way, an "arid" scholasticism could be appropriated (by mysticism, for instance): turn it into a "way" with a certain series of "steps" in the religious "progress" of the individual "subject."

30. Ibid.
31. Dantine, *Justification of the Ungodly*, 24–25.

From a reading of the history of modern Protestant theology, it is apparent that therewith the fate of forensic justification as an "objective" fact is more or less sealed. A temporalized or psychologized *ordo salutis is* all too easily either rationalized as a "pure practical religion" shorn of all "objective" and "theoretical" elements (Kant), or magnified into a religion of "pious feeling" (Schleiermacher), or elongated in a *Heilsgeschichte* (von Hofmann) and finally universalized into a *Geistesgeschichte* (Hegel). I realize that such judgment is somewhat facile and unsubstantiated, but it cannot be gainsaid that such was the course Protestant theology actually took. In all of that, forensic justification could not but get lost.

## SOME CONCLUSIONS AND RUMINATIONS

Justification, if it is to mean anything at all according to the Lutheran tradition, must be forensic in character. Lutheran orthodoxy and indeed Pietism is not to be faulted for maintaining that. That was their finest moment. The fact that it survived in much of the "churchly" tradition in spite of the "academic" tradition has been the sole redeeming feature of the former tradition. The problem is not with forensic justification as such. The problem arises because the tradition has not always fully grasped the radical reversal that Luther himself saw in imputed righteousness, and this led to an increasing isolation of forensic justification from the nature of the Christian life. The result has been either a conception of the Christian life that is at odds with its theology or a theology at odds with the actual course of the Christian life—a highly "unstable" situation, to say the least. If today we are going to "*rescue*" the significance of forensic justification for the Christian life, this can be done only by recapturing the radical reversal Luther saw as entailed in that explosive doctrine. This can be done only if we can proclaim and teach the radical "down-to-earth" nature of the Christian life—a life lived under the power of the "imputed righteousness of Christ" as an eschatological reality breaking into our time, exposing and attacking the totality of sin.

No doubt this will require some adjustment in our thinking about the relationship of law to the Christian life. I have not said much about that and cannot enter into a full discussion so late in this paper. But a few remarks can be ventured. There is no doubt that imputed righteousness bears a dialectical relationship to law. Precisely because imputed righteousness is an absolute gift which is the "end" and *telos* of the law, it establishes the absolute demand of the law as its counterpart. When one settles for less than the imputed righteousness as a total gift, as an eschatological reality, or fails to treat that as the basis for all true sanctification, one will quite likely also make accommodations in the understanding of law. This is the true root of all forms of antinomianism, either overt or covert. The law will have to be adapted to fit one's more or less paltry ideas of human "progress" and possibility.

For Luther, it was precisely the radical doctrine of justification that made possible and established the radical view of the law and the insistence that the law must and will remain "on account of sin" until the final end of the sinner and the appearance of the new being. This was the reason for his objection to Agricola's antinomianism. Antinomianism in one form or another wants to "solve" the problem of law by removing or "changing" it. Luther's insistence was that the law cannot be removed or changed by any mere theoretical arrangement. Rather, the sinner must be changed, and that "change" is from death to life by the grace of God. The objection to a so-called "third use" of the law would be of the same sort. There are of course many problems—semantic and otherwise—surrounding that concept, and I do not wish to go into them here. But the difficulty I see in the light of this paper is that a "third use" of the law proposes an alteration in the doctrine of law to correspond with the view of the Christian life as "change" and immanent moral progress. Nor, if one is seriously to maintain the imputed righteousness as the eschatological power of the new life out of death, can one speak of a "temporal" change in which the Christian "uses" the law in a "third" way. For Luther the sinner must die and be made new; the law is not changed. There can be no accommodations or alterations until the law is fulfilled. The sinner as *totus peccator* is thus attacked by law unto death until the new being arises who actually loves that law, that will of God. Luther thus knows of only two possibilities vis-à-vis law as an expression of the will of God. It is either an "enemy" or a friend but never a more or less "neutral" guide. Which is to say that the will of God for us is either law in the full sense of that word or gospel in the full sense of that word but never a "third" something which is neither.[32]

---

32. Cf. Joest, *Gesetz und Freiheit*, 190ff. Those biblical exegetes who believe themselves to be doing the Old Testament a favor by making its view of law something akin to the "third use" would, I think, from Luther's point of view, be courting a covert antinomianism. Thinking to construct an apology for the Old Testament and the law they

The same interpretation would apply to the New Testament parenesis. It can hardly be maintained that the exhortations of the New Testament taken "*ad literam*" represent any degree of attenuation of the will of God or his "law." If anything, the "stakes" are raised precisely because of the gospel. We are even exhorted to arise from the dead! How can we do that? It cannot therefore be a happy development from a "Lutheran" perspective when the attempt is made to subsume both the "you must, in order that . . ." and the "you may, because . . ." as subspecies under the genus "law."[33] The exhortations are either bad news or good news between which our actual life as *simul iustus et peccator* "resonates" until that day when Christ shall be "all in all," but not something in between.

To be true to a view of the Christian life rooted in the forensic justification of God one must then arrive at a different understanding of the relationship between law and the Christian life. One cannot view the Christian life *ad modem Aristotelis* as an ascent into the rarified air of what the world calls "the spiritual." Rather, it must be viewed as a descent, an incarnation, into the world in service and love. Luther tried to do this with his formula *conscientia in evangelio, caro in lege*. This corresponds exactly to the Christian life as *simul iustus et peccator*. The "conscience" is ruled and captivated by the gospel, the imputed righteousness breaking in from God's eschatological judgment. The "flesh," the empirical life I live in this age, remains however, *in lege*. And that in a double sense. Both in the sense that the law attacks "the flesh" as inimical to the will of God, and also in the sense that under the impulse of the spontaneity and joy fostered by the gospel in the conscience, the empirical life I live in this age is to become the actual "incarnation," the fulfillment of the will of God. Because of the gospel in the conscience, the absolute gift of the imputed righteousness and sanctification coming from God's eschatological "destiny," the Christian is free so that the true battle can be joined "in the flesh." The "new being" in Christ is not, for Luther, a "mystical theologoumenon" without substance, but is to be incarnated in "down-to-earth" fashion in the concrete *vocatio* of the Christian. In this battle, the law of God can be

---

succeed only in robbing it of its majesty and power, its "office." Here also I believe, lies the key to Luther's view of the Old Testament. For him there was nothing finally pejorative in identifying the Old Testament "properly speaking" with majestic, indeed, terrifying "law." Only thus could it gain a status and "office" worthy of and pointing to its counterpart in the New.

33. Ibid., 200.

seen ultimately not as an enemy or as a mere emasculated "guide," but as a true and loved friend. For one should make no mistake about it. The law of God is to be and will be fulfilled. Not, however, by our powers, not by an immanent natural human moral progress, but by the power of the imputed, yes, the forensic righteousness of God.

---

## BIBLIOGRAPHY

Aquinas, Thomas, Saint. *Summa Theologica*. Translated by the Fathers of the English Dominican Province. 3 vols. New York: Benziger, 1947.

Bente, F., editor. *Concordia Triglotta*. St. Louis: Concordia, 1921

Dantine, Wilhelm. *Justification of the Ungodly*. Translated by Eric W. Gritsch and Ruth C, Gritsch. St. Louis: Concordia, 1969.

Elert, Werner. *The Structure of Lutheranism*. Translated by Walter A. Hansen. St. Louis: Concordia, 1962.

Grane, Leif. *Modus loquendi theologicus. Luthers Kampf um die Erneuerung der Theologie (1515–1518)*. Edited by Eberhard Grötzinger. Acta Theolgoica Danica 12. Leiden: Brill, 1975.

Gritsch, Eric W., and Robert W. Jenson. *Lutheranism: The Theological Movement and Its Confessional Writings*. Philadelphia: Fortress, 1976.

Holl, Karl. *Rechtfertigungslehre im Licht der Geschichte des Protestantismus*. 2nd ed. Sammlung Gemeinverständlicher Vorträge und Schriften aus dem Gebeit der Theologie und Religionsgeschichte 45. Tübingen: Mohr/Siebeck, 1922.

Iwand, Hans J. *Um den rechten Glauben: Gesammelte Aufsätze*. Edited by Karl Gerhard Steck. Theologische Bücherei 9. Munich: Kaiser, 1959.

Joest, Wilfried. *Gesetz und Freiheit*. 2nd ed. Göttingen: Vandenhoeck and Ruprecht, 1956.

Knaake, J. F. K. et al., editors. *Luthers Werke, Kritische Gesamtausgabe*. Vol. 34. Weimar: Böhlau, 1883ff.

———. *Luthers Werke, Kritische Gesamtausgabe*. Vol. 39. Weimar: Böhlau, 1883ff.

———. *Luthers Werke, Kritische Gesamtausgabe*. Vol. 40. Weimar: Böhlau, 1883ff.

———. *Luthers Werke, Kritische Gesamtausgabe*. Vol. 56. Weimar: Böhlau, 1883ff.

Luther, Martin. *Lectures on Romans*. Edited and translated by Wilhelm Pauck. Library of Christian Classics 15. Philadelphia: Westminster, 1961.

Pelikan, Jaroslav. "The Origins of the Subject-Object Antithesis in Lutheran Theology." *Concordia Theological Monthly* 21(1950) 94–104.

Schmid, Heinrich. *The Doctrinal Theology of the Evangelical Lutheran Church*. Translated by Charles Hay and Henry Jacobs. 3rd ed. rev. Minneapolis: Augsburg, 1961.

Wilkens, Erwin, editor. *Helsinki 1963*. Berlin: Lutherisches, 1964.

Wolf, Ernst, "Luther—Mein Herr." In *Motive des Glaubens*, edited by Johannes Lehmann, 98–110. Stundenbucher 93. Hamburg: Furche, 1968.

# 5

# Living out of Justification

*Wilfried Härle*

[This is the conclusion of a much longer German essay; its first
sections are here summarized by Mark C. Mattes.]

Current misunderstandings about the doctrine of justification,
including the *Joint Declaration on the Doctrine of Justification*,
can be traced to the failure of the 1963 General Assembly of the
Lutheran World Federation in Helsinki. The Helsinki assembly assumed that for contemporaries, atheistic doubts were far more
pervasive than anxious consciences. The Helsinki assembly failed
in its task to articulate the doctrine's relevance, particularly given
the fact that the doctrine of justification is grounded in the New
Testament and thus retains its authoritative status for us.

Even after an apparent formal ecumenical consensus (the
Joint Declaration), the Roman Catholic Church does not acknowledge justification as the criterion by which to measure all other
doctrines; nor does it affirm the sola fide, works as the fruit of
faith, and the *simul iustus et peccator*, which are all so central
for Protestants. Roman Catholic theologians tend to see justification as one of many metaphors for salvation and hold that the
Lutheran view gives an unwarranted centrality, singularity, and
focus to the metaphor of justification.

Justification is usually taken to be a forensic concept whose
primary metaphorical structure is from the court of law and the
language of guilt and punishment, with God then viewed as a

legislator and judge. This perspective leads to problems. First, the view of God implied in this doctrine seems unacceptable: it burdens and darkens the image of God for many people. Second, its view of humans as all equally guilty is too radical—the concept of guilt is applied far too loosely. Does the doctrine of justification, insofar as it sees Christ as our substitute, judge an innocent man (Jesus) to be guilty, and guilty people to be innocent? Is God then a liar? Third, it raises questions about faith and works. If faith is reckoned to the human, is not faith then a work—in contrast to the Protestant view of faith? However, if it is reckoned to God, then why would faith be called for from the human? In this regard, does not the Protestant view of justification lend itself to a quietism, in which we tend to settle with evil, rather than change the world for the better?

These problems are resolved when justification is expanded beyond a legal metaphor to one of social ordering, when it is understood from its scriptural origin, especially as found in the Old Testament. "Justification" has to do less with righteousness as a quality, and more with right relationships, less with being righteous and more with being right with God and neighbor. Being too bound to the legal metaphor, the Reformation did not unleash the theological, spiritual, and social power of the doctrine of justification.

Why should justification be favored as the chief metaphor over election, vocation, rebirth, or sanctification, when many biblical passages seem to assert or assume the equality of all these metaphors? The uniqueness of this doctrine, by contrast, will be understood only when it is seen as a comprehensive self-interpretation of the Christian faith. For both Paul and Luther, creation out of nothing, the justification of sinners, and the resurrection of the dead are embraced together as structurally identical and reciprocal.

There are three primary ways that the doctrine of justification has been articulated for contemporary men and women: God's love for us despite our sin; acceptance as one is, even acceptance of one's acceptance; and one's worth as separate from one's work.

In the modern secular world, the tendency is thus to translate the concept of justification into self-justification, and thus to absent God from human reflection. This is in stark contrast to the Pauline contention that it is God who justifies and that it is the sinner who is justified. This current problem is partly due to Luther's retention of the Latin juridical term *iustitia* to explain the biblical notions of *sedaqah* and *dikaiosune*. The Latin term is bound to the notion of rights, while the biblical terms signify a comprehensive construction of relationships that entail the social and the cosmic, the synchronic and the diachronic, and the order of social conduct. The Latin concept of *iustitia* is unable to accommodate the Bible's conviction that God stands in favor of sinners, the lost, and even the enemies of God. If this biblical perspective is to be reclaimed, then beyond these legal notions of "justification" and "justice" we must realize that the Bible affirms a relational nexus or community, that error and guilt constrict this community, that God still renews and is loyal to this community, and that the human is made free by relying on this divine loyalty.

The notion of justification is tied to the way in which the Christian faith understands reality. This view of reality is tied to the gospel as the promise of God's nearness, which is unconditional, noncoercive, and effectual as reordering us to God and fellow creatures. From the perspective of the gospel, we can understand existence with the keyword "givenness" (Gegebensein). Givenness entails that our existence is given but also that we must relate to others who likewise exist as a given. This givenness entails a necessary freedom; although we can choose how to relate to our givenness, we cannot choose whether to relate to it. The relationships that constitute human existence pose dangers. God's goal for humans is that relationships be rectified in the face of such dangers. "Being" itself then is relational: this is the ontology appropriate to the doctrine of justification.

The standards of responsibility that pertain to a relational personhood include fulfillment of duties (heteronomy), subjective maxims (autonomy), or fundamental orientations to life (theonomy). In all three perspectives, existence can be seen as encompassing a forum in which one is accountable as one is related to the environment and oneself. Theonomy grounds freedom, in that it limits the claims of heteronomy and autonomy. It is also the grounding of responsibility by specifying the demand within givenness to "take care of" existence. To acknowledge that givenness includes the demand that one relate to oneself as a fundamental life-orientation means that justification, by defini-tion, rules out quietism. Humans, indeed all creatures, are deter-mined for participation in God's lordship. This special worth of humans, however, also entails the possibility of their misery, since humans can ignore, despise, or misuse this possibility. One can reject this divine goal or one can see it as one's own achievement. In the latter path, one attributes such achievement as a claim over against God. Faith, by contrast, indicates a comprehensive trust in the givenness of existence, which includes action in light of the creature's acknowledging God's will for it. Faith implies works (for others and as set by God), but works do not imply faith.

## LIVING OUT OF JUSTIFICATION

BECAUSE THE DOCTRINE OF justification brings into view human ex-istence and all of creation in relationship to its origin, the following statements apply to every aspect of human and creaturely existence. First, where the gospel awakens faith, a new self-understanding arises out of the knowledge of the givenness of one's own existence by God. Second, where the gospel awakens faith, new relationships between humans arise out of the knowledge of the givenness of all human existence by God. Further, where the gospel awakens faith, new societal structures and orders also arise, along with this new self-understanding and interpersonal relation-ships, out of the knowledge of the givenness of all creaturely existence, both past and future.

This threefold meaning of the doctrine of justification for the struc-ture of human relationships can be amplified, although here only briefly.

## RELATING TO ONESELF

As in Paul Tillich's formulation, one can say that the word "justification" spoken in faith implies that a human accepts oneself, as accepted. This affirmation, however, stems not from a self-satisfied self-analysis and ver-dict. Rather, it happens contrafactually, in that it takes into account the ugly aspects of human existence. What is disappointing or unlovable is not suppressed or excused, but allowed to stand. Despite this, justification allows one to accept oneself. This is possible only on the basis of the fun-damental distinction between person and work, which likewise constitute an inseparable unity. This can be described relatively easily in formulas, but upon more rigorous reflection it leads to significant difficulties in theory as well as in practice. Its core lies in this: there is no personhood that is not in some sense determined or even obliged for relationships and therefore to being a "work."

But precisely this extremely narrow and indissoluble connection between person and work refers to a necessary differentiation: this is an irreversible, thus an asymmetrical, relationship. Personhood constitutes the necessity of works, but works do not constitute personhood; rather, they only actualize it. Of course, the person always exists only in the actualization that comes through one's works. In this sense, the doctrine of justification results in three possibilities for the self-understanding and self-relating of the human, which at the same time have the character of tasks and challenges.

First, whoever lives out of justification can and should perceive and accept oneself in one's life story, individual character, and actual experience of self, positively and negatively. However, this possibility and demand is only understood when it silences the praise of oneself in the case of success, and the critique of oneself in the case of defeats. The self-relating of the "justified" human being includes a readiness to accept one's entire life-story, including its "pre-Christian" parts, and the entire spectrum of one's character, including its "unchristian" parts, in the knowledge of the givenness of one's own existence.

Second, whoever lives out of justification can and should perceive and accept oneself according to one's definition. This possibility and demand is only understood when it relates to the definition of all humans as in the image of God as well as the specific definition of one's individual being, with all its possibilities and limitations. Therefore, to the self-relating of the "justified" human belongs also the readiness to take the work upon oneself, which finally consists in nothing other than letting God work upon one.

Third, whoever lives out of justification can and should perceive and accept oneself in the knowledge of the continuing danger of one's self-relationship. Where the message of justification awakens and finds faith, this relationship is made right. But faith itself is threatened and attacked by doubt, error, weakness, mistrust and more; therefore the possibility remains that one's self-relationship will be disturbed. This possibility is first understood when one acknowledges that it also affects the entire structure of relationships, including the relationship to God and the environment in equal degree. The drama of this disturbance in the self-relationship consists in that it encounters the center of human perceiving and relating exactly at the point where it cuts the human off from the truth and thus makes one unable to overlook one's inability to straighten oneself out. Knowledge of this continuing danger in the center of one's person is only bearable by remembering the givenness of the saving definition of one's existence.

## RELATING TO OTHERS

Where the message of justification finds faith, human relationships (and with all other fellow creatures) grow out of the relationship to God in a new, saving perspective. Everything that is valid for one justified human being is equally valid for every other human being. In this perspective there is a fundamental equality among humans that divinely binds them together, so that a "love of God" that excludes a love for one's fellow humans becomes a contradiction (1 John 4:20–21). At the same time, the connection between the love of God and the love of neighbor is still underdefined if it is understood as a merely logical relation. This connection is understood properly when the being of God as such is understood as love (as in 1 John 4:8, 16). It is thus impossible that there could arise a relationship of competition between the love of God and the love of neighbor.

Such a loose relationship between the love of God and the love of neighbor is especially unsuitable because a "love" which is established or done because it is commanded would not be love at all. On this basis, it is understandable that Luther consistently indicated that the connection between faith and love is not a connection of "should," but a connection of "being," as seen especially in the image of a tree and its fruits.

All this shows that when it comes to justification, the human being is defined for one's fellow humans as a matter of joy and pleasure, not an obligation, burden, or annoyance. But just as the negative and unlovable could not be left aside or trivialized in the self-relation of the "justified" human, so too can the negative not be ignored in relationship to one's fellow humans. Here also this possibility and demand can only be perceived and accepted, as indicated by the difference sketched out above between person and work. Here it becomes clear not only that a yes to a person in certain situations can be united with a no to their works, but also that such a no can be a necessary consequence of the "yes" to the person. The closer the relationship of the two people, the clearer this can be.

The difference of degrees and forms of intensity is not a barrier or pragmatic concession regarding human interrelationships in the context of justification, but an integral element of it. That the biblical tradition and with it the entire Christian heritage speaks of love of neighbors and not just of humans is the result of the concrete givenness of existence in its spatial-temporal definition and limitation. The highly intense forms of human relationships, which we designate as friendship or love, include an intensity of emotional encounter, openness, and care which cannot be continually multiplied, but which is singular and unique. Thus is it understandable and suitable if sexual love in its intensity, intimacy, and all-encompassing nature is understood as the earthly analogy to the love of God.

But even the fullest forms of interpersonal relationships will be overburdened and therefore eventually jeopardized if they are unconsciously identified with the original relationship of which they are analogies, and are not differentiated from it. It is not only good but also necessary to be released from all such expectations of salvation. Only this freedom from self-salvation makes it possible that in such relations we can admit that failure, disappointment, and injury will intrude and remain. This can, of course, lead to the recognition that the continuation of a relationship, friendship, partnership, or marriage is incompatible with the determination of one or both partners. Such a relationship must therefore be interrupted or ended with the acceptance of all the injury and pain that is bound up with this incompatibility.

Such disturbance and endangering of interhuman relationships belongs likewise to its givenness, and will always belong to it under the earthly and historical conditions. Sober recognition of this reality underlines by way of contrast what good fortune it is when the joy and pleasures of human relationships are experienced; they too belong to the created definition of humans.

## RELATING TO SOCIETAL STRUCTURES

From the doctrine of justification, it follows that every human being has an inalienable dignity. This dignity is not first acquired by the human through certain abilities or achievements. It is not granted by one's fellow humans or by society, and thus potentially withheld or withdrawn by them. Rather, dignity is given to the human out of one's origin in God as one's definition. It can and must only be acknowledged as an inalienable dignity by the human individual, one's fellow humans, and society. Should this acknowledgment cease, the individual, fellow humans or society can indeed treat an individual as if he or she had no dignity, and were therefore "worthless." However, the dignity given from God, namely, one's definition as the image of God, does not disappear through such treatment, and is not lost through it. But this means that human dignity as the most basic good and highest state of value [as stated in the first article of the German national constitution] is grounded in a dimension (namely, that of origins) that does not stand at the disposal of a nation's constitution or agencies, but on which the nation itself is finally based. Therefore, this criterion is rightly laid out as a standard of judgment about human quality in a national constitution regarding the right of existence for those members of society (especially embryos, children, the sick, the severely handicapped, the old, the dying), who through their own powers of achievement do not and cannot contribute anything to the prosperity of society, but depend for their living at society's expense. However, this criterion becomes problematic when foundational doubts about achievements in society and for society take priority over it. In this case, we lose sight of the fact that only on the basis of achievements brought about by those who are capable, can the existence and quality of life be secured economically for those who themselves are not in the position to make such achievements.

From the doctrine of justification it also follows that every human has freedom. This can be externally restricted under certain circumstances, namely, when the need for human freedom makes demands that are threatening to the existence of other people or to oneself. This freedom, however, presents a necessary choice between possibilities, which is a constitutive element of human existence, and because of this, deserves acknowledgment, protection, and promotion from society. At its innermost core, this freedom is the positive and negative freedom of religion, freedom of faith, and freedom of conscience. It means nothing else than the right to follow one's own insights and certainty in questions about life's fundamental orientation, and to represent them openly. This results from the knowledge that the view of existence as well, which has a foundational character for the orientation of human life, is given and it results indeed in an uncircumventable certainty. This freedom of the individual conscience was and is threatened at different times in various ways and from different sides: by any church or religious society that makes salvation dependent on an assent to its teaching, by any state that does not allow any other opinions but its own, by any society that refuses the undeniability of a fundamental view of existence for every life-orientation, and which defames and marginalizes those who confess such a view. When the Christian church, in the name of the doctrine of justification, speaks up for human freedom, this is only credible when this freedom includes even the right to oppose Christian doctrine, and the right to make apparent mistakes. The freedom of the Spirit, of the Word, and of life, that reigns also in the church itself, is therefore the most effective way the church can show that the societal significance of the freedom meant by the doctrine of justification is to our advantage.

From the doctrine of justification it follows that every human has the right to education. One of the decisive insights resulting from the doctrine of justification was that human dignity consists in one's being defined as in the image of God. However, this definition is neither a determination which leads to its goal by necessity or obligation, nor merely a well-intended wish whose failure is certainly regrettable, but bearable if need be. A definition says something about that which is essential and necessary for the humanity of the human, but it claims no compulsion for reaching this goal. Rather, it tries to win humans over for this goal, to attract but not seduce the human in this direction, so that the movement towards this goal itself becomes a movement of the human heart. It is no accident that the concept of "formation" [Bildung] has its historical-linguistic roots in medieval mysticism regarding the human as the "image" [Bild] of God. The human individual is not simply the image of God, but rather towards it, or on the way. This refers formally to the necessity of an image of the human as the goal of every educational process. This refers structurally to the religious foundation for every educational process that does not limit itself to instrumental knowledge and the acquisition of abilities and skills, but wants to give the human the capability for leading a responsible life. And finally, regarding content, this refers to the necessity of the image of the human, to which the actual constitution (in the sense of reality and determination) of the human becomes correct and corresponds. In light of modern European tendencies toward privatization and the marginalization of religious matters and religious education (which we have increasingly experienced in the last decades), it is an open question whether and how a basic religious dimension of human education can again win some space in the educational systems of our society so that humans do not become driftwood in the stream of time or tiny cogs in the gears of society. Here almost everything will depend on how trustworthy and inviting the educational offerings are, as presented by the church either in its own realm or in the public educational system.

Obviously, the social meaning of the doctrine of justification has only been sketched here with examples such as "dignity," "freedom," and "education." Likewise, these three aspects of living out of justification (self-relationship, interpersonal relationships, societal structures) can only be shown to be advantageous when they are understood not as alternatives, hence not merely as addendums, but as integral to society. The parts cannot be extracted from the Christian image of the human and society without doing damage to the whole. But in its unity and totality, this image can let something be known about the content and the meaning of the doctrine of justification, even in the context of the present living environment.

## CONCLUSION

What is the meaning of the doctrine of justification for the present? It has a foundational existential meaning that must be developed for the present through considerable interpretive effort. It is especially necessary to overcome the forensic language of criminal justice and to win back the basic understanding of the doctrine of justification. With the following presuppositions, its orienting meaning can be shown to be advantageous for the education of human freedom within history, since it leads to a deeper understanding of reality

In the first place, the doctrine makes us perceive reality not as an ensemble of elements that exist by themselves and only come into relationship as a secondary matter, but rather as constitutively relational. With this, the doctrine overcomes an abstract, substance-oriented understanding of reality in favor of a concrete, relational one.

Second, the doctrine shows the world in its constitutive relationship to God as its creative origin. It transcends therefore an understanding of the world that is restricted to the horizon of immanence, but considers the world sub specie aeternitatis, and poses the question in its true sense.

Third, it shows that the human being exists under a promise and definition given to it by God, namely, the definition of being in the image of God. It thus moves beyond the way of seeing the human based on the fact of its being or having become, and refers instead to the dimension of possibility and therefore to an open future.

Fourth, the doctrine reveals that the realization of this definition of the human is radically threatened and put into question through the power of sin, which is aimed at destroying the relationship between humans and God, and thus also the relationships with one's fellow creatures and oneself. The doctrine does not allow the human being to close one's eyes to this destructive power and to deny the reality of sin.

Fifth, justification refers to the promise that God takes the power of the destruction of sin upon himself in Jesus Christ, in that God suffers and thus heals the relationship with his creation. At the same time, the doctrine relieves the human, subjugated by this power of sin, from the impossible venture of wanting to bring this disturbed relationship back to order by its own power.

Sixth, the doctrine identifies the faith that trusts in this promise as the manner in which the relationship of humans to God and thus to one's fellow creatures and to oneself is posed in a new saving perspective. It thus frees good works from any intention toward the good of one's own salvation and lets works be themselves as the fruit of faith.

Finally, justification includes the knowledge that the connection between promise and faith presents a process that never comes to a conclusion within the history of development and the maturation of human life. It leads therefore to a sober perception of oneself and others, and at the same time keeps alive the hope for perfection beyond time.

# 6

# Justification and Reality

*Klaus Schwarzwäller*

JUSTIFICATION IS USUALLY TREATED as if it were purely a single act—the act of being justified by God. As a result, justification becomes a sort of *punctum mathematicum*, having extension neither in space nor in time. Since we live in space and time, however, difficult questions naturally arise and linger with respect to this article, such as the relationship between justification and sanctification, the problem of the third use of the law, living "in" baptism as described in the Small Catechism,[1] and the abiding problem of law and gospel.[2] Answers to these problems, let alone satisfying solutions, are scarce. Indeed, this outcome is unavoidable as long as we deal with the article in the traditional way as, I suspect, seems normal for us. However, Luther saw the article quite differently, especially since from the outset he perceived time as always included in the article. For him this article dealt with nothing abstract but concerned concrete life, or rather *was* life. Consequently, his speaking of the article or doctrine must not be taken in a literal sense of an isolated item but instead hints at a special reality.

This can be seen clearly in the Smalcald Articles, where Luther's treatment is remarkable in at least two respects. First, where we naturally expect a comprehensive abstract of a doctrine, we find only quotations from the Bible, with added remarks such as we usually ascribe to a redactor in

1. "The Small Catechism," *BC* 360:12.
2. See below, n. 5.

Gospel exegesis.[3] It is obvious that Luther is not at all interested in any dogmatic locus or precise definition.[4] Instead he leads us to the heart of the Scriptures and, thus makes us dive, as it were, into what is said there—which is just the opposite of carefully analyzing it and then in a distinct second act seeking to realize it in our lives. To say it pointedly: *Luther does not try to make us understand the Bible, but instead he leads us into it so that our whole way of perceiving and thinking has to be assimilated to the biblical structures.*[5] Second, we are thereby led into the dynamics of life or rather into God's shaping of reality. There is no place on which we can stand and survey a distinctive picture of the whole. Because everything is in flux, it is necessary for us to get into the proper stream—in opposition to all attempts to gain an all-encompassing theory of the whole, which in any case is impossible for us.

We may argue, of course, that in the end we must *know* what the point of the article is. Luther does not object. But he leads us to another level and into a totally different framework than ours. This can be seen quite clearly in his "Disputation concerning Man": "Paul in Romans 3[:28], "We hold that the human is justified by faith apart from works," briefly sums up the definition of the human, saying, 'the human is justified by faith.'"[6]

We rub our eyes: the "human is justified by faith"—this is supposed to be a definition? It is just a subordinate clause, not even a whole sentence, let alone a proposition guided by the rules of definitions![7] Luther was well trained in his era's methods of logic and rules of definition. Even though, as Gerhard Ebeling has shown, this sort of definition sometimes occurred, at this point in the disputation it is really provocative and stirring. As such, its form is either careless, even sloppy, or Luther chose it because it is required by the contents. In this case, it is a part

---

3. Luther, "The Smalcald Articles," *BC* 301:1.

4. The common place that Luther was "no systematician" was done away with nearly one hundred years ago by Karl Holl who on the contrary esteemed him an excellent systematician!

5. As to these "structures" (as I call them here) see my article "Das Geheimnis der Bibel," 23–35.

6. *Hominem iustificari fide.* Translation altered. "The Disputation concerning Man" (1536), Thesis 32, *LW* 34:139; *WA* 39/1:176, 33–35.

7. Which normally are seen in the identification of the *genus proximum* (the proper species) and the *differentia specifia* (the specific difference sc. to all other beings of this species), that is, for example, the definition of human beings as *animal rationale*, i.e., an animal which possesses reason.

of what is intended and thus maintains its specific feature. Since Luther usually worked out his theses with utmost care, we must assume that he proposed it in this special form consciously and deliberately. So let us examine his thesis.

## ✗ THE REALITY OF GOD'S JUSTIFYING THE HUMAN

What is asserted here is that God, and only God, defines us: who we are, who we will be, what is due to us, and what our life weighs. It is God's definition of us that counts, whoever we may be and whatever we have done.[8] God is our judge, the only judge whose judgments are consistent. And as our judge who judges on the basis of the justice of the gospel, which is to grant and to preserve life, he is our redeemer,[9] as Regin Prenter put it, the "Merciful Judge."[10] Thus, neither we ourselves nor anyone else is allowed or has the power to define our lives and their value. Human definitions are only temporary at best, if at all, for we belong not to ourselves but to God.

Since God is always in action, his definition is never static but dynamic throughout. It marks our place within the time granted to us and, thus, within the framework of God's acting, preserving, changing, and shaping our reality.

Our definition is consequently not yet completed but will be finished with our death or, rather, with the Last Judgment.[11] We are in his hands both now and, as is our hope, forever. But this also means that we are given time to do what we want and, thus, can even withdraw from his hands.[12] In any case, the definition and the judgment belong to God regardless of how we chart our path.

The definition presupposes that we are sinners. God does not deal with ideal human beings but with real ones, with sinners, namely, who are erroneous, weak, indolent, sick, bad, malicious, and so on. God turns

8. The Lord's Prayer, "For *thine* is the kingdom . . ."

9. Luther always spoke of the triune God, so that his speech about God always includes Jesus Christ and the Holy Spirit. Speech about God apart from Jesus Christ and the Holy Spirit is speech of the hidden God, and about him we cannot say anything but only tremble with horror and turn back to Jesus Christ.

10. Prenter, *Der barmherzige Richter*.

11. This matches the remark of Claus Westermann that Genesis 1:27 is a predicate of *God's* acting!

12. To show how this matches predestination would need too much space to be treated here.

to us without any preparation or predisposition on our part. He takes us just as we are—impious and lost. As miserable sinners we are real human beings in the eyes of God, whereas, when we try to be good we are but "unhappy and presumptuous gods."[13] Therefore repentance means to turn back to God—as we are and as he seeks us.

To be a human then is not dependent on a special property, attitude or ability of ours. We are humans because God justifies us and not because of things like our wits or weaknesses. At the same time, this shows that justification must not be reduced to so-called "spiritual" features but instead encompasses the whole person.

Once we are embraced by God, as it were, we are being changed. It is a steady process of being formed more and more until God puts an end to it, regardless of whether this makes sense to us or not. But we are not without influence on this process: we may engage in it or refuse to do so.

This engagement is faith. Therefore, faith means leaving oneself in God's hands and following his guidance, or more specifically, following Jesus Christ. To be sure, this is irrespective of our doubts or uncertainties, irrespective also of our advantage or disadvantage. However, it is the faithful acceptance of God's acting upon us—the gracious judge and almighty Father.

Anthropology is widened by this definition. It is now impossible to reduce it to what can be demonstrated or proved by indisputable evidence. Human beings, and humanity as such, transcend our observable and demonstrable world from top to bottom.

Still more, this means a complete inversion of our perception of world and reality as such. All that is demonstrable and self-evident now becomes questionable and uncertain. Everything that is immanent, whether made of concrete or ideas, now begins to falter and grants us no safety. Unless, therefore, we ask for God and his will we will fall victim to ideologies, seductive trends, money, success—or whatever else.

This definition not only keeps us grounded but, at the same time, protects our humanity in that it grants a genuine perception of reality. It is

---

13. "faciens ex infoelicibus et superbis diis homines veros, idest [!] miseros et peccatores" ("Operationes in Psalmos," *WA* 5:128.38–39). Notice this: According to Luther, the true and genuine human being is—a sinner! It is impossible to even enumerate merely the consequences arising from this. This, to be sure, does not mean that human beings were villains or nasty. "Sinner" is not an ontological category, but marks our situation before God instead.

a humbling and sobering definition. At the same time, indeed, it elevates us as people being worked upon by God himself and led to final salvation.

Now that we have clarified various aspects of the so-called *doctrine* of justification in thesis 32 of Luther's "Disputation Concerning Man," we can focus on three of them.

1. Although Luther wrote and discussed it in the academy, this disputation is not reserved merely or exclusively for the academy. The reason for this is not that it was conceived on a metalevel (in current academic parlance). The reason is that it transgresses any academic level because it deals with God, with his doing, and with our human reality. Each of them is totally beyond academic description, let alone any exhaustive investigation. From this it clearly and necessarily follows that dealing with them *theoretically* is more than a bad mistake but really a sign of complete misunderstanding. As can be seen from the unsolvable problems mentioned in the beginning, this does not work, and it cannot work. We may, and indeed must, work on them theoretically at the level of examination, of the adequacy of the language and the terms, the correctness of the argumentation and the logical conclusions, and the necessity of the distinctions, and so on. However, this means that theoretical work makes sense here and is possible only at the façade. The matter itself, however, can be found and realized only through our own lives; we have to *live* it, as it were. Luther once preached against looking too high. "I shall look downward to what God will have. Now he has revealed his will to me through the law and the gospel and has taught me what I am to do, so that I am not to run around and climb up and ask why God does this or that. Let such things wait. But when you have come to faith and true reason and have experienced the cross, then you will understand."[14] Therefore, we have to be aware of two aspects. First, we have to realize that there is an irreversible order: God is acting upon us and by doing theology we only explain or rather unfold conceptually what God has done. Second, this explanation or unfolding needs a special approach lest the matter be altered by the difference of language. For example, I may talk of a certain woman; thus she is, and remains, just a woman and, as in this special case, the very woman I'm talking of. But if my wife is meant then everything has changed, for she is not just a woman; it needs no further elaboration. Correspondingly,

14. WA 16:143.28–33.

if, for example, I write about *notitia—assensus—fiducia*,[15] then even by
the mere words I change both God's acting and aspects of my own life into
things that are to be dealt with as things, as theoretical entities. Through
the mere choice of the wording I thus deny fundamental aspects of what I
am speaking of and, moreover, make it disappear. What remains are mere
theoretical entities or stuff to be treated in the "arts and culture" section
of the newspaper.

2. Once "the human is justified by faith" is stated as a definition of us,
the conclusion can be drawn (and indeed, with regard to Luther himself,
must be drawn) that justification by faith is much more than a special
act of God, but is an attribute of human beings and particularly of believers since they are aware of it. More precisely, it marks the framework
of Christians' lives. Thus, the *punctum mathematicum* criticized in the
beginning may be taken in the sense of the Greek aorist tense, that is, in
the sense that justification cannot and must not be reduced to a single
act but is valid throughout time, whatever may happen. Thus, it matches
the *pro nobis*,[16] which is a Christological attribute: as Jesus Christ died *for
us* once for all, his justification of sinners is valid for sinners throughout
their lifetimes. Thus, all those questions and problems that presuppose a
special succession change their character. Now it is obvious, as was always
implicit, that no temporal order is intended here, and indeed cannot be,
because it would be senseless. The point is the order of the inner logic:
Once I am born and live, I breathe; once I accept the call, I am a pastor and act as such. So, once I am justified, I live and behave and act as
a justified person immediately since this has happened to me; I ask for
God's will and for my neighbor's benefit, pray to God and confess my
faith, and so on. Thus, in a disputation with Melanchthon, Luther sharply
refused the mode of language that the justified "must" do good works. He
objected that this is as senseless as to say that the sun "must" shine or that
three plus seven "must" equal ten. "For it is not that the sun "must" shine,
but it does so naturally without any command, because it is created for
this very purpose. Thus, a good tree produces good fruit. Three and seven
already equal ten and do not need to become ten. We are not speaking
here about what should be but about what is the case already. Or you

---

15. "Taking notice—assenting—trusting in it," that is, the gospel.

16. "For us" in the sense of "on our behalf" or "to our benefit."

might understand the distinction: If it's the sun, then it shall shine; if you are believer, then you shall do good deeds."[17]

To make it more clear, one might say that *justification is the sphere or element in which the believer's life is led.* Thus anything he or she does or does not do is traced by this fundamental situation. And this happens, apart from or rather without our knowledge and perception, provided we keep asking for the Lord and his will.

3. Luther's thinking was shaped by the Bible and its structures. Although he was brought up and trained in Scholastic theology, he never did theology as if he stood in front of a cabinet and pulled the contents out of different drawers, for example, justification from one drawer and sanctification from another and God's law from still another. Theologically he had no cabinet or closet at all but was living before the face of God and thus kept together what was torn apart by theological distinctions. So it goes without saying that any speaking of "God" was actually appealing to the Holy Trinity. Conversely, this means that in what he commonly called his "teaching" on justification, he naturally also "taught" of the Father and the Holy Spirit, of the Father who is *our Father* and of the Holy Spirit who effectuates our renewal. This is valid particularly with respect to faith: "But we assert that faith is a work of divine promise or the gift of the Holy Spirit which indeed is necessary for the fulfillment of the law, but it is not attained by the law or any work. But this gift which is granted to us renews the person thoroughly and without ceasing, so that the person does new works, yet the new works do not produce a new person."[18]

I will omit lengthy argumentation and offer this conclusion: Other than the static way of perception that evokes the question of how the justified person will now live a holy life, Luther recognizes that we now live precisely because of justification, in and under the guidance of the Holy Spirit. Therefore, we do not need to be urged to do this or ask for that but instead can leave ourselves to this guidance and follow it. This guidance makes us aware of God's will and our neighbors' needs—and, correspondingly, saddens us when we fail to perceive or do it. It is through this guidance that we are free from the law; we do not try to match the

---

17. *WA TR* 6:153.8–13, #6727. A few paragraphs prior to this Luther most drastically underlines what he means: "When the guy to be hanged saw the people running and scurrying to the gallows, he said, 'I'll be there, too.'" *WA TR* 6:152.19–21.

18. *WA TR* 6:152.31–36, #6727.

law but are urged by God the Holy Spirit to be aware of its contents and to be eager to do it even *before* we have become aware of it or its wording.[19]

The interpretation of the Ten Commandments in the Small Catechism can shine an explanatory light on this. The commandments mark the boundaries *within* which we are free to do God's will and the knowledge of which keeps us from trespassing. And since he is our Father, we may return to him if we fall into sin. Just as we do not love our children because they are well behaved but because they are *our kids*, so God does not love us because we behave, but he loves us instead as sinners whom he justifies so that we may glorify him.

## "THE LUCK OF ARRIVING AT REALITY"

In 1990 Gerhard O. Forde asserted that *Theology is for Proclamation.*[20] This proposition is valid not because of the author's piety or because it favors the religious expectations of those who distrust academic theology. It is valid because it follows from the matter itself. To put it in Luther's words: "The proper subject of theology is the human being guilty of sin and condemned, and God the Justifier and Savior of the sinner."[21] To deal with this theoretically or primarily in terms of the academy means that we thereby miss what we think we are explaining and that we deny our own claim in the very moment it is proposed. For it implies that those who deal with this very topic make statements, or confessions, or explications *of their own person*—unless they deny being sinners at all. In this case, theology is simply nonsense or a mere game of marbles and may be done correspondingly. Why not? But it would be mere foolishness or a joke to take such "theology" seriously. According to Luther's proposition, however, doing theology means or rather unfolds what is meant by

19. This is exactly what is meant in the Sermon on the Mount, Matthew 5:20. For the righteousness of the Scribes and Pharisees was focused on the fulfillment of the law, word by word; but the "better righteousness" is "per-fect" (Matt 5:48), namely (the original meaning of the word in this connection), "unlimited" commitment of the person to God's will.

20. Forde, *Theology Is for Proclamation.*

21. "Nam Theologiae proprium subiectum est homo peccati reus ac perditus et Deus iustificans ac salvator hominis peccatoris. He continues, Quicquid extra hoc subiectum in Theologia quaeritur aut disputatur, est error et venenum" ("Whatever is asked or discussed in theology outside this subject is error and poison.") ("Ennaratio Psalmi LI, 1532," *WA* 40/2:328.17–20; *LW* 12:311.

these words: sinner, guilty, lost, justifying, savior and, last but not least, God. This presupposes, as already mentioned, that one has come to "faith and to true reason" and has "experienced the cross" in order not to speak about colors as a blind person. And perhaps it is not unnecessary to recall that the Lord did not tell us to ponder the gospel or to theorize about it but to "go, therefore, and teach all nations." It is not only stupid but rather blasphemous to think that Jesus died on the cross in order to provide a basis for theological research—a main concern of Søren Kierkegaard.

Genuine theology requires, at the same time, that we be clear about its aim. At this point, all theologians throughout history agree with the Bible that the aim of all our doing and acting and our lives as such is the praise and the glory of God. To put a spin on it, God's aim is not, as some Lutheran traditions seem to suggest, the salvation of the sinner, as if the Holy Trinity rotated around the welfare of sinful humanity precisely in order to satisfy our spiritual self-centeredness. The aim of our lives is not to be saved or, as some argue, to get into heaven. The aim of our lives is to honor God by doing his will.[22] And, by justifying the sinful creature God maintains his glory: that he is almighty and gracious.

To return to Forde's claim, once you take seriously and really understand the Bible and, correspondingly, realize what Luther's description includes, you cannot escape the consequence that theology has its *raison d'être* and, at the same time, is determined by its aim, that is, the glory of God. It was Anselm who, in picking up a strand in Augustine's theology, established an approach to theology that sought God's praise in its intellectual necessity. This resulted in the necessity for reason to declare God's existence as we see in his ontological proof of God's existence.[23] Thereafter, the tradition developed into a philosophical theology. In its origin, this theology was embedded in the monastic framework with its hours of praise; it was the reflection of what fills and forms life beyond the liturgy.

But once theology freed itself from this boundary and became its own subject, its aim changed, albeit without denying the traditional one. It now found its expression in rationality and intellectual lucidity. Additionally, since the eighteenth century a rising positivism has progressively pervaded the whole of the academy, including theology. Thus,

22. Matthew 6:33!

23. His proof is mostly known as the demonstration that no higher entity can be thought of but only God (*quo maius cogitari nequit*), but this is, as it were, only the run-up to his main point: that it is impossible and inconsistent to deny him.

the actual goal in the academy has shifted to a sort of rationality that is expressed in terms of positivism, that is, of demonstrable evidence or at least obvious probability. I do not need to draw this out; it is clear that in this horizon Forde's assertion needs to be made even if it sounds strange and perhaps awkward in the current academic climate. Yet Forde's proposition as a matter of fact is a call both to the requirements of theology and also to the genuine tradition of theological work and research.

This includes, of course, that any control over teaching and preaching "the article" of justification by faith cannot, and must not, end by stating dogmatic correctness or identification of this "article" in a sermon. This way of proving or challenging "the right doctrine" has become obsolete and, indeed, amounts to merely sham fighting. Once "theology is for proclamation" and its "proper matter is the human being guilty of sin and lost and God justifying and being savior of the sinner," then preaching the gospel, that is, explicating and outlining justification by faith, is *to lead into the very reality created through God justifying us and to establish or even to root us there.* Or, to put it another way, it is to confirm our lives within the sphere of the wonder that God himself, in Jesus Christ, is loving and redeeming us. But how are we to weigh this, to check it, to guarantee its adequacy, or to judge its inadequacy? Once this is excluded in terms of traditional examination of a doctrine, we grasp a little bit of the reality of the Holy Spirit and of the specific rules for how to live and to move in it. The possible objection at this point that a valid control is, thus, impossible can be met by the insight of a learned and experienced person who wrote: "The Holy Spirit is no Skeptic, and it is not doubts or mere opinions that he has written on our hearts, but assertions more sure and certain than life itself and all experience."[24] This means that only the Holy Spirit himself can and does control our acting and speaking and that, correspondingly, his control can be assessed and genuinely taken up only by people who are led by this very same Holy Spirit. Yes, this does indeed lead into a spiritual sphere in the strong sense of the word, a sphere that is beyond the control of any academic means or tools. As the first statement about God is that he defines us, so the first thing to say about the Holy Spirit is that he judges our academic judgments.[25] But of course, this is an offense to the academy and cannot be tolerated!

24. Luther, *BW* (*LW* 33:24; [*De servo arbitrio* 1525], WA 18:605. 32–34.

25. I vividly have in mind the debate on Gerhard von Rad's typological interpretation of the Old Testament when famous scholars had the alarming feeling that thus—the

These are theoretical reflections. In order to show what it means and how it works I will provide an example, a sermon on 1 Cor 12:12–27 by Pastor Susanne Zingel from October of 2008.[26]

Grace to you and peace from him who was and is and will come.

Dear Congregation,[27]

"Many members, one body" is a familiar image, a well-known text. It sounds so familiar that at first it doesn't stir anybody up from his armchair. Many members—one body: we've heard this before. It's a commonplace that everything belongs together and is interconnected with one another. And if we were able to live accordingly, our world would look differently. However, this insight simply becomes boring when it is changed into a moral appeal such as "you ought to behave as one body" or "you ought to have sympathy when one member is suffering" or "you ought to rejoice when another rejoices."

But Paul does not come off as offering morals. For him, the body of Christ is a real experience. He suffers when the Corinthians quarrel; he weeps for lost brothers and sisters; his heart thrills to receive good news; he awaits and is gladdened by each messenger; he prays without ceasing; he is never indifferent.

Paul really is connected with his sisters and brothers (we have no clue whether or not they felt good about this). In any case, today we all are involved too. The current financial crisis shakes all the suppositions on which modern society is erected. This shows that everything is netted together and interwoven. No country, no bank, and no household stands for itself alone.

But this raises the question: what sort of spirit connects us, what sort of medium? The point is not only damage to material

---

ineffable horror of—a "pneumatic exegesis" was being introduced in academic theology. Whereas, many years later, a New Testament scholar put the things in the correct academic order claiming that hermeneutics prepare the way for the Holy Spirit and help him. I am quite sure that the Holy Spirit is deeply grateful for this help granted to him by learned men!

26. She is Pastor at Keitum (on the Island of Sylt). She gave me this sermon of October 12—which was just at hand—to be quoted in this article as an example. (She approved my translation.) I add three remarks: this sermon can be understood properly only within the whole worship service. Second, the sermon is a speech, not a writing; this ought to be kept in mind, and will be noticeable. For obviously the thread of argument and the emphases depend on the preacher's voice. Finally, it is neither meant nor seen to be a paradigm.

27. The usual way of addressing the congregation in a German sermon (*Liebe Gemeinde*).

things. We also know that friendship can end over questions of money: friends soon become enemies,[28] brothers and sisters become heirs at odds. It is terrifying just how quickly new conflicts arise. Great Britain froze all Icelandic accounts with reference to the anti-terror laws! Just that quickly do peaceful neighbors fall out with one another.

Yet it was money that has brought everything into flux. Everyone believed that it was possible to become wealthy. And smart people had their money work for themselves; one didn't have to do anything. Now the image of a living thing is relevant. If all banks now anxiously withhold their money, this is as if all organs keep back the blood that has supplied them, even if the heart pumps its best. What however is the core here and how is it connected with us who really do have a living heart? What sort of heart is beating where all participate in the game because they see the chance to become wealthy in a short time? Money is the one thing, but although it appears strange, belief[29] is stronger. For the whole thing is based on belief and on stories. All over the world people told stories about boldness, risk, and fortune. And people believed in them. They gained profits that many of them had never had in their hands before. Not just numbers stimulated this feeling. Instead, one told another, and they believed. Trust is the key word. It is a word with religious impact. A study of the Organization for Economic Cooperation and Development from 2005 gives evidence that 50 percent of the investors in hedge funds were unable to offer a correct description of these funds. At the same time however they estimated their knowledge of the financial market to be good or excellent. They were convinced that the explanation of financial products was unproblematic for them. It is hard to realize that people only believed and trusted, that they made their decisions on mere speculative basis.

The most important thing is to regain trust, the politicians say. But the question is, reasonable trust in what? Since all had striven after riches and felt comfortable about this, now the goal is to get cushioned by the state. Those who were the loudest in calling for free development now are at the head of those requesting support for the banks and companies by the state.

In preaching we are interwoven with this; that is no news. For "all one body we"[30] even though many members. The one cannot

28. Reference to a German proverb: "Beim Geld hört die Freundschaft auf."

29. In German "faith" and "believe" are the same word: *Glaube*. This ambiguity allows for punning.

30. *Lutheran Book of Worship*, hymn 509, verse 2.

be without the other, and what is striking one hurts all. The point is to support one another. The conflict at Corinth was challenging. There was a rich upper class, wealthy Christians who said that they were independent, that togetherness is a good idea, that new life in Christ is a feeling, is like poetry, and not from this world. Thus they went on celebrating their festivities. Sometimes the poor joined them. So one shared a piece of bread and offered a little wine, said a prayer, sang a hymn and continued to be independent—the one rich and the others slaves.

Paul sees that, in this situation, the congregation of Jesus Christ is at the point of failing. For the history and story[31] of Jesus Christ is not ornamental; it is impossible to embody it like a motto. It is rather a small light; this story is continually being told and connects people in a silly hope of riches and abundance and luck beyond any profit at the stock exchange.

## IT IS THE LUCK OF ARRIVING AT REALITY

For surely this is reality: anything breathing and living is connected through the Spirit of God's creative power. The congregation of Jesus Christ accepts this and quite consciously takes part in it. We know that we are not in paradise, but where two or three gather together it is possible that the door of heaven is opening. Each participant is able to contribute something. As to this, there are stories which happened here: Rhythm: The Dance of the Tides. Royston Maldoom and Simon Rattle performed a Stravinsky ballet. Royston Maldoom was in Sylt and, during their vacation, sixty children rehearsed here and danced—ebb and flow, in tandem with one another, and they joined together, totally as one body, on the stage, all participating and giving away their tickets as gifts. This does happen.

Or two weeks ago we had a big playground celebration. All the children helped and they wanted to do so. And not without good reason. Of kids Jesus says, "Unless you change and become like children, you will never enter the kingdom of heaven." And, "Whosoever does not receive the kingdom of God as a little child will never enter it." But when you receive the gospel as a child, you will be right in the middle of it, and it will seem like a fairy tale, like a remote story, yet it is true, and we are in it. Every slight sign of kindness and of love hidden in the smallest detail shows the right track. And God will keep us on that track, and his peace,

31. In German "history" and "story" are the same word: *Geschichte*. The context determines the meaning.

"which surpasses all understanding shall keep your hearts and minds through Jesus Christ," our Lord. Amen.

We take a step back and have a theoretical look at what we, alas, only have read but not heard. In this sermon we are led into reality, into the reality as we perceive it day by day in our surroundings and from the newspapers and television. Indeed, the reality which God creates in our "normal" reality, thus converting this normality into an unreal chimera, is mostly unknown and unnoted. Yet it cannot be denied, for it proves itself through many small or big things. To be sure, it also cannot be demonstrated, yet only a fool would be bold enough to contest it. There is no question, neither in this sermon nor at all, why God does it, how he achieves it, and where it is to be found in any case, and what are the conditions by which we become aware of it—let alone the many usual questions of this sort, which is our daily bread in the academy. This reminds me of Gerhard Forde stressing Luther's thesis 21, "A theology of glory calls evil good and good evil. A theology of the cross calls a thing what it actually is."[32] This is the case here. No "why?", "how?" and "wherefore?" but simply taking God's acting as real and, therefore, instead of pondering on it, living in and with what God is doing and introducing the hearer into this framework. To put it bluntly, I am well trained in dogmatics and its subtleties, and I am well aware of the fact that, in terms of precise dogmatics, this sermon appears rather questionable. But above all, I realize that if I examined this sermon in this usual way, I would miss it and miss it the more to the degree that my analysis is more precise. Because its point is that it just yanks us in or rather places us into God's reality which has come in Jesus Christ, which is in, with, and under our everyday reality, and makes us see the light of God's reality and makes us also see the shadows now visible to our eyes.[33] Finally, it goes without

---

32. *Theologus gloriae dicit malum bonum et bonum malum, Theologus crucis dicit id quod res est.* "Heidelberg Disputation, 1518" (*LW* 31:40; *WA* 1:354.21–22.

33. For this is, in short, the point of this sermon: There is no point to be reported! Rather it leads us straight into our complicated reality and opens our eyes so that we become aware of the inconsistence of our normal sense and perception, become aware of the heavy weight of things one can neither buy nor produce, and, above all, become aware of the work of the triune God interfering with what is going on amongst us: that he widens up our reality through facts and events and perspectives that fall apart from our usual framework, that he is acting, that this frees us and makes us discern new ways. To sum this up: It is the description of how our eyes are opened and our lives freed in that we begin to grasp the "real" reality, created through Jesus Christ. To arrive at this level, indeed, is good luck.

saying that one single" sermon can neither explain nor outline the whole reality that God creates among us. If we are good preachers, we *might* possibly be granted the gift of showing one single strand of it throughout our lifetime —if at all. To realize this is the beginning of understanding the "article" of justification by faith, for then we begin leaving ourselves to God to guide and act upon us.

## GOD JUSTIFYING DEFINES REALITY

It is one thing to deal with justification by faith in research or in dogmatics or in order to explain it in the academy. This, of course, has its right and necessity. But one must never forget that this is only talk *about* but never *of* justification itself. It is a way of coming to grips with it intellectually. It is quite another thing to deal with justification by faith itself, that is, to speak of what God grants us and acts upon us. In this case none of the relevant keywords need occur, yet it may be a complete and consistent description of it. More precisely, it is the report of our being transferred into a new reality which penetrates our current reality and of being given the capacity to become aware of it and gain our orientation in it. And this is that new reality in dogmatic terms: That human is justified by faith, by faith in Jesus Christ, as Pastor Zingel's sermon illustrates.

With all of this in mind we now can draw several conclusions. First, justification by faith makes us realize that we are loved sinners, that we are God's beloved enemies. In short, we are lost people under God's grace. So is the world as a whole. Whatever we see, achieve, possess, or try to do is lost; even the tanks of the dictators or the riches of the bankers are doomed to decay. And whatever good deeds I myself do cannot set aside this predicament; they may truly be good deeds or they may only seem so. For this is not the point. The point is this: Who am I in God's eyes? And he responds, "You are my enemy whom I love and therefore lead to salvation. So leave yourself in my hands; my will is known and found in Jesus Christ. Then you will be my child and my friend and will not have to sustain yourself. As my child and my friend you need not be concerned about your own person. Thus you are free to look around and to concentrate on others and things outside your own person and its interest."[34]

---

34. This is the reason why Hans Joachim Iwand insisted on the bondage of the will and declared it the presupposition of any ethics.

Second, as God's child and friend—which of course is totally unexpected and no less unmerited—I am aware of many things which I and others normally pass by. For example, Zingel's sermon offers the insight that commerce and trade depend on much more than money; they fundamentally depend on confidence which is something one can neither produce nor buy. Or it makes us think of the inflation of words, of cheap and empty words spread all over the world. This provokes the question of which word, after all, can be not empty but trustworthy and, additionally, how we can know or become certain which word is trustworthy. To the point, this leads to the insight that without God's Word present there are only mere words. And what is God's Word? Once more, as the result of long and complicated reflections and argumentation, I can clearly say: it is the word that justifies the sinners for Christ's sake. This directs our eyes to an unusual way of perception. We should not take our normal reality as deceptive or mere shadows,[35] thus declaring our world and its reality as imagination or a disappearing illusion of heavenly reality, as is often done in a Platonic tradition. Rather we now perceive reality to be much more than we are able to see *and* that this "more" marks the decisive quality of our world and time. This "more" is God's will, his acting, his redemptive work. And this, to be sure, is real among us. It has come "down to earth" and is no heavenly archetype. "The Word became flesh, and lived among us" (John 1:14). It is in this very event that his glory has become visible for us. Consequently we discern God's hand even there, where normally only "change and decay in all around"[36] is to be seen and where death seems to have the final say.

Third, the human as justified by faith is happening now. It is, as it were, the seal on our lives and world. The God who defines reality and leads his creation to the aims he desires to be fulfilled is no mere heavenly or spiritual thing or a matter which occurs "only in faith." It coins and traces reality—"e'en though it be a cross that raiseth me."[37] As Christ by his resurrection warrants, God is opening a *thereafter* when all things have collapsed, are broken down or come to a final end. For although it is true that death *is* death, real death, and that destruction *is* destruction,

35. Jesus Christ did not die on the cross on behalf of an illusory world or mere shadows of human beings! On the contrary, his passion and death, his suffering and blood ensure us of the true reality of our world and all we see in it. So it is to be taken seriously.

36. *Lutheran Book of Worship*, hymn 272, verse 3.

37. "Nearer My God to Thee," *Service Book and Hymnal*, hymn 577, verse 1.

true destruction, it is even more true and certain that God and his possibilities are by no means limited by our borders. By definition justification by faith implies that we keep connected with Christ, as in life, so equally in death, and as in death, so equally in resurrection. It is here that Paul's statement has its framework and rings most true, "If for this life only we have hoped in Christ, we are of all people most to be pitied" (1 Cor 15:19). For now it is obvious that this sentence is neither a mere claim nor the call to wait for a better "beyond," but that it explains the dimensions of reality and its substance. This substance is neither vague nor does it blur in uncertainty, but can be said in clear words: God, in Jesus Christ, makes the final and valid statement about our lives: we are lost sinners, but now God's children and friends forever.

I return once more to Zingel's sermon and how it speaks of "the luck to arrive at reality." Reality is made and sustained by God and is by no means as narrow as our brains, eyes, and hands perceive it. It has the dimensions of God's will and work. We enter this wider reality of God and his glory by leaving ourselves to Jesus Christ. All that follows then is no longer an issue for us. Now God himself takes care of it.

*I am grateful to colleagues Ken Jones, Mark Mattes, and Paul Rorem for smoothing and improving my English, and for supplying the references in English editions.*

## BIBLIOGRAPHY

Forde, Gerhard O. *Theology Is for Proclamation*. Minneapolis: Fortress, 1990.
"Hymn 272." In *LBW*.
"Hymn 509." In *LBW*.
Knaake, J. F. K. et al., editors. *WA* 16. Weimar: Böhlau, 1883ff.
Luther, Martin. *The Bondage of the Will*. In *LW* 33.
———. *The Bondage of the Will*. In *WA* 18.
———. "Disputation Concerning Man, 1536." In *LW* 34.
———. "Disputation Concerning Man, 1536." In *WA* 39.
———. "Ennaratio Psalmi LI, 1532." In *LW* 12.
———. "Ennaratio Psalmi LI, 1532." In *WA* 40.
———. "Heidelberg Disputation, 1518." In *LW* 31:.
———. "Heidelberg Disputation, 1518." In *WA* 1.
———. "Operationes in Psalmos." In *WA* 5.
———. *Table Talk* (*WATR*), In *Luthers Werke, Kritische Gesamtausgabe*, edited by J. F. K. Knaake et al. Vol. 18. Weimar: Böhlau, 1883ff. Vol. 6.

————. "Nearer My God to Thee." In *Service Book and Hymnal*. Hymn 577.

————. "The Smalcald Articles." In *BC*.

————. "The Small Catechism." In *BC*.

Prenter, Regin. *Der barmherzige Richter*. Aarhus: Universitetsforlaget, 1961.

Schwarzwäller, Klaus. "Das Geheimnis der Bibel." In *Theologie und Gemeinde. Beiträge zu Bibel, Gottesdienst, Predigt und Seelsorge*, edited by Heinz-Dieter Neef, 23–35. Stuttgart: Calwer, 2006.

Weber, Max. *Personal Knowledge*. London: Routledge & Kegan Paul, 1958.

# Part Two

## PREACHING

# 7

# Categorical Preaching

## *Steven D. Paulson*

WHEN THEOLOGY OPERATES OUT of its center, justification by faith alone, the first result is that theology is *for* preaching. After all, if it is by if faith alone, the immediate question is: "then how do I get that faith?" The answer is simple and profound: God sends a preacher. Yet that simple answer annoys the world to no end. If faith comes by preaching, and preaching by a preacher, then faith is not like a decision, leap, understanding or effort of my own, it *awaits another*. But waiting for a preacher is like waiting for Godot. What if he never comes? What if I don't like him when he arrives? And what do I do in the meantime? Waiting to receive freedom that we do not have seems worse than the slavery we do have, just as years in the Sinai made the Israelites think fondly about Egypt. No wonder so few apparently believe—getting faith is out of their hands in the realm of historical accidents that reasonable human beings spend their days trying to avoid, just as they try to avoid a car accident or hail storm.

When Paul said, "Faith comes by hearing" (Romans 10), he answered the question of how one gets a gracious God, but opened a much larger Pandora's box. Out flew divine *election and predestination*—two things more dreadful to sinners than their own disbelief in God. What God does with preachers is the answer to *the* theological question: "Why do the nations conspire and the peoples plot in vain . . . against the Lord and his anointed?" (Psalm 2).This explains why it is the denial of faith that provides most people with their best sense of freedom; doubt gives them a sense of security, and the comfort of rejecting the magnificent terror of divine election. The wonder is not that there are so few Christians in Christendom, but that there are any at all.

## PREACHING IS AN ACCIDENT

If preaching gives faith, it does so far too selectively to be trusted. Preaching is by nature historical, specific, here and now, personal, direct, and either occurs in time and space or does not occur at all. By its nature, preaching denies pure subjectivity. It is a real, objective phenomenon, like a car accident that happens without one's intention, desire or will. It is also external like a criminal sentence from a court judge, and even more life changing to my subjectivity because of its objectivity. It is the abject removal of freedom as defined by the law, and as such, preaching is experienced by its hearers as the robbery of their greatest hope until a new, greater freedom without coercion from the law takes hold. The minute a true preacher arrives is the moment that I die as a hearer—as an idealist, as a potentialist, as a nostalgist and even as one who is learning how to "live in the moment." The arrival of a preacher means the end of my attempt at self-selection out of the horde of individuals populating the planet, who says to God and the world, "pick me, it only makes sense." It also devastates any hope placed in the law as a way to give life, meaning, or a goal to reach—whether that law is "within" as Kant inferred, or outside in the state, art, religion and philosophy as Hegel surmised, or runs through biological transmutation like an invisible and blind hand as for Darwin.

When the Apostle Paul preached he put a particular *person*, born of woman, born under the law (Gal 4:4), exactly where lost and seeking sinners put Moses's law or the law in their consciences. The dreams of sinners include simple things such as that one day they will finish cleaning the garage and restore order or that their children will all be successful doctors, or the much more complicated dreams of Kant that one day we will all live in a kingdom of ends inspired by duty! So when true preachers arrive on the scene and replace the dream of a *catholic* law by the reality of a *parochial* preacher there is a terrible consequence that Scripture calls *death*. Paul preached a person, not a pure, spiritual, holy, divine law, and the trouble has never ceased because of it.

Persons, unlike laws, do not wait for you to self-select, they intrude upon you and impose themselves upon you in a way the law never would. A person, unlike the law, loves and hates, and in so doing "selects" persons in the same way that a man or woman selects a mate. When it comes to God selecting a mate, we call it "election." That much may be quite pleasantly received, as it was more or less for Samuel, David or Solomon, that is, as long as we believe that God manages to choose wisely. But the reason for God's *personal* selection lies outside us; we do not choose, God does. God's choice also, and terrifyingly, lies outside the universal, natural code of law that otherwise is the very best thing in life itself because it preserves that life. We have no rationale for the selection done by Jesus, although God knows we have tried to explain why, for example, Peter's betrayal was forgiven and Judas's was not, or why Jacob and not Esau received God's blessing. It does not matter if that law is written on tablets of stone or on the human heart; the shock of God setting *law* aside for a *person* who selects lawlessly, even his only begotten Son, is beyond (or shall we say beneath?) all philosophical wisdom and the reasonable search for signs according to God's ordering of history. Although the preacher's election has always been troubling from the time of Adam and Eve, the self-named modern world has laid down its gauntlet before God at just this point—reason does not allow righteousness to arrive accidentally through preaching. As Lessing put it, accidental truths of history cannot ever be absolute truths of reason. Thus, in order to be truly free we must be free from one specific thing: from a preacher. To be free from a preacher is to be left alone in a universe of eternal, universal law in which one is either optimistic about discovering and enjoying (classical enlightenment teaching as in Kant), or one becomes pessimistic about its discovery and resigned to election by "nature" in the postmodernism inspired by Spinoza. In either case the modern and postmodern worlds are constructed precisely to reject preaching on the basis of the fear of divine election and the bondage of the will that election reveals.

Preaching is the DNA structure of the gospel that selects who shall inherit eternal life, and so if you are determined to preach, you will do so in the face of the world's worst nightmare: that eternal life hangs upon an historical contingency of an alien person's choice that excludes self-selection and is absolutely lawless. What are we left with, but only the whims of this particular person, Jesus of Nazareth? If that is not bad enough, this person, Jesus, believes himself to have been universally wronged, and may well be correct in that assumption, from what we know about his cross; he is therefore primed for revenge according to the simplest laws of nature or by the law of Israel into which he was born. What hope is there in that?

To get a sense of what is meant by preaching in this way, consider that the Apostle Paul spent little or no time thinking according to the strange category Christians called "conversion," which begins with a false premise about Jews and is usually confused about what makes a sinner sinful. The Apostle Paul did not so much convert as have his vocation changed from a scribe to a preacher. Moreover, the change was violent to his person, such a change in vocation also meant a total death to the old man. A scribe deals with the law alone and that in terms of what is written. Writing's conservation of being, of what originally was and will so remain, or even writing's cohort that tries to make what is written "live" by translation into new contexts, was Paul's prior occupation as defender of God. Paul, however, was called out of this work to become a *preacher* for whom the living word beyond the law was set to be the falling and rising of many—his vocation radically changed and so the old Paul was dead leaving only the Christian.

Preaching both the law and gospel is a unique and unsettling occupation. It is the work of withdrawing another person's freedom in relation to the law in order to give a freedom apart from the law in faith itself. The withdrawal of freedom is a terrible thing to behold, and is naturally opposed with every animal instinct for survival. This requires preachers to recognize how their work systematically emerges out of the doctrine of election, and election is the worst human spectacle imaginable. To take up this vocation is to enter this fearful spectacle of preaching, and to ask, if God indeed does use this means to withdraw freedom according to the law, and to give freedom apart from the law: How, then, should a person preach? What does a preacher actually say? How do you know if you have a true preacher or not?

## THE CATEGORICAL AND THE DREAM OF DEFERRING

There are many competitors for the term "preaching," and for that reason the Confessors always had to add a modifier like "true" or "pure" or "right" to preaching. In his final work, *The Captivation of the Will*, Gerhard Forde suggested that we consider the term "categorical preaching" which Luther used to distinguish a preacher from a mere scribe or sophist (persuasive, earnest public speaker).[1] True preaching bestows two very different words from God that are called by shorthand *law and gospel,* whose effect is the withdrawal of legal freedom and God's eternal election. Categorical preaching assumes that one can deliver this specific, divine dialectic that Paul describes bluntly: the letter kills and the Spirit gives life (2 Corinthians 3).

This way of speaking starts in the strangest place imaginable. It is an utterly unique speech event that delivers its words directly to bound wills who naturally reject them, but who nevertheless undergo those words passively and passionately on account of the Holy Spirit. The word "categorical" identifies both the content of the preaching, and also the nature of the deaf hearers to whom we preach. Christ is given as crucified to people who cannot hear because they *will* not hear, in other words, in order to elect the unelectable. Categorical preachers are not just playing to a tough audience; they are speaking to people who literally cannot hear them. This is why preaching categorically has no locus in ancient texts of rhetoric, and cannot even find its proper place in modern speech-act theory or the current fascination with the differences between writing and speaking.

Martin Luther used the term "categorical" to describe preaching while he was in the middle of a key argument against the prototypical postmodern skeptic, Desiderius Erasmus. Luther was demonstrating the single, continuous argument in Scripture that everything with a future belongs to Christ, and all else is consigned to the devil's destruction, which distinguishes between old and new, law and gospel. Luther recognized that the argument is categorical, not just an isolated "Paulinism," and so the Gospel of John makes the same argument: "Moreover, since Christ is said to be "the way, the truth, and the life" (John 14:6), and that *categorically,* so that whatever is not Christ is not the way, but error, not truth, but untruth, not life, but death, it follows of necessity that "freewill" inasmuch as it neither is Christ, nor is in Christ, is fast bound in error, and untruth, and death."[2]

The term that I am using adjectively, *categorical* preaching, is in Luther's Latin a prepositional phrase: *per contentionem* and as such func-

---

1. Forde, *The Captivation of the Will,* 77–79.
2. Luther, *BW,* 307.

tions to position or to *relate* words, in this case *Christ* and *truth* (way and life). The particular relation is contentious, as the Anglicized Latin still communicates to us, not between Christ and truth, but because preaching excludes from truth any other than Christ. Using this word of Christ is like a lead wolf in a pack possessing his territory precisely because this territory—truth, life, and way—is in dispute, contested for, under strife and so must be re-possessed. It was the repeated mistake of Erasmus, and is that of any modern skeptic, to think that truth, way, and life describe neutral territory liable to scientific investigation without ideology. The reality is that wherever there is a crack in life there are hundreds of thousands of wedges, as Charles Darwin once described it, trying to insert themselves. Preachers and their preaching contend for possessed space, as Paul did, "by categorical statement and comprehensive contrast; so that not only the natural force of words and the actual flow of speech, but also that which comes before and after, the whole surrounding context, and the scope, and the contents of his entire argument, unite to prove what his meaning is: Paul intends to say that apart from faith in Christ there is nothing but sin and condemnation."[3]

As usual, Luther refused to beat around the bush. The problem the world has with preachers is that they not only give strange and culturally local ideas like any after-dinner speaker might, but they proceed to elect sinners, which is to say they remove the free will. They do this categorically, that means *not hypothetically* and completely *without any condition*. Giving Christ sucks the air out for anything else, especially the free will. But is not the free will what religion is supposed to uphold? No. Free will is a synonym for death, since whatever it is, it is demonstrably not the person of Jesus Christ. Christ is life, and what is not life is death. Preachers destroy the myth of free will, which has become the ultimate hope, and this surgical removal is precisely why no one can hear them. This contentious preaching situation is what the philosopher Derrida calls "*differance*" whose special motive is to defer or delay the final judgment, especially if such delay leaves us with nothing but the "experience of the law" as our only hope. No one *wills* to hear true preachers, no one desires or wants to hear them, since what preachers say does not fall into the category of things people hope will defer God's arrival to claim everything. Those who are awaiting a preacher, that is the dying, do not

---

3. Ibid., 299.

want preachers when they arrive. Just like when a person meets a bear in the woods, the arrival of a preacher causes a hearer to delay, detour and postpone, hoping that the fearful presence will recede and leave only a trace of his appearance in order to tell a really good story later of how one nearly died—but did not. In fact, this delaying is what has appeared in recent philosophy as the meaning of "narrative" or "metanarrative"; it stretches out time as if the final judgment had not already occurred, so that the myth remains of having time to prepare for the End by means of a free will. Free will is, we could say, in the wrong category for God to love, bless, and give it eternal life. When the preacher arrives Christ arrives to choose his own, and as a result everything else comes to an end, including the free will. Whatever is not Christ is sin and condemnation. This, the world cannot stand and so is the reason why the First Commandment includes *fear* before *love*. It will help preachers to understand what this means for their work, since what they generate initially is the animal instinct of delay and fear.

"Categorical" means that everything the preacher says falls into one "category" or another—whether the preacher knows it or not. The categories are not plural, to our endless dismay, since our fondest tactic to delay the final judgment is to imagine that God is a pluralist in a decidedly noncontingent (monistic) way. We hope that when it comes to salvation all sorts of "ways" ultimately "converge" as Teilhard de Chardin liked to put it, under a large and generous catholic umbrella. Not so for God. The categories of preaching are God's own, and they are not one or three or more, but exactly two. Moreover, the two are mutually exclusive: either P or not P. Good or evil. Christ or not Christ. Heaven or hell. A preacher's job is to predicate properly so the categories can go to work.

When Luther made his argument with Erasmus, he showed what happened when the categorical syllogism was applied correctly. By this he did not mean that a preacher ever tried to convince a disbeliever by a mere rational proof, but he did mean to give the preacher a sense of the resistance of reason to the logic of preaching, and the reason to keep preaching in the midst of disaster. We could perhaps say that as a science, as a logic, preaching is extraordinarily simple. The difficulty is not in what to say, but to whom you are speaking. There the art becomes complex since sin sets itself in direct opposition to true preaching. Preaching truly sets out Christ, the subject with the proper predicate in this way: Jesus

Christ alone justifies. Free will is not Jesus Christ. Therefore, free will does not justify.

We could, and must eventually, substitute any and every subject in the world below and heavens above for "free will" such as the "Angel Gabriel is not Christ," or "the categorical imperative is not Christ," or even "the visible church is not Christ," and the major premise of the syllogism would work the same way. It gets downright frightening how categorical the negation here is. Try, for example, substituting your own name, or your fondest hope.

When we switch the *subject* of our inquiry to *ourselves* or to the heavenly Father, and take up *Christ as predicate* then we get right down to the heart of the matter. Even the very best thing in life, the most salutary doctrine of life—the law itself—is not Christ. Scripture normally says this by comparing Christ to Moses, and concluding: "the law was given through Moses; grace and truth came through Jesus Christ" (John 1:17). This marks the radical basis of preaching Christ. When you preach Christ categorically, you are preaching the distinction of the law and the gospel. The syllogism is this: no law is ever the gospel.

## PREDICATING CHRIST

Such categories immediately set off every warning signal. Is not this what we call "black and white" thinking? Are not such opposing categories a childish and harmful inability to think in the real world of ambiguous grays? The modern world and its postmodern appendix is a fantastic effort to overcome this truth, to become not "either/or" but "both/and"— to change the dialectic so that all the parts fit into a greater whole, or so that thesis and antithesis are overcome in a higher synthesis, or so that some decision of pure subjectivity awaits you. In actuality, the situation for preaching is much worse even than the possibility of putting things into neat boxes. A categorical preacher does not assume that something is either black or white (one or another substance or quality), but preachers set out the premise that a thing is very specifically either Christ or not. How odd! If a person said, "The paper is white," whiteness would then be predicated of the paper. That makes sense to us, since this is what subjects and predicates in a sentence are for. The predicate is to help identify the subject. But what Luther meant was that the key to the art of preaching is whether or not the preacher applies the predicate *Christ* to her or his subject at any moment. Is this not intolerable narrowing—things are either Christ or not Christ? Indeed it is, but only if a sermon is taken to be the exchange of ideas between a speaker and hearer, or a revelation of what God decided prior to and outside of time, or a proposal for your free will to adopt.[4]

Yet even the preacher who really wants to preach Christ (and not merely muse about the latest theological trends) is left with a real difficulty. Predicating Christ is harder than it sounds. One could say that "God is Christ," and try to make of this a quality like "whiteness" or color so that Christ would then be something like "christness"— meaning certain ideas or qualities that accompany Christ would then apply to divinity, like "love" or "forbearance." If you predicated in that way you would then excite people to imitate one of Christ's many worthy qualities or at least to be influenced by him. In this mode, the common fashion today is to tell people that Christ accepts us as we are so we ought to accept others as they are. In the end, despite whatever intent the preacher had, and however many times Christ was mentioned, the sermon would end up predicating "not Christ" to everything. In place of the incarnate man, Jesus Christ, the preacher puts a "Christ idea." Most "preaching" in churches never does any more than this, it makes Christ into an idea to imitate, and so the speaking is merely an exchange of religious ideas with the hearers that one hopes will help them transcend their earthly problems.

Christ is not a category of ideas or laws, but is the unique, incarnate, historical, individual who came down from above in a permanent act of interference in his own creation. When that sacramental Christ is predicated in preaching, then hearers have nothing left but to conclude, to their horror or joy, that they have *no other God than this man Jesus Christ.*5 It may surprise you how seldom this happens, especially in people who talk endlessly about Jesus and his Christness.

---

4. Lutherans are historically known for the caution of Protestant christocentrism that does not understand the first article and God's work in creation. This was notably applied by Lutherans to Karl Barth in the likes of Hermann Sasse and Gustaf Wingren, among others, but of course the real problem was not the tension between first and second articles of the Creed, theocentrism vs. christocentrism. The real problem is precisely what we are unpacking here, that is, the distinction between law and gospel.

5. Formula of Concord, Solid Declaration VIII, 81, quoting Luther from "The Great Confession Concerning the Holy Supper," *BC* 631.

## GOD HIDING AND REVEALING: NOT-CHRIST AND CHRIST

If we decide (as the Old Adam must), that the predicate "Christ" does not really work, since it is too constrictive for God, then of course we will necessarily be predicating "not-Christ" to God, which presents another set of problems—especially if you are one who has come under the experience of law and failed to justify yourself. God either comes as preached or not, in Christ or outside Christ. Since the true *subject* of preaching (the one speaking) is God, we must attend to what this God wants. God desires preachers specifically to predicate Christ of him, as Paul says, "God was in Christ reconciling the world to himself" (2 Corinthians 5). That means that in any grammatical sentence a preacher will necessarily end up predicating *Christ* of God, or not. What comes out of preachers may be full of religion, and still predicate not-Christ.

Now what does it mean to give God the predicate not-Christ? What are we really doing if we balk at giving Jesus Christ to people because we are convinced they cannot hear him anyway, or we come to believe it is best to give an attribute or quality of Christ instead of the whole person? *God not-Christ* is a divine power whose intentions you do not know, but who judges all. In fact, if you spend any time with this God you would swear he, she or it is out to get you, and is even now removing your free will in relation to the law. In that case it would be much better, it would feel like release and freedom, to cease predicating anything at all of God. Secularism's secret power is this faux-gospel that refrains from speaking for God out of a self-interested humility that eschews the categorical proclamation. Most people hide behind the screen of mystery when it comes to God, since such divine things simply cannot be known, and so it is better to leave them to mystics, higher spiritual authorities, or the insane.

But God is relentless. If you listen to God's words in Scripture, God-without-Christ is a death sentence already delivered. Such a God is the Last Judgment that only awaits your personal execution. The normal reaction to God not-Christ is to delay and run. But successful running from God, as Jonah learned, requires not only a *get away,* but a place to *get to.* A gracious God is nowhere to be found unless God gives a specific word, and as Romans 3 describes it, this word is given only when and where God so chooses. The Jews received God's words, his oracles; the Gentiles did not. The Jews were near God; the Gentiles far away. God either "is" without words or "comes to you" with words. You can spend countless hours convincing people that God is good and merciful in himself, and still end up predicating not-Christ to God. When preachers assure you, for example, that God had nothing to do with a death, they are predicating not-Christ of God. If preachers predicate God without Christ, they must be able to identify precisely where he is mercy—not only in himself, but *for you*. Otherwise you leave people with a Last Judgment that is already made and a long silence afterward while they wait for the other shoe to drop. A successful escape from God requires that you be able to run from God-without-words to God-with-words. Hence, Luther's dictum: finding a gracious God. But this is not a pilgrimage of holiness into the beatific vision, but a flight for survival under terrible duress whose end comes only if a preacher gives Christ's benefits while you are on the run. For that there is no law and no possibility of becoming righteous in yourself, there is only the contingency of whether the preacher arrives or not. The chances of that happening seem ridiculously small and peculiar.

Any other "subject" than God with which preaching deals will also bear either the predicate Christ or not-Christ, so that if you decide one day to address "the human condition" in a sermon, the key, likewise, is how you predicate Christ—whether you are saying the human "is Christ" or "is not-Christ." The one is alive; the other is judged dead already. The one is raised; the other eternally judged. The one is in heaven; the other is in hell. This is how so many preachers get confused about who exactly is dead and who is alive when they are speaking, since taking a person's pulse gives no clue to their actual condition before God. The truths and mistakes of Feuerbach lie in this matter: God is whatever you believe, and so you are the *creatrix divinitatis,* not in essence, but in relation to yourself. Someone like Cyril of Alexandra used to say "in the economy" of God.

Faith is the new locus of the Reformation, as Luther kept repeating, which philosophy and science does not know. Because those sciences are premised on the law alone, they know nothing of faith. In fact, faith is excluded because it deals entirely with the contingent—whether a true preacher arrives or not, and science is specifically charged with the elimination of the contingent. To deal directly and honestly with faith, with true hope for yourself in the end, then either you will believe God's words and have your faith given to you, or you will create a not-Christ God. The trick is not to run to this unpreached God, but from him. Freedom is not creating a silent God to worship, or a God who speaks just like you do, or the attempt to peer through a trace or sign to the mystery of God behind all things. Those are the bondage of will—they captivate the will by saying that there is a much bigger world of great possibilities out there beyond the narrow matter of "Christ" or "not-Christ." Freedom of faith is the absolute contingency of getting the God who is gracious to you, the God who forgives your own personal deicide and creates trust that those words of forgiveness survive the death of the law—for you specifically.

The two predicating categories "Christ" and "not-Christ could possibly be tolerated by sinners if Christ is only an idea, principle, or character to imitate or be influenced by. But that is not what categorical preaching means by Christ. Christ did not become incarnate as "humankind," or "humanity," as if those were viable "categories" for him to enter into outside his normal category of divinity. Nor does he represent an *idea* of grace or love, but he came as a particular person with a history or "timeline," if you like. More to the point, Christ is crucified and his crucifixion was not a mistake, he was murdered for sinners' sakes, and therein is the trouble. He, himself, is the way, truth and life. John's use of this in the "I am" sayings, brings the point home: "*I am*" means he alone "is," and therefore you "*are not*" Christ. Christ spoke there in what the church teachers called his *hypostasis,* his unique individuality and difference from all others, which has become historical and not only the distinction between Creator and creature. That produced an insuperable problem for all sinners seeking justification by some other means than the preacher who brings that man Jesus—all alone.

Sinners immediately reject the basic premise of preaching that all things are either Christ or not-Christ and take shelter in plurality's secret inner monism, like Adam and Eve hiding behind a leaf. This is why we make fun of people who categorize in twos; like the old joke: there are two kinds of people, those who think there are two kinds of people and those who do not. The humor is self-protection that reveals the truth under the guise of ridicule. Reason surmises that, since there are so many things in the world that just are not Christ, like fish in the sea and Hindus in India and possible life on Mars, that one would have to sacrifice too much that is good in order to believe this business about Jesus being "the One." Charles Darwin purportedly rejected his Christian faith prior to the *Beagle* voyage, not because of what he discovered on the Galapagos Islands but because he could not theoretically bear a world in which eternal life is determined by the exclusivity of Christ and the contingency of hearing a preacher—something akin to the very contingency that he was about to rediscover in another place and location, in the mystery of heredity, but this time presumably without God to blame. That reason for rejecting Christ alone as our salvation makes sense when you realize that things did not go well for Jesus in his "time on earth" and if we listened to his story truly, our own stories would already be over and done with. Where Christ is predicated, old time—my time—is over. The Judgment is past. So, here is the captivation of the will that preachers are facing. When everything is distinguished by the categories Christ and not-Christ, sinners quickly get the gist of the message that *they are in the wrong category,* and are out of possibility, so they do whatever it takes to deny the truth. What a jolt to discover that one is not Christ and therefore without any righteousness in oneself.

## INTERMEDIATE PREACHING

The blind search for alternatives to the categories "Christ" and "not-Christ" leads to what Luther called "*something intermediate . . . which, of itself, would be neither evil nor good, neither Christ's nor Satan's, neither true nor false, neither alive nor dead, neither something nor nothing (perhaps).*"[6] The devil is always something "intermediate." Seeking "something intermediate" is deadly since it marginalizes Christ so that we need not live in the wrong category. Christ must be shoved over to make room for some other mediator who preserves our own time. The search for a softer "mean between the extremes" of the two categories leads to absenting Christ (at least partially) in order to create an imaginary "space" by which to escape final judgment. Once Christ is absent, sinners put their "highest and best" in the vacuum—free will. Preachers need to know that this is the secret tool of sinners who have Christ breathing down their necks—the delay tactic is to "defer presence" and so substitute for Christ a mere sign whose user is the free will. Jews seeking signs and Gentiles seeking wisdom are two versions of keeping Christ at bay so as to make him pursuable, something to aim at, all the while convincing us that the Last Judgment has not already occurred.

When a preacher who lays out the true syllogism arrives, it terrifies us, since it is the public declaration of the final judgment (which is, after all, what these "categories" mean). Final judgment means the delay

---

6. Luther, *BW* 307.

is over, leaving the judged to pine for some past dream of mediation or synthesis. After all, we reason, "it takes two to tango." I'll admit my part of the problem in my life if God admits his! This strikes us as common sense, since earthly life is largely occupied with mediations in relationships, and of course everyone knows that successful politics practices the art of compromise. Religious extremists cause terrorism and violence in the world so that moderating types like to "imagine there's no heaven, no religion too." The modern world itself was really an experiment, a bet, that the hoped-for intermediate "something" between Christ and Satan was the *universal intuition of the law within.* The so-called postmodern world has now laid its bet that the intermediate something is the human *ability to adapt* to the hard rule of law outside, to survive and evolve—which is more chaste, perhaps, but no less determined to locate freedom in an elongated human will. Love of duty or love of fate, Kant or Nietzsche, place your bet and take the consequences—none of which can be worse than Christ, and waiting around to see if you get to have a preacher, so it appears.

Whatever else this yields, it creates the kind of intermediate preaching that we are drowning in today. Current pulpit rhetoric has, to its temporal credit, a modesty about it, a kind of reduced expectation. We even call preaching by tepid names like "meditation," or preachers announce they "would like to share some thoughts." Yet, the pattern of give and take, or seeking the mean between extremes, that works elsewhere in our lives is not sufficient for our relationship to the all-worker God. God wants more. The relationship between Creator and creatures must deal with what Scripture calls *a jealous* God who does not compromise or meet us on middle ground. This God deals in totals because he wants all of you, not part, and will not compromise one iota on the law. To get this he sends all of Christ, not part of Christ, and when that happens preaching cannot give Christ in small doses to keep a sick patient alive. What we are after here is the eschatological end matter—what finally justifies. How can we stand before God at the Final Judgment? How do we get over the primal fear of contingency and election when we notice that some hear and some do not? In fact, it seems to reduce everything to the "miracle" of accidental truths of history, which Lessing taught us cannot be trusted to last a whole eternity. What if I wait and wait and no preacher comes? What if I once received a preacher, but then the Spirit was withdrawn and I must wait again? Who can live like this day after day in a world of accidents and chance events that He outside my own will?

Categorical preaching deals cleanly with these questions that swirl around a preacher by saying: "you cannot, Christ can—in fact he already has." But the cost is too high for the Old Adam, who goes searching for a scheme that leaves him more time in which to become righteous in the self rather than wait around to see if a righteous God will miraculously appear. Most preachers and congregations opt for the dream of intermediate preaching.

Lutherans are miles behind most American churches in perfecting intermediate preaching. Since the outcome is disastrous anyway we might take pride in this fact, but once we enter the dusk of night in which all cows are gray we ought at least to attend to the professionals in the area. For that, let's recall a quintessential American event.

## EMERSON AT CHURCH

One winter day almost two hundred years ago, Ralph Waldo Emerson went to church. Why he went to church that day was a mystery, even to himself, since things had gotten so bad with Christianity that, as one of his friends told him, "On Sundays it seems wicked to go to church." Christians all over America were "signing off," dropping out of the church, because it did not answer their most basic questions or, as we say it today, "meet their needs." For this reason, Emerson reflected on that winter day in his classic "Divinity School Address (Harvard)" July 15, 1838. He thought of church as "Historical Christianity, suckled in a creed outworn," or what most people today call "organized religion." Organized religion lacked "soul," especially in a period of religious decline like his own in which the old, believing Puritans were long gone. For Emerson, there were only two reasons left to go to church at all. One was to join the democratic collection of Americans called out by the Sabbath tradition from their daily toils, habits, and class distinctions into the cheerful contemplation that they were, after all, *something more.* The Sabbath could be the best day of your week when it *lifted* you to the transcendent along with everyone else, whether you were a coal miner or college professor.

The other reason to go to church was for the preaching—"the speech of man to men" as Emerson liked to say—that great old institution brought over to our shores by the dissenting Protestants who nearly burst at the seams to preach since they were forbidden the pulpit in Europe (often enough by Lutherans!).[7] Even if you no longer got a good Puritan sermon from the likes of Cotton Mather, you could still hope to hear some stoical morality by the less gifted subsequent generation.

The particular day Emerson went to this church, the old democratic Sabbath seemed to be working just fine—all classes and types were mingling there—but what really flunked his ecclesial test was the preaching; it was simply vulgar. The pulpit, he said, was "usurped by a formalist" who preached dry doctrine about what others believed once upon a time. Emerson heard tradition's rundown on the way things used to be. He got, he says, the "usual," the "second hand," the historical, what *Paul* or *Wesley* believed, instead of the "necessary, eternal" truths of the law. Bad as the doctrine was, when it was over things got worse. What followed in the sermon was the inevitable request for contributions to foreign missionaries in order to foist on some poor, sodded primitives a thousand miles away what he as a Christian was barely able to endure here—more bad preaching about dead white males by dead white males! Then the preacher concluded with, "come back next Sunday and we'll run through the same thing again," and a paltry invitation to the Lord's Supper with its "hollow, dry, creaking formality"—a ritual of ancient sacrifice in the form of metaphors.[8] I hate to agree with Emerson on much here, but when Christ gets absented in order to make room for a sign that can be interpreted in endless, pluralistic ways (the secret of the old Mass Canon and modern Eucharistic prayers) it is true that even the Sacrament becomes hollow and dry.

In any case, on that famous old day, Emerson got bored. While the preacher preached, he looked out the church window and saw the falling snow of a winter storm. Then he thought to himself a nearly eternal thought—"the snowstorm is real, the preacher merely spectral." The snowstorm outside was life and power and excitement and—well, it was Nature! Nature never forgets what is most essential about itself—the "ought," the *law,* the divine necessity of life. Snowflakes fall down, as they ought, and do so without resistance. What Emerson wanted from his preacher was something of that snowfall—it was what he called "life." He wanted the preacher to discharge "the great and perpetual office of the

---

7. Emerson, "The Divinity School Address," 91.

8. Ibid, 86.

preacher,"[9] which was the means to convey the joy of the law from one man to another, to "beget a desire" for doing what is right. In other words, for Emerson preaching was persuasion of the will, whose test was the "power to charm and command the soul," so that we "find pleasure and honor in obeying." There you go, you preachers, your job is to charm the soul into finding pleasure in obeying the law. The law and free will always seem to be the very best "intermediates" between Christ and not-Christ.

To charm another soul the preacher needs a style of "friendship," not "formality." So as Emerson sat there preferring the silent "preaching" of the snowstorm to the bluster of his minister, he wished the preacher would excite him with the law, lift up, "entertain," as he says.[10] To preach *friendly not formally* meant the preacher needed to express his own soul in terms of his own, personal experience of life. God's best work is the law, and the preacher works his charm when he presents the *law as a positive, personal experience.* So he complained of his dreary preacher:

> Not one fact in all his experience, had he yet imported into his doctrine . . . Not a line did he draw out of real history. The true preacher can be known by this, that he deals out to the people *his* life . . . But of the bad preacher, it could not be told from his sermon, what area of the world he fell in; whether he had a father or a child; whether he was a freeholder or a pauper; whether he was a citizen or a countryman, or any other fact of his biography. It seemed strange that the people should come to church. It seems as if their houses were very unentertaining, that they should prefer this thoughtless clamor.[11]

This is what Emerson calls "preaching unworthily." If people come to church at all, it must mean they have no entertainment at home. The preacher should inspire us by drawing on his own inner resources, so that we in turn can draw on ours. What are those inner resources? The ability to endure what seems unendurable, to get through a "rugged crisis," at which times our true angel-selves are shown—so that when tested by fire we can rise above. Spirit is not found in revelations of the past, the external word, and so the preacher does not bring something we do not already have. Since we have law within, we have God within. Emerson wanted the preacher to help him discover his own inner prophet: "Yourself a newborn

9. Ibid., 84.

10. Ibid., 85.

11. Ibid.

bard of the Holy Ghost," and such new prophets of the Spirit are meant to chart new, untrodden paths to make of this world a better place to live.[12] Preachers should help us find better laws by which to live, laws that live eternally within.

A preacher is a bad preacher, for the quintessential American, Emerson, when the law comes out as something that must be imitated from outside, like when he tells you that there are Wesleys and Oberlins or for that matter even Jesus Christs to follow. Instead, the joy of the law is to be an *inventor,* to do what is natural to one. Soulful Americans do not *imitate,* they *invent.* They do not find the spirit in Bibles or Christs of long ago—they find the universal law within. Without this spiritual excitement "parishes are signing off," and so we have what Emerson called a decaying and declining church. Our preachers have no soul; they do not express what is in them, and so cannot excite "soul" in anyone else. They make Jesus's own gospel "not glad." The preacher, in the end, must tell us to trust our own hearts where one finds the great and divine "Ought." Otherwise your God is a tyrant, your law someone else's, and your own invented hope will be crushed.

This most American of arguments desires Nature's snow, not a preacher who ends the law. What Emerson wanted, what we all want, is to get rid of preachers entirely, once and for all. Preachers drag down, not lift up. They give us *their* opinions instead of listening to *ours.* They bring an external word, instead of turning us into ourselves to find the truth.[13] They make us experience the law as a burden, not a joy! They are contingent, and freedom lies in the eternal, invincible. The problem with the gospel in the end is that its subject is not "me," and so Emerson finally gets to the real issue when he said that Christian preaching "dwells, with noxious ex-aggeration about the *person* of Jesus."[14] When preaching dwells on Christ's person, rather than his principles, it always comes back to one boring thing: it speaks as if the future is over and done with. No more possibility. Time is already up. Jesus is the end of the law, and so of me. Judgment is

---

12. Ibid., 89.

13. Truth "cannot be received at second hand . . .What he announces, I must find true in me, or wholly reject; and on his word, or as his second, be he who he may, I can accept nothing." No "secondary" faith for me! No bestowed, given, external word for me! Preachers must in the end go; even if they are needed as a "temporary crutch until I am healed" (ibid., 79).

14. Ibid., 81.

over. Such preachers "come to speak of the revelation as somewhat long ago given and done, as if God were dead." Well, there is the trouble. God is dead in this old world, once and for all. And all history can do is point fingers. Who wants to hear that *preparation* and even *perseverance* for the Last Judgment is fruitless, that the Final Judgment is over? The only thing that American glory, enthusiasm, and transcendence then required in order to become completely decadent was to take away Emerson's faith in the universality of the law. Without that old enlightenment belief in universal law, whatever is inside a person is understood to be utterly unique and different, and as uniquely posited it must be expressed in its plurality to the outside world in order to make each individual "free." The "holy office" of preaching is moved inside, eaten alive, and so anyone who attempts to preach either the law or its end in Jesus Christ is in for an eschatological, end-time fight with those great numbers who are "signing off" from categorical preachers who refuse to confirm that the hearers are, after all, God themselves. Instead of Christ crucified, and the forgiveness of sins "categorically," we want friendly preachers expressing their experience of life soulfully so as to excite the desire to heroic acts that overcome obstacles and find joy not in outward material, but in the inner spirit—which is the perfect, progressing, life-giving, inventive law itself.[15]

## THE RADICAL GOSPEL AND THE END OF HISTORY

Our problem with preaching is the problem of every age. The intermediate between Christ and not-Christ produces a search for the hidden God within. Luther called it enthusiasm. Seeking God within is what sinners do who do not want a word from God who is outside them, judging them. Enthusiasts do not like categorical preaching. They prefer the excitement of a preacher who "deals out to the people *his* life," or for those even more advanced in inner searching, they prefer the silent preaching of the falling

---

15. It is true that bad preaching produced this response of Emerson's in the first place. In particular it resulted from the very bad attempt of finding an intermediate by teaching both predestination and the third use of the law as the mind of God himself that forced this debacle upon us. When preaching became the substitution of Christ's merit for ours, and left us with the imitation of Christ, who can stand hearing time and again how much better than you is your brother? Preaching that fell into the external law alone is usually answered by demanding the end to preaching the law with its proper predication of "not Christ." One theological enthusiasm in Puritanism begets an even greater and opposite theological enthusiasm like Emerson's.

snow. All we need in order to find Divinity and our happiness is time and a map! God's hiddenness then becomes something of an adventure like a robust mountain climb rather than a second shoe waiting to fall on us.

Preaching to bound wills means that the dream of being a potential-ist, an optimist or pessimist, a delayer and denier is over. *God died* by a homicide that was religious, state sponsored, and irrevocable, and this historical accident changed everything. God has an accusation to bring, that the sin against the Holy Spirit has been committed with universal complicity. Humans are not right; in fact, they are irredeemable and un-forgivable by any measure of justice or any leniency of mercy. The wages of sin is death, so the sinner must die. Categorical preaching concedes no neutrality to the will nor does it concede that the will has any time remaining to change itself once the preacher arrives. That means preach-ing is always *preaching to the dead.*

There is no other rhetoric in the world that assumes bound wills who cannot hear because they *will* not to hear and so willing *cannot* hear. Preaching is therefore utterly unique as categorical speech, not as some supernatural form of communication called "revelation," but precisely because it does the impossible in the most down-to-earth way—it gives something that cannot be heard unless God creates a new person to hear it. Preaching also *raises the dead.*

Passing on this categorical preaching has always been difficult. It must be done, as with Paul and the apostles, through the crucified body. In his inaugural essay for the second series of *Lutheran Quarterly,* Gerhard Forde made some suggestions as to how to preach what he there called "the Radical Gospel."[16] First, he argued that it is always *proclama-tion and not theology* that justifies by faith alone. Theology has as its goal to get preachers to preach categorically. Theology does not accept that its work, like that of philosophy, is to eliminate contingency, but to multiply it. Talking *about* forgiveness must give way to actually *giving* it—thus the-ology is for preaching, and preaching elects historically.

Second, radical or categorical preaching must not compromise with sinners by becoming only "a repair job." It speaks without any conditions about what death is—death is whatever is not-Christ. You and I are in the wrong category, but the gospel is a new creation because Christ forgives through preaching.

16. Forde, "Radical Lutheranism," 13–16. See also this volume 15–30.

In this way a third matter emerges in categorical preaching: everything is marked by the distinction between what is preached and not preached, new and old. "Everything" includes yourself, the world, God—everything and everyone bears this distinction. Instead of living life so as *not to die* (what the world pushes us to do) we proclaim what it means to *die so that we truly live*.

That inverted world has been forcefully opposed, as we might guess, by the largest powers this world can muster: the devil, the fallen world, and our own sinful selves. These have aligned themselves from the beginning to oppose Christ, and when they saw their own demise in the cross, they went after the next best thing: the down-to-earth preacher of Christ. The entirety of history, in the form of ideas or acts, is the attempt to rid ourselves of contingency, as Hegel knew, which means nothing other than ridding ourselves of categorical preachers.[17] This is actually the secret, or the cunning of history, which hides its violence by supporting the life of many other forms of rhetoric. Getting rid of contingency means eliminating God's choice, which comes, as Hegel knew, in historical form in the act of preaching Christ categorically. History in all of its parts and scope is made by sinners refusing to let God elect anyone, including themselves—in order to overcome the fear that some may hear and others not. Even in its most ideal moments, history is deeply material, and the material is the most tangible, earthly rebellion that seeks to destroy God's preaching office. Christ has no place or time according to this worldly scheme. After all, if you are getting rid of preachers, you must get rid of the preacher par excellence, the one who spoke "as one who has authority," that is, the preacher who himself became the preached (Bultmann). Christ the Savior is downright dangerous to a will seeking to embrace either duty or fate—the two options of modern and postmodern worlds.

Christ was murdered in order to stop all preaching and election. The cross failed to do this, despite all human efforts, and now that Christ cannot be killed again, the next best thing is to execute the ambassadorial preacher. Sometimes blood is spilled again and we call it martyrdom, but more often it is easier to execute a preacher in a bloodless coup. If the preacher can be enticed to give something else than Christ as the proper predicate for the true Subject, the Creator, then a death occurs with no apparent violence. It seems like the perfect crime. Just predicate some-

17. "The sole aim of philosophical inquiry is to eliminate the contingent" (Hegel, *Lectures on the Philosophy of World History: Introduction*, 28).

thing other of God than Christ—you have the freedom to say whatever you want, do you not? Consequently, the largest offenders against God's mission on earth are preachers themselves.

The formula for bad preaching is simple, you mix law and gospel and come out with a law that sounds like the gospel in its excessive religiosity like: "Grace means unconditional acceptance of your good creation," or even "acceptance of your acceptance while unacceptable," "Try, but if you fail God will not condemn." "The Gospel is free, now all you need to do is join God's mission and spread it." "God is love, so there is no law," or "Christ stands for no barriers or divisions." Most especially, bad preaching offers Christ as a principle or a sign that is supposed to influence you to become like him as measured by the law. The intermediate mixups in preaching are many and common.

Categorical preaching takes place in the "bright light" of the distinction of law and gospel. It understands that Christ is present as Lord of his church as the one whom we crucified. Otherwise, one makes of Scripture a self-justification: "Choose me Lord, it only makes sense!" Categorical preaching assumes that God's Word always meets a bound, addicted, captivated will that refuses the truth that there is either Christ or not Christ, that no other hope or future exists.

The content of preaching is summarized in the chief article of justification by faith alone, and can be given in a nutshell this way: Jesus Christ, our God and Lord was put to death for our trespasses and raised again for our justification (Paul in Romans 4:25). You killed him; the Father raised him (Peter in Acts 2). Jesus says, "I am the way, the truth and the life, no one comes to the Father but by me" (John 14). The law kills, the Spirit gives life (Paul in 2 Corinthians 3). Jesus said to them again, "Peace be with you. As the Father has sent me, so I send you." When he had said this, he breathed on them and said to them, "Receive the Holy Spirit. If you forgive the sins of any, they are forgiven them; if you retain the sins of any, they are retained" (John 20).

## POTENT FORGIVENESS

A sermon first tells the basic story of the man Jesus Christ: that he is God, that he came down from heaven incarnate as this particular person rather than an ideal cause, and that this man preached to elect the ungodly outside the law. For this he was killed, sacrificed, and even became a curse for us. He became contingent among those who refused God's own contingent mercy. The Father raised him up as Lord of a new kingdom, which he will never leave, and so he sits in judgment over all. That judgment is already made, but there is potent forgiveness, which is the resurrection of the dead. Receiving that forgiveness from a preacher as an external word is the way you "find" a gracious God—or better, that he finds you. This God speaks and so creates a new person who enters a new kingdom or world. Everything following this cross is thus categorically either Christ or not-Christ, belonging to Christ or not. Preaching elects, first by counting the trespass and denying the righteousness of the hearer, and then by creating anew.

If it is clear that the free will is not Christ, then neither is the law Jesus Christ, which is the hardest blow of all. Sin sees Christ as intolerably narrow; faith receives Christ as the fullness of life eternal. Categorical preaching is therefore the true worship of God in Christ that makes it possible to worship the unpreached God by running away because it gives the one place you can run to, Christ himself and alone. Getting rid of such a preacher leaves you with a God whose will you know in general, but you never know what he thinks about you in particular. Getting a righteous, gracious God happens through preaching so that the categories Christ and not-Christ do not remain abstractions, but are actually *predicated, given for you.* Most amazingly, they are predicated of us not because of what is in us; which is to say that getting a gracious God is none other than the act of forgiving the unforgivable apart from their contrition or guilt or mending of ways—on account of Christ alone. But forgiveness does not mean that the person remains more or less the same. It radically breaks the person eternally between old and new, dead and raised. By this "the true worship has now been restored, that is, the preaching of the Word of God, by which God is truly made known and honored."[18]

True preachers know the difference between heaven and hell, death and life, because they know a little something about Christ. They know we have no other God than Christ. Eliminating this announcement is the end of contingency, accidents, election, fate and all the world's fears only in one sense: all have fallen short of the glory of God. What we all need is a *new contingency* to enter the world that the world knows not of, and so he has. We need Christ who chose sinners in what can only be called the

---

18. Luther, "Psalm 2," *LW* 12:4.

most blessed contingency ever to happen to a person, better than dumb luck or winning the lottery or surviving an earthquake, namely, to have some preacher predicate Christ of me. Not even the great Aristotle would know how to categorize me then, other than to say that this is really, truly new—unprecedented, unrepeatable, neither scientific or metaphysical, and unheard of until now. When you have such a gracious God, being filled by grace in your old self becomes irrelevant. Categorical preaching to a lost cause is the only thing that honors God as the one who justifies himself by justifying me, for in that reconciliation the crucified Christ has become all in all. That is worth the wait.

## BIBLIOGRAPHY

Emerson, Ralph Waldo. "The Divinity School Address." In *Essays & Lectures*, 77–92. Library of America 15. New York: Classics of the U.S., distributed by Viking, 1983.

Forde, Gerhard O. *The Captivation of the Will: Luther vs. Erasmus and Bondage*. Edited by Steven Paulson. Lutheran Quarterly Books. Grand Rapids: Eerdmans, 2005.

———. "Radical Lutheranism." In *A More Radical Gospel: Essays on Eschatology, Authority, Atonement, and Ecumenism*, edited by Mark C. Mattes and Steven D. Paulson, 3–16. Lutheran Quarterly Books. Grand Rapids: Eerdmans, 2004.

"Formula of Concord: Solid Declaration." In *BC*.

Hegel, G. W. F. *Lectures on the Philosophy of World History: Introduction, Reason in History*. Translated by H. B. Nesbit. Cambridge Studies in the History and Theory of Politics. Cambridge: Cambridge University Press, 1975.

Luther, Martin. *On the Bondage of the Will* (*BW*). Translated by J. I. Packer and O. R. Johnston. Westwood, NJ: Revell, 1957.

———. "Psalm 2." In *LW* 12.

# 8

# Preaching the Sacraments

*Gerhard O. Forde*

## THE SACRAMENT OF PREACHING

BEFORE WE CAN GET on to the matter of preaching the sacraments it is necessary to say something about preaching itself. So I have titled this first part "The Sacrament of Preaching." I take this title because my thesis is that we would do well to take our cue for preaching from what we do in the sacraments: We *do* something. We *wash* people. We *give* Christ to them. I remember a heated discussion once in which a theological professor was arguing with students who complained that teaching Christian doctrine with the aim of convincing was "brainwashing." The professor replied without flinching, "We do not wash just their brains, we wash their whole bodies!" In the sacraments, that is, we do not just *explain* Christ or the gospel, or *describe* faith, or give instructions about how to get salvation, or whatever (though we may well do all of that), we just give it, do it, flat out, unconditionally. One of the most persistent problems in this regard is that what is said in the sermon is all too often quite at odds with what we do in the sacraments. If we give unconditionally in the sacraments we are likely to take it back or put conditions on it in the sermon and leave our people completely confused. We are likely to imply in our preaching that the gift is not really what it is cracked up to be so now they better get *really* serious. We are tempted to operate like the TV "evangelists" who warn us not to depend on baptism. The upshot of that is that people are cut adrift between Word and sacrament so that their allegiance to one or the other is reduced to a matter of taste or "preference."

So something of a split develops in the Christian camp. On the one hand the preaching of the Word undercuts the sacraments. On the other hand there seems to be a growing antipathy to the preached Word (the "excessive wordiness" of our worship) and in some circles at least, a growing appreciation for sacraments. For the most part, preaching gets a bad name. Preaching is equivalent to scolding or haranguing. "Do not preach at me!" we yell, when all else fails. I expect that one reason people are coming more and more to prefer sacraments is that there you have to become a giver, like it or not. You cannot deny your role, the role of ministry. The rubrics direct you to it and will not let you escape. You actually have to work at it to avoid it or louse it up—though I suppose one can manage that too if one tries! Some, alas, actually succeed! But is there not something of a judgment on us in that people on the fringes, for whatever reason, whatever vestigial remains of faith might be there, are still willing, even anxious, to have their babies baptized, but hesitate or even resist allowing us to holler at them? Indeed, we find ourselves in a kind of Catch 22: they do not want to hear the preaching because likely as not it will take away what is given in the sacrament, and at the same time they have such a poor understanding of the sacraments because they never hear them preached. Of late, there seems to be a move afoot to remedy matters by restricting access to or taking the sacraments away from them altogether! A curious way to solve our problems, I should think!

At any rate, preaching on the sacraments is not likely to do much good if the preaching itself is at odds with what goes on in the sacraments. So we need first to talk about preaching itself as a sacrament, an instance in which one does basically the same thing as one does in those other instances which we have come to term "the sacraments," baptism and the Lord's Supper. It was Regin Prenter, I believe, who always insisted that for Luther the basic reform move over against the medieval tradition was not, as with most of Protestantism, to "spiritualize" the sacraments, to reduce them to handy illustrations or symbolizations of a spiritual communication that supposedly takes place only by words, internally in the mind, from "spirit" to "spirit." Luther's move, we might say, was not to "wordify" the sacrament, but rather to sacramentalize the Word. The preaching of the Word, that is, is to do the same thing as the sacrament—to give Christ and all his blessings. Indeed, since the Word is Christ, preaching is "pouring Christ into our ears" just as in the sacraments we are baptized into him, and he is poured into our mouths. We have tended to overlook or forget the fact that the Christ whose body and blood is really present in the Supper is also really present in the speaking of the Word. Preaching is to be understood as a sacramental event.

So we can do no better in thinking about preaching than to take our cue from the sacraments. To preach is to give Christ to the hearer, to do the sacrament to them. Now that, of course, is easily said. But the question is, how do we do it? How do we do something with words? What can we do? In the sacraments we can wash them or give them a bit of bread and some wine. We can do something. But what can we do with words?

Now the Lutheran tradition has had a lot to say about what to do with words. Indeed, one could say that theology itself in this tradition is largely instruction on what to do with words in preaching, how to make them come out right, do what they are supposed to do. The much maligned, caricatured, and misunderstood art of distinguishing between law and gospel is simply a matter of learning what to do with the words. That distinction is the outcome of centuries of wrestling with the problem going back all the way to the New Testament, signaled especially by St. Paul's struggles with the matter and his insistence in 2 Corinthians 3:6 that the letter, the written code, kills, but the Spirit gives life. The claim that the letter kills but the Spirit gives life is an assertion in unmistakable terms about what words can actually do. They can kill and make alive, they put to death the old and call the new to life in Christ. The art of distinguishing between law and gospel is simply the attempt to reclaim in the living present this active, sacramental functioning of the words for the preaching of the church. "The letter kills but the Spirit gives life" translates into "the law kills, but the gospel gives life."

This kind of consideration can help us with our questions about how to preach sacramentally, how to give Christ to the hearers, to do something with the words. When I myself try to put all the pieces of the tradition together in a view of preaching that takes its cue from the sacraments, I come up with what I fear is something of a barbarism: Preaching is doing the text to the hearers. *Doing* the text, not merely explaining it (though that will be involved), not merely exegeting the text (though that is presupposed and indispensable), not merely describing or prescribing what Christians are supposed to do (though that will no doubt result).

Preaching in a sacramental fashion is *doing* to the hearers what the text authorizes you to do to them.

Before I go on to talk about what such doing the text to the hearers involves, it is important to consider what it does not mean, because that is most often where our problem lies. Just the task of understanding an ancient text of course confronts us with a number of severe difficulties in and of itself. But *preaching* or applying an ancient text raises the ante much higher. How do we bridge the time gap between then and now? Or as the question most often comes down, how do we make the text *relevant* to our time? The overwhelming, well nigh incurable tendency we have is to run to some sort of translation, to try to make the text relevant by translating it into more viable terms, either of a more "timeless" metaphysical sort (something that is *always* true like eternal ideas or doctrines or laws) or, since such esoterica are in disfavor today, into more contemporary terms and stories. How many sermons do not begin with some anecdote or "experience" from "real life" so as to set the stage for proving its relevance in some fashion or other? Personally, I have just about reached a state of complete despair over this constantly repeated, dreary approach to the matter. You can just bet the preacher spent most of the week looking for some such handle to sneak the text onto the scene—and little time actually exegeting the text itself? So when you come home and ask yourself whether anything was really said about the text, the answer most likely would have to be that the preacher was too preoccupied with being relevant and so never really got around to it!

Always, it seems, the text has to be translated into *our* terms, twisted to fit what we call our "needs." In the old days, before the Reformation put a stop to it, they were at least more open and above board about it. They had a method for doing it and that afforded at least some restraint on the nonsense that could be perpetrated even if it was not always terribly successful. They called it "spiritual interpretation." Usually it is referred to as the allegorical method. Even though the Reformation tried to shut down this entire enterprise and suggest other ways of interpreting and preaching the text, it seems simply to have gone underground only to emerge unrecognized (because it is now without a name) particularly in our preaching. The historical method has pretty much banished allegory from interpretation and exegesis, but because that method suggests no effective substitute when we come to preaching, the old monkey business surfaces again in all sorts of nefarious ways.

We tend to become allegorists. The secret of allegory is that it translates the text into "another story," *allo agoreuo*. "Other-speak" would probably be a good translation for "allegory," something like George Orwell's "newspeak." Basically what happens is not that the story of the text invades our lives or changes them but rather that we change the text to fit *our* story. Or we become tropologists. Tropology was also part of the method of spiritual exegesis and had to do with the moral application of the text—what we are to do about it. Often, in our impatience to be relevant we feel the pressure to translate the text into something to do. Little ever comes of it, of course. Confident that they have gotten their expected scolding, people go home to Sunday dinner and watch the game on television. But at least we preachers can supposedly salve our consciences with the comfort that we have once again managed the marvelous feat of translating the text into some handy moralisms and so accomplished the duty everyone expected of us!

The general result of these misadventures is that preaching does not proceed in sacramental fashion. Instead of *doing* the text to the hearers, preachers at best only *explain* it, no doubt with as many clever and appealing illustrations as one can muster. Or one describes the Christian life, or prescribes what we are to do. The text becomes the occasion for us to do something, if, perchance, that something can be demonstrated to be relevant to our "needs." The text does not do anything to us to change us or incorporate us in its story; rather the text is changed to fit our story. The Word becomes mere information or description or instruction. Thus instead of being a sacrament, the Word becomes an occasion for us to exercise our powers; it becomes a law, perhaps inevitably a club with which to beat people.

We have had much fuss in the church about the relationship between preaching and sacrament. We pride ourselves in being a church of the Word and get nervous about stressing the sacraments to the degree that the priority of the Word is threatened. But we have to be cannier about sorting out the problem here. If the Word we preach does not do anything, if it is not sacramental, then it is only meet, right, and salutary that sacraments come to the fore as the only really viable mediators of the grace of God. This actually happened in ancient and medieval times, when the Word became really just doctrinal or moral instruction. The sacraments became the only available and reliable means of grace. But that development brought with it no little distortion in the understanding of grace. When sacraments are not preached they can degenerate into religious automats for dispensing a substantialized grace. Sacraments too, that is, are removed from the story of the text and fall into a different story. But then, of course, we only compound the felony if in righteous zeal for the preached Word we proceed to exalt a preaching that is not sacramental over the sacraments. Exalting a nonsacramental Word over the sacraments will only mean the complete bowdlerization of everything. The sacraments too will then degenerate into religious tea parties. That is to say, the sacraments too will eventually succumb to allegory, "other-speak," be translated into our story. The Holy Communion, for instance, will become merely our communion, our "fellowship," our "celebration" of whatever it is we think we have to celebrate. When the passing of the peace is supposed to take place what you get is, "Hi there, my name is George," rather than the Peace of the Lord! It all degenerates, as Luther already scornfully remarked on one occasion, into a parish fair. Word and sacrament will stand or fall together.

By now we have circled around our prey long enough, I think. It is time to pounce and go for the jugular. What is the sacrament of preaching? How does one *do* the text to the hearers? Now we come to the difficult business akin to lecturing on swimming. Eventually the only way out will be to try some concrete examples, look at some texts and develop what doing such texts might mean. That is always tricky, of course. Preaching styles are often highly individualized and differ a great deal. One runs the risk of a certain arrogance by suggesting one's own as an example to be emulated. But there is finally no way out of doing it if I am to convey some idea of what I am harping about. So I shall make some attempts to do just that.

Before we proceed to the examples, however, a couple of general remarks are in order. First, if one is going to preach in sacramental fashion, do the text to the hearer, one has, of course, to pay close attention to the text. That should go without saying, but since it seems seldom to be done, one must keep on saying it. Doing the text, furthermore, involves paying attention to the text in a quite specific manner: looking to see what the text actually *did* and is supposed to do, and therefore what it authorizes you to do. One must see what it did and then re-aim it to do the same thing in the present to the assembled hearers. Usually the text itself gives you the clues. The texts usually involve highly charged dramatic situations in which the Word of God is cutting into people's lives. It will tell you that they were amazed, shocked, incensed, or even took up stones to kill, or marveled, or glorified God, and so on. Jesus got killed for saying those things. Doing the text again should provide a rather interesting agenda!

Second, doing the text involves wielding the text so as to do what is supposed to be done if the letter, or law, kills and the Spirit gives life. Doing the text may help us around some of the perpetual problems we seem to have with the business about law and gospel. We seem always to get ourselves into a bind where we do not do very well with it. We apply it in too wooden a fashion or turn it into psychological gimmickry where first so much law is applied to frighten and then gospel applied to comfort—and on the other hand we do not do very well without it. Sermons degenerate into exegetical lectures at best, or at worst little talks of a popular religious sort on how to cope with "life's problems." Which is to say that when we do not concern ourselves with the difference between law and gospel all we do is preach the law—usually without any teeth in it, but law nevertheless.

We tend to get all tangled up in arguments about whether to preach the law or not. Are people not already sufficiently burdened by it? Do they not encounter it all the time in the general rot and despair of daily life in contemporary society? So the questions go. Preaching the law effectively is indeed one of the most difficult tasks of all. The idea of doing the text may afford some help. For that means that the law is precisely the cutting edge of the text itself, the way the text cuts into our lives. One does not have to scratch around for some law external to the text to preach, look for some "relevant" story or experience or analysis of the current morass to convince of the text's importance. One should seek to preach the law of *the text*. The law is simply the cutting edge of the gospel and is usually immediately to hand in the text itself in the form of the hard saying, the offensive announcement, the cutting remark, the crucial incident, that sets the whole matter rolling. Doing the text involves taking that and running with it, using it to kill the old and then turning it about so that it can, in the end, be heard as gospel. Doing the text involves using the Word to kill and make alive. Perhaps if we get some idea of what that means we will approach preaching as a sacramental event, doing something, not always and forever trying to turn the text into something to do.

To see what that might mean let us look at a couple of texts. The first is the one about the hidden treasure in Matthew 13:44. I like to use this as an example because it was in a struggle over what to do with this text that the idea of doing the text first struck me. The kingdom of heaven, we are told, is like treasure hidden in a field, which a man found and covers up; then in his joy he goes and sells all that he has and buys that field. As with most gospel texts, it is actually rather difficult to turn this into a law text, turn it into something to do. But I expect we can manage it if we work hard enough at it! In itself, of course, the text hardly proposes something to do to gain the kingdom of heaven and makes no sense at all in such terms. It is just a story about the absolute surprise of stumbling onto hidden treasure, and makes the claim that gaining the kingdom of heaven is like that. But how could that possibly be "relevant" to anything? Law theologians, as we shall call them for short, have to find some way to invest the strange words with a "meaning" we can buy into, some way to translate them into something for us to do. Thus I suppose our law theologian might say something like this: "If you plow your field faithfully, if you really stick to it day after day, if you think positively and really believe in your possibilities and refuse to surrender to negative thoughts, and so on, someday, somewhere, you too might find your treasure." Plowing the field seems the most immediate way you could work in something to do. If you plod along faithfully like a good old workhorse, maybe you too will get yours. Life has its little surprises after all. The kingdom of heaven comes to those who think positively and stick with it. Some day your ship too will come in! You can turn the text into such "Little Engine That Could" theology.

Or there is, of course, that bit about selling all. Now *there is* something to really sink your teeth into, something to do! The price is, alas, a bit higher than I expect we would be prepared to pay! But it is something to *do* at least! If you want to get your treasure, you will have to sell all. You really have to get serious now. Renounce everything, the lusts of the flesh, the pleasures of materialistic society, and so forth. The only trouble is that according to the text it was at his joy at having already found the treasure that the man went and sold all. The action sprang from his joy; it was not a condition for arriving at his joy. In general, it is pretty difficult to make anything but complete hash of such texts by turning them into something to do.

For the disturbing, perhaps even shockingly irresponsible thing about the text is that the man in the first instance did not *do* anything to deserve or earn the treasure. He did not plan for it, he did not strive for it, he did not earn it, nothing. He just stumbled onto it one fine day quite by "accident." You feel about him, perhaps, much like you feel about someone who wins a lottery or a sweepstakes. Lucky stiff! What did he ever do to deserve that? The unspoken resentment is always there: "When, oh when, do I ever in this unfair and cruel world get mine?"

Now it seems to me that the preacher who wants to *do* such a text to the hearers would have to sail right into the storm here and drive home precisely the shocking nature of this surprise. The "law" here, the letter that kills, is precisely the shock, the unfairness of it all. It is the cutting edge of the gospel. There is nothing to do. Here God is at work, no one else. Nothing avails. One certainly cannot end the discourse by exhorting the congregation to go out and find some hidden treasure! Hidden treasure just is not that available—as though I could resolve while shaving in the morning that today I am going to find some hidden treasure! In the text we are told that the man covered it up after he found it. It even sounds rather unethical. Apparently it was not even his field! It is truly hidden treasure and it stays that way, hidden even under apparently questionable behavior. I expect the very hiddenness here is related to the fact that Jesus spoke in parables so that those whose ears have become fat shall not hear, and those who think they know shall not know, to exclude completely the notion that here there is anything to do. There is nothing. The treasure belongs to God; it is hidden; it is an absolute surprise. Just imagine how that must have hit in a society where all those parties had their formulas for getting into or realizing the kingdom! Some said keeping the law would do it. Some said retreating into the desert to practice righteousness and wait was the key. Others said they must revolt against Roman overlords, and so on. But here it is said that the kingdom is like hidden treasure that a man just stumbled onto. Just think of that!

Now, however, the text has you in a corner. Now what can you do? If the treasure belongs to God, if it is impenetrably hidden, what can you do? Where does the preacher go from here? When I arrived at this point and was struggling with what to say it suddenly dawned on me that that was just the point, there was not anything I could do, no way out, nothing to which I could point. And so there was only one course of action left: I could only give them the treasure! Do it to them! I could only surprise them absolutely by daring to say to the hearers, "You lucky stiffs, you have stumbled onto it here and now because I am here to say that Jesus died and went into the blackness of death and still overcame for you. I am here to say your sins are forgiven! There it is! The hidden treasure! The kingdom of heaven. The preacher has to have the audacity to exercise the office of ministry, the audacity to believe that the very moment of the preaching is itself the sacrament, the audacity to claim that from all eternity God has been preparing for just this very moment and thus to say, "Here it is, it is for you!" The preaching itself is the treasure, the sacramental moment. Now when this is clear, when one is absolutely surprised by that, what is left but to sell all in joy? Sell all your reservations, your false freedom, your investment in your prejudices and paltry goods, your "status-quo-ism." There is a new day coming! Sell out! When the text is done somehow in this fashion it seems to me the words might actually function as the hidden treasure, be sacramental themselves.

Or take a text like the parable of the Laborers in the Vineyard (Matthew 20:1–16). Again *there is* the shocking fact that when it came down to the final reckoning, they all got the same. The preacher would have to uphold the scandal of that. How can one run any kind of business that way? How, for that matter, could such proceedings be held up as a model for justice? We like to do that a lot with Jesus these days! Is there any way one could turn the parable into something to do? One might, I suppose, try to recoup something by saying that at least the last workers did show up to do a little anyway! But that is hardly likely to encourage appropriate behavior! That they all got the same was bad enough, of course, but the reply of the keeper of the vineyard to their indignant questions about justice is the absolute coup de grâce. (I like that French expression for ending the matter in this case: stroke of grace, i.e., a "mercy killing!") "Can I not do what I want with what is my own?" What can we do about that?

Here we can only sail right into the storm once again, take what the text authorizes us to do and do it to the hearers. More and more I believe we should proceed by just taking the hard saying like that, the key assertion, and put it right up front, leading from that rather than from some cute illustration or story that is supposed to be "relevant" but would just get in the way anyway. We have to face the fact that the gospel is just not relevant to the "old Adam," and nothing we can do can make it so. The old is to be killed in order that the new may arise. Is not that the point of the hard saying? "Can I not do what I want with what is my own?" I would be inclined to start right out with that and drive home, what an awful and frightening thing that is. What can we do about that? How can we possibly get on with such a master? Where does it leave us? That is the law, the letter that kills, the cutting edge of the text. But after doing it as letter that kills, one would have to turn it around so that in the end it would be gospel, be a sacrament. One would have to have the audacity to turn it around and say that our only real hope lies just in the fact that he does do just what he wants with what is his own and that he is doing it *here and now* in the moment of the absolution, the moment of the preaching itself, the moment of baptism and the Supper. The preacher must see the proclamation itself as a sacrament, the moment when what the text authorizes is actually to be done once again in the living *present, not* just explained or talked about. "Can I not do what I want with what is my own?" That is a terrifying thought and *nothing,* absolutely *nothing* can relieve the terror of it unless it is true that right here and now in the sacrament of preaching, of baptism, of the Supper he is doing exactly what he wants. Unless the preacher has the guts actually to say that, all is lost and the sermon will degenerate into a more or less hopeless attempt to explain or apologize for such an unjust and unreasonable God. The *preacher must* simply have the courage to say, "I am here to tell you that you are his own and that you can thank your lucky stars that they all got the same because that is all we can count on in the end. For this God has decided to do something utterly and absolutely wild! He has decided to give you his own here and now. I am sent to tell you that."

In some such fashion as that I would seek to do the text to the hearers, to make the preaching itself a sacrament, the moment when the divine deed is done. Preaching today, it seems to me, lacks nothing so much as simply the vision and the courage to do that. If preaching is not itself a sacrament in this fashion, it degenerates into mere instruction or cheap psychologizing. When this happens the sacraments too gradually degenerate into automats for dispensing a mysterious quantity called "grace" that has lost its relation to the gospel story.

## PREACHING THE SACRAMENTS

A student once told me that he asked his pastor why he never preached on baptism. The pastor replied, "I guess because I do not think I myself could preach a whole sermon about that." I do not know whether the pastor was sincere but the remark does indicate a rather serious state of affairs and probably reflects something of the way things actually are. We indeed *do* the sacraments, thank God, but rarely outside of a few stabs at instruction do we talk about them and, I expect, almost never *preach* them. Preaching them is here to be taken in the sense indicated above: not merely talking *about* them but *preaching* them. In the old days, we are told, only those properly initiated, that is, those who really knew what was going on, could participate in the "Holy Mysteries." Nowadays, it seems, virtually everybody participates readily, but few know what is supposed to be going on. Sacraments seem to be held in high esteem, but they tend to remain "mysteries" in a profane sense, a kind of conundrum. Nobody knows what they are for or about. Perhaps the only reason they are preferred in many circles today is that they are at least better than a good deal of the nonsacramental preaching that goes on.

But if people do not know what sacraments are for or what they are about, we must raise some questions about the preaching. How shall they hear without a preacher? No doubt we have overcompensated for the days when participation in the sacraments was contingent upon a rather highly intellectualized grasp of the doctrine *about* the sacraments. The result seems to have been that preaching the sacraments too has been silenced. If people, as we are constantly warned these days, have a poor grasp of the gift given in baptism, for instance, it would seem that the first and most positive move we could make is to preach baptism. It has always seemed at least questionable to me to attempt alleviation of the contemporary difficulty with the so-called indiscriminate practice of infant baptism by restricting the practice. If people do not know what it is, perhaps we ought first to try preaching it more and then see what happens. For centuries there seems to have been a kind of conspiracy of silence in the pulpit about the sacraments. Could it be, perhaps, a covert reflection of the age-old competition between pulpit and font/altar and that this competition plays itself out in the silence of the pulpit about the sacraments? Is the preacher in us jealous, perhaps, about the sacraments? Do we fear that sacraments may undercut what we work so hard to estab-lish with our words? Listening to many so-called "evangelical" preachers who like to remind us that sacraments are not to be depended upon, one could get such an impression. Could the "altar call" for instance, be the culmination of this jealousy, when upon arriving at the altar what you receive is not Christ but a personal encounter with the "evangelist" or his representatives?

In any case, we ought to be forewarned that a battle between Word and sacrament is one the preacher is not likely to win. Increasing preference for sacraments maybe just a sign of that. But if it is a battle, it must at all costs be headed off. It can only end in disaster, for both Word and sacrament, preacher and priest. Without a sacramental understanding of the Word, preaching degenerates into mere information; without preaching, sacraments degenerate into "magic."

So let us talk of *preaching* the sacraments. Our talk must be of preaching the sacraments, not merely talking about them. This means in the first instance preaching the sacraments as *gospel,* not as springboards for ethical exhortation (though they may be that too) since that is not where our problem lies. The task is to preach the sacraments as a gospel Word for us, a Word which cuts into our lives, puts the old to death and raises up the new. So preaching the sacraments cannot be just explaining them or even just talking about what they are supposed to do, though some of that may incidentally be involved. If preaching, as I have already tried to suggest, is doing the text to the hearer, then in this case the "text" is the sacramental deed, the visible, tangible Word, and preaching must then be the somewhat exacting and tricky task of doing the visible Word to the recipient in such a way that the audible and visible simply go hand in hand, or better, hand in glove. It must be apparent that there is no competition and that the spoken and the visible Word complement each other perfectly, supporting and reinforcing each other so that together they save us.

Preaching the sacraments involves us in the tricky task of doing a visible word by means of an audible word. No doubt one could get rather tangled up in a linguistic jungle were one to attempt sorting out all the issues involved. But perhaps here we can leave the mental gymnastics behind and approach the matter just by considering the traditional problems that arise in thinking about the relation between the benefits of the preached Word and those of the sacraments. Here we come immediately to the old problem of the inner versus the outer, the "spirit" versus the external "sign," or however one wants to put that.

The basic problem with the preached word is that it goes within and rattles around in the psyche where it can, *ubi et quando visum est deo* (when and where it pleases God), set things right, but also, alas, where it can, *ubi et quando visum est diabolo!* (when and where it pleases the devil!), create all kinds of havoc. We have an incurable tendency to collapse inwardly upon ourselves all the time, to feed on our own innards. We are, as the Augustinian tradition that Luther imbibed rightly saw, *curvatus in se,* all turned inward upon ourselves. We have a desperate time getting out at all. I may be coaxed out on occasion but like the nervous groundhog I will be frightened, perhaps by my own shadow, and that is the last you will see of me for some time. All it takes is some little word, some slight mistake, some nuance, glance, gesture. It is like reading books on psychology about some quirk or nasty disorder and constantly reading oneself into the picture.

My internal self constantly defeats or swallows up the word coming from without. The preacher says, "Your sins are forgiven," and tries to explain what a marvelous thing that is. But I say, "It could not really be me that is being talked about." Either I do not find it particularly "relevant" to my "needs," or I can find no guarantee that I am really intended by such words. In particular, I just do not see all those marvelous things happening "within" that the preacher is always blowing about. The preacher says, "Now if we really believe this, then such and such will result. But then I am driven inside again. Do I *really* believe? Deep down, sincerely, absolutely, truly? What would that even mean, for goodness sake? I get caught in all that adverbial theology. You must learn to think positively, affirmatively, to brighten the corner where you are, to celebrate, be joyful or remorseful, and goodness knows what else. Anything and everything can just drive me relentlessly into myself, no matter how well meaning it may be. "Witnessing" about one's marvelous experiences or preaching about joy and possibility thinking can be the worst of all, something like people who are constantly bragging about their sexual prowess. It just turns everyone inward, wondering if anything like that could ever happen to them. The inner self can be, and most of the time is, a sticky quagmire in which we get hopelessly mired, a bottomless well into which we are forever falling, falling.

In John Bunyan's *Pilgrim's Progress* the first mishap Christian endures on his way to the Celestial City is getting mired in the Slough of Despond. When the man called Help comes to the rescue, he asks Christian what he is doing in such a place. "Sir," says Christian, "I was bid go this way by a man called Evangelist, who directed me also to yonder gate, that I might escape the wrath to come; and as I was going thither, I fell in here." When Christian asks why the place was not mended so that poor travelers on the way from the City of Destruction might go with more security, Help gives him a very interesting answer.

> This miry slough is such a place as cannot be mended; it is the descent whither the scum and filth that attends conviction for sin doth continually run, and therefore it is called the Slough of Despond; for still, as the sinner is awakened about his lost condition, there ariseth in his soul many fears, and doubts, and discouraging apprehensions, which all of them get together, and settle in this place. And this is the reason of the badness of the ground.
>
> It is not the pleasure of the King that this place should remain so bad. His labourers also have by the direction of His Majesty's surveyors, been for above these sixteen hundred years employed about this patch of ground, if perhaps it might have been mended: yea, and to my knowledge, said he, here have been swallowed up at least twenty thousand cart-loads, yea, millions of wholesome instructions, that have been brought from all places of the King's dominions, and they that can tell, say they are the best materials to make good ground of the place, if so be it might have been mended, but it is the Slough of Despond still, and so will be when they have done what they can.[1]

Twenty thousand cartloads, millions of wholesome instructions! Just think of it, all those sermons, all that counseling! But the Slough of Despond remains just the Slough of Despond and cannot really be mended. The inner self remains forever just that sort of quagmire.

This problem of the inner life, of subjectivity, means that we should be aware of the limits of the audible word and that it is just at this point that "Help" must come, something "from the outside," what Luther called the "alien Word," the "alien faith," the "alien justice." The "alien" in this case means it is something that comes entirely from without. The irreducible externality, the givenness of the sacrament, is the seal on the truth of the proclamation. The devil, Luther always maintained, is the master of subjectivity; the heart and the conscience are his playground. He can make a nefarious and poisonous brew out of the finest sermon. I expect anyone who has preached much is well aware of that! As a matter of fact, in the Smalcald Articles, Luther describes the Fall itself as the enticement of the human race in Adam and Eve away from the external Word to subjectivity, "enthusiasm" (God-within-ism).

> All this is the old devil and old serpent who made enthusiasts of Adam and Eve. He led them from the external Word of God to spiritualizing and to their own imaginations . . . In short, enthusi-

---

1. Bunyan, *Pilgrim's Progress*, 24–25.

asm clings to Adam and his descendants from the beginning to the end of the world. It is a poison implanted and inoculated in man by the old dragon, and it is the source, strength and power of all heresy, including that of the papacy and Mohamet. Accordingly we should and must constantly maintain that God will not deal with us except through his external Word and Sacrament. Whatever is attributed to the Spirit apart from such Word and Sacrament is of the devil.[2]

The devil, however, is ultimately powerless against the "alien Word," the absolutely "from-without" word, the visible word. It has happened and even the devil can do nothing about that. And that is precisely what must be insisted upon in preaching in spite of all difficulty and objection. Remember an episode from *All in the Family*? Archie Bunker insists on having the baby baptized and plans to take it secretly if necessary to have it done. His son-in-law Michael protests that he does not want the baby baptized.

Archie retorts, "What's the matter, you were baptized, weren't you?"

"Yes," Michael says, "but I renounce my baptism."

Archie astutely replies, "You cannot do that. You can renounce your belly button, but it's still there!" In spite of all the nonsense, Archie is a better theologian than most of us on that point. It is an alien word. It has happened, and there is nothing we can do about that. No doubt that is one of the things that rankle. That is part of the offense. Just so it also stands against the devil because he can do nothing about it either. In the end that may be our only defense. When Luther was demolished by the devil in his *Anfechtungen,* unable to escape wallowing around in his own subjectivity, he could at last only cry out, "I am baptized!" The word from without, the alien word, at the last may be all we have.

Indeed, there is a strain in Luther's theology at this point that is puzzling and perhaps even disconcerting to us so-called moderns. It sticks out in instances where Luther is even willing to suggest that infants are saved by the faith and prayer of the church. But it does not have to do only with infants because Luther can even say the same about himself. He applies the word, "He saved others, himself he cannot save," to his own situation. "I have saved others, but I cannot save myself," he can say. By that he means that he cannot of his own power free himself from

2. BC 322–23; BC/T 312–13.

his doubt and *Anfechtungen,* his own self-wrought righteousness seeps through his hands like water, the conscience does not hold its ground. Therefore, Luther says, I can be saved only by another, by the preaching, intercession, sacraments, and communion of the church. In his sermon on "Preparation for Communion (1518)" Luther could go so far as to say, "If faith fails you, then grasp the last chance. Let yourself be carried to church like a child and speak without fear to the Lord Christ: I am unworthy, but I cast myself on the faith of the church—or another believer. However it is with me, Oh Lord, I will be obedient to your church, which commands me to go to communion. Even if I have nothing else, I bring you this obedience."[3] Then, Luther says, believe truly that you do not go unworthily to the Lord's Table. The faith of the church will carry you, the adult, and not leave you in the lurch any more than the little child who is baptized and saved by virtue of alien faith.

But now this turn of the matter from the inner to the outer, the audible to the visible, from subjectivity to objectivity, a "proper" to an "alien" word, does of course raise another set of problems for preaching the sacraments. The alien word can indeed save from the Slough of Despond, it is not without a certain peril of its own—for the old Adam, at least. It is, after all, an *alien* word, like a strange comet from some other realm. While it helps against the devil because he can do nothing about it, it rankles us as old beings because we can do nothing about it either. The peril is that because we can do nothing about it, we may conclude as old beings that we need do nothing about it. What we encounter is the age-old problem of the objective validity and efficacy of the sacraments, the question of the *ex opere operato,* in popular parlance, the question of sacramental "magic." The problem particularly for preaching the sacraments is that what we say about the alien word, the *ex opere operato,* the "magic" seems to save us from our subjectivity only in turn to be a severe threat to it. It rankles that we, like the devil, can do nothing about its sheer givenness. The "magic," so-called, threatens to overpower, to bypass our subjectivity, our "moral selfhood" altogether.

This was, it is to be recalled, a basic problem at the time of the Reformation. The big objection was to the medieval idea that sacraments "worked" just by being done as long as the individual did not object. Protestants objected that this implied a kind of "magic." Most of

3. Luther, *WA* 1:333.13–26.

Protestantism tried to solve the problem of magic by simply rejecting the objectivity, the externality, of the sacraments in favor of preaching understood as a word addressed to our subjectivity, our inner "decision." The sacraments degenerated into symbols of what goes on within, signs of our dedication and the like. Thus the Word basically disappeared into the inner reaches of the soul, rarely to be heard from again, gradually degenerating into pop psychology and greeting card sentimentality.

The question of how one preaches the sacrament, how one preaches the visible word, what one does about the objectivity, the sign, the elements, becomes an important test case, a crisis for preaching itself. For if, as in most of Protestantism, preaching steps in to *domesticate* the alien, to attempt merely to return sovereignty to our threatened subjectivity so as to leave us in control, then all is lost for both preaching and the sacrament. For then preaching enters into *competition* with the sacrament, and loses its own character as a sacramental word at the same time as it robs the sacrament of its alien power. It is fatal for preaching itself to compete with sacraments, to attempt to domesticate the "magic." By and large this is what has happened in modern Protestantism, if not Christianity in general. And it can happen all too easily in Lutheranism just by default where there is a conspiracy of silence about sacraments from the pulpit.

For the Lutheran Reformation had a quite different kind of solution to the problem of the alienness: the "magic," the *ex opere operato* of the sacraments. The problem for Luther was not the alienness as such, the objectivity, the "from-withoutness." The problem, Luther always said, was that the medieval tradition did not give proper place to *faith* as the only possible aim of and receptacle for what sacraments have to give. In the quite correct and laudable zeal to guarantee objectivity and givenness so that the sacrament did not *depend* on faith, the medieval tradition tended to neglect the fact that the very point of the objectivity was to *create* faith, to aim for faith, and that faith was the only possible way a sacrament could be received. Dogmatic assertions are made *about* the sacraments to guarantee their objectivity and efficacy which descriptively may be quite true, but nevertheless do not work at all if there is no delivery system. It is like a gift without either the giving or the card. The problem lies exactly in the question of the preaching of the sacraments. The Word and the sign must go together.

Luther did not complain about the alienness of the sacrament, the objectivity, and not even what moderns call the "magic" of it. I have a colleague who likes to say, "Let's face it, sacraments *are* magic." The real question is whose magic is it? Ours or God's? Luther's objection to the *ex opere operato* was not to the idea that the sacraments work *on us* just by being done, but that they had become means put in our hands whereby we could work on God. Magic, that is, becomes reprehensible if it is understood as a means put in our hands by which we can control or manipulate God. When there is no appropriate delivery system, no preaching, the direction of the "magic" gets reversed. Sacraments are understood not as things God does to change us, but as things *we* do to change God. They become means for priestly manipulation of the gods, and subsequently also of the laity. This can be repaired, not by denying the alienness or removing the objectivity or even the "magic," but only by reversing the direction. This has to be made clear in the teaching, of course, but it can actually be done preeminently in the preaching. The preaching, the Word, has to make unmistakable that it is *for you.*

Preaching the sacrament, that is, if it is to be the doing of the visible word to the hearer, must therefore do that text to the hearer in the same way that the audible word does. The preaching of the sacrament, that is, must not domesticate the alien word, not chicken out on it, but just drive it home. It must in the first instance have the cutting edge of the law, the letter that kills the old Adam in us, cuts into our lives. The very alienness of the sign does that. The water of baptism, after all, is out first to drown the old Adam, not to coddle or be nice to us. The preaching of the sacrament cannot back off from the danger, the offense, involved here. The very thing the old Adam finds reprehensible is what is going to save us in the end. If the sacraments are going to create faith precisely by drawing us out of the quagmire of subjectivity, the Slough of Despond, then they shall have to be preached first of all as just the alien word that sounds the death knell to the self that always collapses into itself like a black hole. It is just that alien word that draws us out again into the freedom of faith.

Luther found a new way to affirm that sacraments save us. True, they do not save us "automatically," as though that could happen without our knowing it. They do not work like a magic potion or a medicine or a vitamin pill. Such things work with or without our necessarily being involved. But sacraments save us because they work on us to create faith, just as the audible word does. They give us something to believe, as Luther said. The sacrament, that is, works to create the faith that receives it. But this can occur only when it is properly done and preached, called and recalled to mind. Not that they work secret magic without us, carry out some hidden agenda unknown to us, but that their indubitable alienness continues to work on us in the preaching of them to put to death the old inwardly directed being and raise up the new, turned outward to God. That is what it means to say that baptism, for instance, is not just a once-upon-a-time act, but a continuing act, a matter of daily renewal. Preaching baptism is the quite alien act that kills and makes alive in the renewal. It is quite correct to say, of course, that sacraments are not efficacious without faith. But the faith spoken of is precisely faith in the sacramental deed itself, the faith created by the sacrament. The case is not, as with most modern Protestantism, that one has to go *somewhere else* and get something called faith to qualify for participation and so come back to get it. No, the faith that receives the sacrament is faith in the sacrament created by the sacrament itself as Word and sign.

Further, in driving home the very alienness of the sacrament, the troublesome and persistent question of the place of the elements also gets a different theological cast and use for preaching. Where sacraments are understood as a kind of magic potion, the words become incantation that are somehow supposed to "change" the elements, to make them "holy." The words need not be addressed to the hearers at all. Or where sacraments are understood as sacred analogies or symbolic actions, one rummages about trying to conjure up the symbolic significance of the elements and signs. One talks about the "nature" of water, or the crushing of the grape and the grinding of the wheat, the symbolic significance of eating, and so on. One tries to ameliorate the alienness, the stubborn materiality and externality of the elements by explaining them or changing them via the verbal symbol system. One tries, you might say, to have the elements swallowed up by the words, obliterated by or disappear into the words. Perhaps it is the sacramental equivalent of allegorizing: the elements are changed to fit our story, not *vice versa*. But the elements will not disappear into some other story. One is reminded of the old argument about whether the body and blood of Christ are changed by the human digestive system when the bread and wine are devoured. Luther aptly replied, as did the Fathers, by saying that *our* bodies are changed, not Christ's. The elements stay in their own story. Indeed, the stubborn persistence of the outward and material is itself both attack on our incurable inwardness at the same time as it is to be comfort.

Luther always liked to insist, furthermore, that the elements, the outward signs, belong intrinsically to the story. God, he said, never gives Word or Commandment without something outward or material.[4] This precisely is part of the attack on our unfaith, our turning inward upon ourselves. When discussing why it is useful to believe that Christ's body is present in the bread, Luther (though first entering a disclaimer about the place of such "why" questions because the Christian is simply to take God at his Word) says that the first benefit is "that clever, arrogant spirits and reason be blinded and disgraced in order that the proud may stumble and fall and never partake of Christ's supper, and on the other hand, that the humble may be warned and may arise and alone partake of the Supper, as St. Simeon says (Luke 2:34), 'This child is set for the fall and rising of many in Israel.'"[5] The elements themselves participate in the attack on our pride and bring us down to eating "humble pie." Just as the water drowns, so the bread and wine bring down the pride. It is, to sum up, a great and mighty offense that I, great religious being that I am, should be reduced to depending for my eternal salvation on eating a bit of bread and drinking a sip of wine.

Perhaps we have gone about matters in quite the wrong way in the business of relating word and element. We have asked what the words do to the elements, expecting, no doubt, that they raise the elements to some lofty spiritual heights. They change them into heavenly substances or elevate them into lofty symbolic systems. Perhaps we ought rather to ask what the elements do to the words. Perhaps it is just as much the case that the elements help to bring the words down to earth. At any rate, it is obvious that it is vitally important for preaching the sacraments that here the very alienness, the materiality of the outward, finds its place and use in a story quite different from our general inward and upward spiritual flight. It is obvious that for someone like Luther, at least, that story is the story of Jesus, the despised and crucified one who was nevertheless raised, the one who brings eschatological hope. In baptism one is baptized into that story. In the Supper one participates in its end and its hope. "As often as you eat this bread and drink this cup you proclaim the Lord's death until he comes." The elements stubbornly refuse to be removed from that story and thus they participate in it and, in fact, do that story to us. I expect that

4. *LW* 37:135.
5. Ibid., 131.

is what it should mean to say that the elements are "consecrated." They find their place in the eschatological story and do it to us in the form of the promise. Indeed, one should say that they find their true place in the story, a place that was lost with the fall. Water no longer washes us clean because we have turned inward upon ourselves where the water can no longer touch us. But here it is true once again, back in its true story, the washing of regeneration. One day it will once again be all we need to be clean. A bit of bread and a sip of wine no longer satisfies us here. It no longer gives life. Bread is what we fight for, defend ourselves for, die and kill for. We call it ours. But here it is taken from us and put back where it belongs. "This bread," says the Lord, "is mine and I mean to have it back. This is my body." And it is free. And so it shall be in the end.

Preaching in such fashion might alleviate current worry about the use of the sacraments in the church. Just as with complaint about the risk of free grace we worry whether practice may not be too liberal. Do we baptize too indiscriminately? Are we too open in communion? No doubt we must take care that practice does not undercut, cheapen, or mock the gift. But we also need to remember that the alien justice of God given unconditionally does throw us into a perpetual crisis. When the *sola gratia* does not seem to work to our satisfaction, the temptation is always to retreat and make it not quite *sola*. When we get nervous about "cheap grace" the remedy seems to be to make it at least a little expensive—bargain basement, maybe, but at least not cheap. But then the battle is lost. When confronted by the perpetual crisis of God's liberality we must simply forge right ahead and become even more radical about the *sola*. Grace is indeed not cheap. It is free! But the radicalization must be carried out precisely in the preaching. Grace full and free must always be preached so that it kills and makes alive. If it is cheapened to coddle the old Adam, that is indeed bad enough. But if one tries subsequently to remedy the cheapness by making it expensive, that is absolute disaster. The only cure for cheap grace is radical grace. And this can be done only in the preaching of it, doing the text to the hearers.

There is cause for alarm, I have come to think, in a church where one wonders whether the gospel is being preached anyway, where nervous pastors and theologians are anxious to take steps to remedy supposed misuse of the sacraments merely by withholding or restricting them—in effect, raising the price. If the remedy for cheap grace is not raising the price, but rather radicalizing it to free grace, then could it not be that a large part of the remedy for misuse and misunderstanding of the sacraments lies also in radicalizing them precisely through the proper preaching of them? I just do not believe it possible today to convey the right message by arbitrary restriction of practice. It will always be interpreted as clerical highhandedness and legalism. I suspect the only weapon we have left in this battle is the preaching itself. So it is imperative that we take steps to use it properly.

But how shall we do it? No doubt sacraments should find their way into a good many sermons if not all of them. When there is a baptism or a baptism Sunday there should be a specific baptismal sermon. Perhaps the best way to close out this essay is to offer again some concrete suggestions and experiments to exemplify what I have been talking about.

I begin with baptism. If baptism is to be preached in accord with what I have been saying, it should be preached as the unrelenting and unconditional divine yes that cuts off our inward flight at every point, lays the old to rest, and calls forth the new. It would probably go something as follows. Baptism regenerates, it works forgiveness of sins, life, and salvation. But how can it do that? Simply by being what it is, a washing with water that cannot be erased together with the speaking of the promise, the creative word, the divine yes spoken over us, spoken to us from the outside, from the beginning, the first and the last word about us, the word calling us to life out of our death "in Adam." "You are mine," says the Lord God. "You always have been and always will be." But that, of course, is incredible. Maybe even frightening. Thus all the questions come tumbling out, all of them attempts to take the gift and retreat inside, protests of the old Adam and Eve who know themselves to be under radical attack in their inner bastions.

But in the preaching all the questions must be countered relentlessly by the divine yes. Is baptism enough? Yes! It works forgiveness of sins, life, and salvation. Live in that and hear it again each day. Believe that it is enough and that is certainly enough! Would it have all that significance even if I were only a baby and did not know what was going on? Yes, because it was *God* who spoke that yes over you. God is *God*. What about my response? Are you saying that I do not even have to respond? Now that, of course, is the trickiest question of all in the old Adam's arsenal. It too can only be countered ultimately with what is perhaps an equally tricky yes. Yes, I am saying you do not have to respond. What is the matter, do you not want to? It is the old Adam who can only think in dreary terms of *have* to and ask stupid questions about it. The old is through, drowned in the water. If you think it is a matter of *have* to, forget it! Here we are calling forth the new who simply wants to! This is the divine yes calling to our yes in the Spirit. "Awake thou that sleepest and arise from the dead!" Come out of your stinking tomb! But, but, do you mean to say I am not free to reject? Yes. I should hope so! What in the world do you want to do that for? How could you call such rejection freedom? To reject must be only the most horrible form of bondage. It certainly is not "freedom"! Does that not mean that God is taking a great risk? Yes indeed. But he takes it nevertheless, even unto death. Are you saying, "Once saved, always saved"? Yes. What is wrong with that? I am counting on it, aren't you? It is the divine yes, God's Word. You do not mean that grace is irresistible, do you? Yes. I find it to be so, do you not? To be sure, grace is not force. Grace is just grace and as such it is by definition "irresistible," I expect! Does that not mean it could be grossly misunderstood, misused, and abused? Yes, I expect it does. But God suffered all the abuse to bring it to light. Is that not what it's all about? Should God, as Luther could put it, call off his goodness for the sake of the ungodly? If so, who at all would be saved?

The answer, you see, is yes, yes, yes. It is God's yes, and he will go on saying it until finally you die of it and begin to whisper, "Amen! So be it, Lord!" Baptism *does* regenerate. Of course this is dangerous business! So-called evangelicals will howl about sacramentalism and object vociferously to the "magic" of such externalism. And they are quite right to do so if sacraments are only analogies or allegories of our inner life. If sacraments, that is, leave the old subject intact we could not speak like this or put such confidence in sacraments. Either we must preach them so they kill the old Adam and Eve or we'd better forget them. A sacrament that has all the objective validity we want to claim for it and still leaves the old subject intact is only an invitation to disaster.

As short experiments on the Lord's Supper, I offer some sermons preached in our seminary chapel. They give some indication, I hope, of what I have been talking about. Also, I expect, since they were preached in a seminary chapel one presupposes some things one would not for the ordinary parish.

## TEXT: JOHN 6:35. "I AM THE BREAD OF LIFE"

When your life and mine come down at last to bread and wine, will it be for us the sacrament of his presence? We had thought, perhaps, that we were destined for grander things. We had thought, no doubt, that we should have been eligible for the food of the gods, some celestial elixir perhaps, or at least something capable of "turning us on" or sending us on a trip somewhere, even if it did not turn out to be very far after all. For everyone knows that religion has to do with grand things, being transported, perhaps, to some Elysian fields, some never-never land, some heaven or other, through the food of the gods? Yet here we are, gathered around a hunk of bread and a bit of wine. Is that not strange? Are there not more relevant sacramental substances on the market?

I suppose that in our disappointment, or even despair, we have been tempted to make something more of the bread and wine than just bread and wine. We have told ourselves that it is mysteriously changed into something else, some heavenly substance, or perhaps that it symbolizes a much more important transaction that goes on elsewhere—maybe even in the "depths" of our souls. We have wanted to make it worthy, to promote it, make it worthy of our exalted religious sensibilities. But here it is, just bread and wine. And there is a kind of stubborn persistence in its being just what it is.

Now it may just be that the point, or at least a large part of it, is just that. It may just be that it is the voice of creation, this earth, calling us back from our excursions elsewhere, and that it is here that we will find our Lord and each other. Luther says in one instance with characteristic bluntness that "God used bread and wine in order that the proud may stumble and fall and never partake of Christ's Supper; and on the other hand that the humble may be warned and may arise and partake." Offensive? Perhaps. And yet perhaps it has to be. Because I expect that for most of us it is a long way down here to just bread and wine. It takes some dying. But our Lord is here calling to us, calling us back to our true home. Calling to us out of his sacrifice unto death to a sacrifice that will meet and unite with his. He gives us bread and wine and says to us, "Take, eat and drink. It is good bread and wine. Your sins are forgiven." And when we heed his call, eat bread and drink wine, taste its indubitable reality, we will get an inkling of what he meant when he said, "I am the bread of life." For down here you will find him. And not only him, but yourself and all your brothers and sisters. Eat and drink, rejoice, for you have come home!

Here is a second experiment, preached some time ago during the Watergate affair. The text was 1 Corinthians 11:23–26.

## TEXT: 1 CORINTHIANS 11:23–26. "TO RECLAIM HIS OWN"

We meet here today amid the tangled skein of tapes with sections erased, resignations and firings high and low, lies and deceptions, unkept promises and broken truces, wars, injustices, hunger, and poverty, to see if we can once again clear a little space amid the clutter to partake of the Supper of our Lord. And what should it be for us in the midst of all this turmoil of body, soul, and spirit? Well, it is for us what it has always been. Nothing can upset or erase these words. The context in which they were first spoken is not unlike that in which we find ourselves today. It means that God is for you all the way to the end.

We might, I suppose, be tempted to turn that into cheap and easy comfort. God is for me? So what is new, Reverend? A comfort perhaps, that enables us to make peace with what is happening all about us, or at least just to endure it until it all blows over and we have shuffled off this mortal coil for more pleasant climes. But it is not, of course, that simple. For the fact that God is for us in such a fashion as we have here is in many ways rather uncomfortable. It would have been better if he had not gotten quite so close, if he had stayed in heaven where he could do no more harm. But he did not. He has come to be for you. He has come to claim his own back again, come into this place where bread and wine go to the highest bidder, where people's lives and reputations are peddled for it, where clever ones kill and cheat for it while the less clever and the innocent suffer and starve and die. He has come into this world and by his sovereign act taken this bread from us and said, "This is my body, my blood, and it is free." He comes to reclaim his own and to give it to us as a foretaste of the way things are going to be. Here is real bread and wine, real because he has reclaimed it; taken it out of our fallen story back into his own story; in, with, and under it is his body and blood and thus it is without price. Bread and wine are what they were meant to be and will be again one day.

Yes, God is for you, all the way to the end, for you in *his* way, with his goal in mind. That is not cheap comfort but it is ultimate comfort. And does this not speak to us amid the clutter of the day? Does not this ultimate comfort discomfort us about the world we see around us? Can we eat this bread and still look away from those for whom bread is too high priced? Can we eat this bread without price and still tolerate the liars and cheaters who traffic in people's lives? I put the question to you and invite you to come and meet the God who is for you, eat this real bread and drink this real wine. Fear not! For he has great things in store and one day, one day, this Supper alone will be left and all the clutter gone. Amen!

My third and last experiment is on John 6:53, the discourse on eating the flesh and drinking the blood of the Son of Man which shocked many of Jesus's own disciples to the extent that they went away and no longer went with him. It is a classic example of the way the preaching of the sacrament does cut into our lives to kill and give the possibility of life.

## TEXT: JOHN 6:53. "COME OUT, COME OUT WHEREVER YOU ARE!"

"Truly I say to you, unless you eat the flesh of the Son of Man and drink His blood, you have no life in you." It is of course preposterous, is it not, that we, great religious and indeed "spiritual" beings, aspiring virtuosi in the realm of beautiful abstractions, experts in the domain of inner feelings, and thus masters at avoiding the issue and stalling off the end, preposterous that we should be bidden to depend for our eternal well-being and salvation on eating a bit of bread and drinking a sip of wine? This is a hard saying. Who can hear it? It is indeed enough to drive a person away. But then where or to whom shall we go? Shall we then, as is our wont, turn inward upon ourselves to that enticing realm of pure ideas and warm feelings for some final assurance and consolation? Ah, but the inner self, however much it is indeed to be cultivated can in this regard be a quagmire, a bottomless pit. Our forebears in the faith have warned us about that. We are, they have said, *curvatus in se,* all turned inward upon ourselves so that we have a desperate time getting out again. We are called out, but like that stiff tapioca pudding we used to get when we were children, we keep snapping back again, disappearing into ourselves.

Do you really—I mean really, deep down, in the "ground of your being"—believe? Are you *really* sincere? Have you got the Spirit? How can you tell? So the questions turn upon the inward self. How shall I answer? Indeed, what is all that supposed to mean, after all? (At this point in the sermon I inserted the section about the Slough of Despond quoted earlier in this essay.) The inner self is a quagmire, a Slough of Despond from which there is no escape. Not without Help. "Lord, to whom shall we go?" Is there anyone? Is there anything "out there" at all to help us? Well, there is this preposterous and astounding word: Whoever eats my flesh and drinks my blood has eternal life, and I will raise them up on the last day. You can count on that. Just think on it! That's all there is to it! Come out, come out, wherever you are. The game is over! Repent and believe it. It will save you!

## CONCLUSION

I do not know how successful these very short experiments are. Some are not so radical as others. But I think you can get a glimpse of what I was trying to do. I was trying to do the visible word to the hearers, to preach the sacraments in such a way that they are not undercut and thus in such a way that they might actually be a means of grace, that we might come to trust them as a sheer gift which actually saves us, calls us out of the darkness of our own inner selves into the glorious light of God's salvation.

## BIBLIOGRAPHY

Bunyan, John. *Pilgrim's Progress*. New York: Grosset & Dunlap, 1961.
Luther, Martin. "Preparation for Communion, 1518." In *WA* 1.
———. "Smalcald Articles." In *BC*.
———. "Smalcald Articles." In *BC/T*.
Pelikan, Jaroslav, and Helmut Lehman, editors. *LW* 37. St. Louis: Concordia, 1955.

# 9

# Absolution: Systematic Considerations

*Gerhard O. Forde*

T HERE IS A RATHER delightful story about a bothersome pious Roman Catholic lady who kept claiming to her priest that she had regular visions of Jesus. The priest was doubtful of the genuineness of such visions and was hard pressed to get her off his back. So he devised what he thought was a sure test to put her off. "The next time you have a vision," he said, "you ask Jesus what sins I confessed in my last confession." So some time later she returned and claimed another vision. "Did you ask him what sins I confessed?" the priest inquired. "Yes, I did," said the lady. "What did he say, then?" said the priest. She replied, "He said he forgot!" I do not know that that has anything particular to say about the theme of this essay but I do think it one of the nicer stories I have heard about absolution. And perhaps it does introduce the subject at least and some of its problems. The priest was not helped in his curiosity about the delivery system but he was reminded of the unshakeable theological truth behind absolution: Remember not, O Lord, our sins.

Our theme is absolution, the actual concrete act of forgiving sin, the exercise of the office of the keys, as it was called, the actual turning of the key in the lock, so to speak. I take it to be my task to introduce the theme by considering some of the systematic presuppositions and questions appropriate to it. To that end, I begin by absolving myself from all responsibility for or guilt toward it. To do this I would like to begin with a kind of play on words that shall serve as a thesis for my deliberations: *The only solution to the problem of the absolute is actual absolution.* Or, otherwise put, absolution, the concrete act of forgiving sin, from me to you in the name of the crucified and risen Jesus Christ here in the living present, is the *only* solution to the systematic problem of the absoluteness of God. What I want to claim here therefore in these systematic considerations is that absolution is not only the solution to the "subjective" problems of guilt, but also and perhaps above all the solution to the systematic problems arising from God's absoluteness.

So I shall begin my deliberations with a discussion of absolution and the absolute, and then turn secondly to absolution and the absolved (the believer) and then try to conclude with some observations about the scope and relevance of such absolution.

## ABSOLUTION AND THE ABSOLUTE

God, to use Robert Jenson's *bon mot,* is by platitudinous definition absolute. And of course, that is just the problem. To return to our play on words, it is interesting and significant for us to note that this name of God, the absolute, is actually derived from *absolve.* Its Latin cognate and predecessor, *absolutus,* is simply the past participle of *absolvere,* to loose from, to set free, to be disengaged. God, so to speak, as the absolute, is the preeminently "absolved" one. Nothing can be laid to God's charge. The list of meanings for absolute that one can find in Webster's large dictionary is imposing: 1) freed, disengaged; 2) free from imperfection; 3) free from mixture, simple, pure; 4) free from limit, restriction, qualification; 5) determined in itself, not relational, independent; 6) Logic: not relative; 7) Philosophy: not dependent on anything else, not affected by anything outside itself, fundamental, intrinsic, unqualified, self-contained and self-sufficient, free from error natural to human perception, and so on. Just to go down the list is to realize that when we deal with the absolute and with absolution we are dealing with theological dynamite. No doubt that is why there has been such fear of these things in the history of the church.

God is absolute, free. That is the systematic problem. We cannot get on with such a God, with an absolute who is "absolved" from all charge, free, disengaged, independent, and all such. An absolute God is the "end" of us. Such a God leaves us no room, no freedom, destroys us. We see this particularly, I suppose, when we come up against the concepts of divine, that is, absolute, predestination and election. If the absolutely free, disengaged, unlimited one predestines and elects, what room, what freedom does that leave us? As long as we try to tangle with the absolute directly, to wrestle with God in the abstract, or, as Luther put it, try to peer into the things of the *deus absconditus,* it leaves us with *absolutely* nothing, no freedom, apparently, nowhere to move. If God is absolute, that is, determined in himself, then we are, it would seem, likewise simply determined. To the degree that God is free, we are unfree. So we tell ourselves. And so we must turn against the absolute God. We simply cannot take such a God. We will not take such a God. This turning against the absolute is something we must and will do. The fact that we must and will do this describes exactly, I believe, what Luther meant by the bondage of the will.

There is a very subtle problem here that is often missed, I think. It is not the absoluteness of God *as such* that *really* binds us, but rather our *reaction* to the idea, the mask, the threat that hangs over us expressed in the concept of absoluteness: the superiority, the priority, the very godness of God. In the day-to-day world in which we live and move, the absoluteness of God does not directly appear to restrict anyone's freedom in actuality. We do pretty much as we please within natural limits. As Luther put it, if we must talk about free choice, we can say we are free in those things "beneath us." Whatever you may think or believe about the absoluteness of God, it does not necessarily make all that much difference in your day-to-day choices. You may be a determinist and I a libertarian, but we both decide to go to lunch and choose what to eat, and God at least apparently does not interfere. Which is to say, I suppose, that as long as I do not think or worry about the absoluteness of God, I get along quite swimmingly—in the realm of things below me. The absoluteness of God does not *actually* restrict me. *Quod supra nos nihil ad nos.* "What is above us is nothing to us." The problem, however, comes when I do think and worry about God, about the absolute—as I expect I inevitably will and must. Death enters the picture. I am not absolute. I begin to worry about whether the absolute is actually pulling the strings secretly, or has actually preset my destiny. "We are not puppets, are we?" So the agonized protest goes. The problem comes, that is, when we turn from those things beneath us to those things above us. Since we do not comprehend the ways of God, the ways of "the absolute," since it appears to us that we could only be determined by such a God, we can only turn away from such a God in one way or another. This turning away, this reaction, the fact that we must and will do this, that is our bondage. We are bound to say no to the absolute. We can and will do no other. That is to say, we are bound to say no to the hidden God, the abstract God, who is, of course, the only God we know apart from Christ. In other words, we flee a theoretical loss of freedom into a real one. We flee the threat of the absolute, an apparent determinism, say, into a real one. We flee the threat of the absolute, an apparent determinism, say, into a real bondage under the law. The sting of death is sin and the strength of sin is the law. Since we claim the freedom to determine our destiny over against the absolute, we are left to save ourselves. Then we must see to it ourselves. There is no absolution. We go out of the frying pan into the fire.

The problem of the absolute simply drives us into bondage. To go out of the frying pan into the fire is not an *option,* not a choice. It is something we must and will do. We are bound to do it. We are not forced to do it. It is a matter of the bondage of the will, not the forcing of the will, or the determinism of the will. It is not, you see, a matter of what we can or cannot do in the abstract. We often get caught playing that game of hide-and-seek with the absolute, arguing about whether or not we have or do not have something called "free choice of the will," or discussing what we can or cannot do. That is not the question. The question is what we will actually do when we come up against "the absolute." Will is originally a future tense verb, not a noun. When we go abstract and theoretical we try to make a substantive out of it and talk about it as though it were a thing we *have* and can push this way or that. So we indulge, as Luther said, in a lot of fictitious talk. The question, however, is what we will do when the crunch comes. "Before the cock crows, you will deny me thrice." "No," Peter said, "I will not." Uh-huh. What will we, when we come up against the absolute? That is the question. The natural will will not will God to be God. Rather, he wills himself to be God, and God not to be.

The only solution to the problem of the absolute is absolution. That is my thesis. That is to say that the only solution to this systematic problem is the *pastoral* one, the move from the abstract to the concrete, from the hidden to the revealed God, from, we might say, the lectern to the pulpit, font, and altar. Only if the absolute actually absolves here and now can our bondage be broken and we be *saved.* However, in this regard it seems that since Luther, in general, and certainly more particularly in recent times, the theological world has been gun-shy if not downright skeptical of this fact. In the absolution controversy it was considered Popish nonsense and error. Instead of seeing absolution as the solution to the absolute, theology seems rather to have stuck more to the lecterns, to the old, old fantasy that theology itself could solve the problem. Theology then only becomes the further enactment of our bondage. That is, instead of seeing that the only solution is to move to the pulpit, font, and altar, theologians (and indeed the pastors they taught as well) thought the problem could be solved in the study, the classroom, at the lectern, or pious folk, in the heart. Thus instead of moving from the absolute to absolution, theology undertook the dissolution of the absolute. The problem of the absolute is to be solved by dissolving, dismantling, cutting down, reducing the absolute to manageable proportions. If the absolute is bothersome just remodel him, cut him down to size, make him more or less just one of the boys or girls. This move has today reached almost epidemic proportions. Everyone proposes to "do something" about the absoluteness of God. As Ronald Goetz pointed out in a *Christian Century* article,[1] the idea of the suffering and limited God has become virtually a new orthodoxy in our day—and the battle has been won virtually, without a shot being fired. Everyone seems obliged to fall all over themselves to explain away the absolute, the timelessness, the wrath, the impassibility, the aseity of God. Process theologians seem to say that God is not absolute yet, but is, apparently, working on it. Perhaps this only means that where absolution is denied the absolute has to be as well. Do we believe in *God* anymore?

Where absolution is effectually denied, sin, too, must also be denied. Sin will, of course, have to be explained away or treated with therapy rather than absolved. If it were not so tragic, it would be comical to follow the way our church bureaucracies and management committees crank out papers assuring us that this or that tragedy, disease, or addiction, or consequences of a lifestyle are not really evidence of the wrath of God. Just think, is it not comforting to be told by a specially appointed task force that the AIDS tragedy that hangs over society is not an indication of the wrath of God? Perhaps it is too bad that the people of Sodom and Gomorrah did not have the *Lutheran Standard* to comfort them! Imagine the prophets announcing that the Babylonian captivity was not a manifestation of the wrath and judgment of God but just an unfortunate and inconvenient instance where the balance of political powers was temporarily displaced and was working itself back to a new and different equilibrium! If one

1. Goetz, "The Suffering God," 385–89.

gets unduly upset about it, what one needs is a little therapy! A student prefaced his paper on sin this last term with a cartoon depicting people sitting around in hell with the flames licking about, where one person was saying to the other, "What I am in here for is no longer a sin!" Since we have apparently taken the road of explaining sin away or changing the list rather than absolving it, perhaps we should at least have the good grace to declare it retroactive! Consider the Baptist convention that decided infant baptism was not a sin and moved to make it retroactive.

The refusal to realize that absolution is the only solution to the problem of the absolute has meant that theology has stayed more or less in the classroom and become an increasingly "abstract" and "academic," theoretical business of watering down the absolute and dissolving it. A curious and confusing situation arises where academic theologies try to be pastoral by undercutting the need for or practice of absolution. The modern split between theory and practice relates to this, certainly. God is reconciled to us in the *theory,* and the practice is just a matter of "applying" the theory in cute and popularized ways. If you do not get it, you are wrongheaded. Pastoral practice is then predominantly therapy, not absolution. The absolute has been dissolved and sin explained away. If you still labor under the illusion that you are a sinner, what you need is therapy, counseling, a new self-image, a new sense of self-worth, and so forth; but not absolution. Thus the people wander like sheep without a shepherd.

The only solution to the problem of the absolute is actual absolution, the concrete act of forgiving, through the external word. If the post-Reformation church had realized this, the story and shape of modern theology would have been vastly different. But the way of absolution is a costly and dangerous business. The barebones systematic logic is to absolve the other, to set the other free unconditionally; the absolute can only die. And, on the other hand, to be absolved, to be set free, the one bound to its own rejection of the absolute must die in order to be made new. The way of absolution, that is, for both God and the sinner, goes through death. It is costly and dangerous, costly to God and dangerous for the sinner. I expect the reason why modern theology has been so skittish about the way of absolution is just this cost and this danger. Let us look at it a bit more in detail.

For absolution to take place the abstract absolute can only and must die, and get out of the way. The point is that God cannot forgive in the abstract. God cannot be merciful in the abstract. God is "in general" merciful. Why? Precisely, I expect, because of God's absoluteness. The *idea* that God, as absolute, is one who will have mercy on whom he will have mercy, is of course, most threatening of all. For then we are left wondering who it is upon whom he will have mercy—left with the threat of the absolute as predestining, electing one. The *idea* that the absolute is forgiving in general is hardly of help to anyone and is usually just frightening. It recoils on us: God is forgiving, what is the matter with you? You have to learn how to claim the promise. It leads to a sentimentalizing view of God, or to the threat of "universalism." God, the absolute, cannot be merciful, or more accurately, cannot actually *have mercy on you* in the abstract. Thus Luther: apart from Christ God is wrathful, hidden, not distinguishable from Satan. For the absolute is simply absolute and as such free, disengaged. The absolute, that is, is removed, absent from us. The only solution for the problem of absence is, of course, presence, the external word coming to us. To have mercy, he must actually come and be present among us. To absolve he must be here. He must say it, do it, "to you." The only solution to the question of predestination, to the question of upon whom he will have mercy, is if he comes to say it: "You are the one." "Your sins are forgiven."

But this "solution" to the problem of the absolute is, of course, preposterous. How can anyone who comes among us, anyone here, actually forgive sins, actually absolve? As we read in the Gospels, Jesus was deemed blasphemous. His listeners protested, "Who can forgive sins but God [the absolute] alone?" The problem with Jesus was that he freely forgave really wicked people! In other words, it is far safer if forgiveness is reserved for the realm of the absolute, if it remains an idea, an abstraction. Perhaps God, who is free, who has nothing to lose, God in his heaven can forgive, but certainly not here. Forgiveness cannot work here. Certainly not if it is free, a setting loose, an *ab-solvere*. Forgiveness simply cannot work here. It is too disruptive of the way we must run things. How can you run a business, or a country, or even a temple or a church on forgiveness? The appearance, the actual presence of the absolute as absolver among us is just too explosive and dangerous a business. We cannot have it. For the absolute, even an absolver is the end.

What then can God do? He could, I suppose, draw back, compromise his determination to have mercy on whom he will have mercy by placing conditions on his forgiving. He could say, "Come on now folks, be nice, will you not please change your ways and accept my forgiveness?" "Will you not please exercise your free choice and decide for me?" Ah, but then he would surrender to us. His absoluteness would be dissolved in conditionalism. Thus, precisely in order to retain his absoluteness as presence, to be the absolute as absolver, he goes to his death. He knows that we as bound sinners will not be absolved, and he will not be anything other than the absolver. So he dies for us. He refuses to give in to our conditionalism, refuses *absolutely* to be the abstract God of wrath for us. He dies, crying "Father forgive them," and the resurrection is his vindication, the vindication of his determination, his absolute self-determination to be the absolver. Thus God in Christ solves the problem of his own absoluteness by insisting on *being* the absolver, concrete, here and now unto death, and vindicates this by the resurrection. He insists on being the absolver, not an idea, but an actual presence, a person who comes to say it, to do it in the concrete: to say, you are the one, you are forgiven, flat-out, unconditional, startling, new. "I will have mercy on whom I will have mercy." Absolution is the solution to the absolute! There is the systematic of Christology for preaching—God (the absolute, the end) is repeated in the absolution.

But of course, that was all a long time ago. It lapses into the past. Perhaps where once it was said "Who can forgive sins but God alone?" we now might be tempted to say, "Who can forgive sins like that but Jesus?" After all, he knew the hearts of people, and all that comes with that. But how can we forgive? So it all might lapse, once again, into past history. Once upon a time there was absolution, but now no longer. But if we let it so lapse, we forget the Spirit. The risen Lord in John's Gospel breathes on his disciples and commands them to go and do it, to carry the presence forward in the absolution. Since Jesus has been raised, since the unconditional absolver has been vindicated, the absolution is to go on. Absolution remains the only solution to the question of the absolute. The followers of Jesus are to be absolvers. Why can we not ever get that through our heads? Pastors, particularly, are to exercise the office publicly, ordered to do it right out there in the open, make public argument for it and do it. They are primarily absolvers. We always seem to think we have a thousand better ways to reconcile the absolute to ways of mortals. Students and pastors often ask about that other part about binding people's sins—are not we supposed to do that too? Yes, we need to consider that too—but not here. That is not my assignment, I think. Here it might be appropriate to remark that we seem naturally to be pretty good at that! Ironically that is what we mostly do anyway and unwittingly when we think we have better ways to solve the problem of the absolute than actual absolution!

## ABSOLUTION AND THE ABSOLVED: THE QUESTION OF THE BELIEVER

Now we cannot conclude this exercise without turning to the question the absolved, the believer, the workings of absolution on the "you" to whom it is addressed. Here we deal with the danger to the sinner. Actual absolution has, of course, always been considered a dangerous business. When Jesus absolved the paralytic, we are told, the crowds "were afraid, and glorified God who had given such power to men." It has always seemed presumptuous for humans to claim such power, and dangerous to use it, and certainly to use it too indiscriminately. So it would seem, the church has always found it necessary to bring the danger under control. To use an image from atomic physics, they have always tried to put rods in the reactor to get some kind of controlled energy flow, one that they could control, that is, rather than have it blow all at once. If it were to do that, it might just make all things new.

Before the Reformation, the practice was developed of doling out absolution to approved candidates only after private and carefully monitored confession and assignment of appropriate penance. The church was only a closet absolver! Luther's Reformation did not reject the idea of private confession and absolution, but tried to excise the ecclesiastical monitoring and control, the conditionalism to which it had fallen prey. What was helpful about it was the one-to-one doing of the absolution. Thus, Luther said that private confession was to be retained *because* of the *absolution,* not because of the confession as such, or its compulsory nature, or the need to demonstrate proper penance. What is to be loosed from its Babylonian captivity is the absolution. Doing it one-to-one, privately, is thus a beautiful and primary paradigm of just what absolution essentially is: the concrete I-to-you, setting the bound will free, unconditionally. But basically, Luther's move was even more daring than that. He took the absolution and "went public" with it in the preaching of the gospel. He came out of the closet, so to speak. The liturgy, sermon, and the sacrament are basically a public absolution. That is its heart and soul.

But somehow after the Reformation this confident assertion of absolution was always considered too dangerous. Surely, it was thought, the sinner will take advantage of it. If things go wrong, if sinners step up the fever of their sinning, if liberty becomes the excuse for license, if antinomianism threatens, and so on, all the way down to the present day with the complaint about the lack of concern for social justice, surely it must be unconditional, open absolution that is at fault. Curiously the gospel and absolution are the first candidates for blame when things go wrong! As Luther already put it in the argument with Erasmus: Was not the world always full of war, deceit, violence, quarreling, and iniquity? "Yet now that the gospel has come, men start blaming the world's wickedness onto it— when the truth is, rather, that the good gospel brings the world's wickedness to light; for without the gospel the world dwelt in its own darkness. So do the uneducated blame education for the fact that as education spreads, their own ignorance becomes apparent. Such are the thanks we return for the word of life and salvation."[2]

Unfortunately the charge seems to stick. Absolution is too dangerous in a world of sinners. So steps are invariably taken to bring the danger under control. At least proper penance must be demanded before absolution can be granted. Absolution is made conditional, at least on demonstration of proper penance, and the deep fog begins to roll in once again. Conditional absolution is, of course, just the practical counterpart to the dissolution of the absolute by theoretical manipulation. Somehow it seems awfully difficult to get that unconditional absolution out into the open. As Luther wrote, "They fled this morning star as though their lives depended on it." So we have had, especially among Norwegian Americans, arguments about whether public and unconditional absolution is appropriate. The pietistically inclined always suspected it was popish chicanery and that it simply ran roughshod over the need for personal conversion and repentance.

Of course, those who feared that unconditional absolution was dangerous were quite right in spite of themselves. The problem was that they did not see that if the right to absolve unconditionally costs the absolute a death, it also spells death for the sinner. All the problems with and fears about unconditional absolution are rooted in the fact that after the Reformation the prevalent tendency was to work with the wrong anthropological paradigm. They thought of the sinner as a continuously existing subject who was only *altered* by sin for the worse, as well as for the better by grace. The human was a substance whose qualities were changed. They thought in terms of *change*, not in terms of death and resurrection. Absolution is "dangerous" if it is just granted flat out to a sinner who has not "changed"

---

2. *BW* 94; *LW* 33:55.

in any noticeable way. So it could be granted only conditionally. The only other alternative in such a system would be to say that absolution freely granted, publicly, unconditionally, must mean the blanket absolution of the whole world, changed or not. Some of the Norwegians who wanted to counter conditional absolution thus found themselves willy-nilly espousing "the justification of the world," the next step to universalism. In other words, absolution simply relapses once again into a universal, an idea. It disappears again into the absolutist heaven.

The problem was and still is that we work with the wrong paradigm, the wrong theological anthropology. The sinner is not just changed. Rather, the sinner must die to be made new. The paradigm is death and resurrection, not just changing the qualities of a continuously existing subject. Unconditional absolution is indeed dangerous for the sinner. It means the death of the sinner one way or another. Either the sinner will try to appropriate it on his or her own conditions as a sop to the self, and go to that death which is eternal, or the unconditional absolution will itself put to death the old and raise up the new in faith to new life.

Yes, it is a dangerous business for sinners. It spells death, and it gives new life. But what we need is precisely to see that. What we need to do, I believe, is not to chicken out, not to compromise, and fiddle away while the City of God burns (this time!), but precisely to forge ahead in uncompromising fashion. The only solution to the problem of the absolute is absolution. It is, of course, quite consequently and necessarily therefore, also the only salvation for the sinner. The absolute dies to become the absolver; to be absolved is therefore to be saved, to die to the old and be raised to the newness of life. It is the purpose of theology, therefore, to lead us to see that and to drive us to do the absolution authorized by the crucified and risen one, actually to break the silence of eternity and say it: Your sins are forgiven for Jesus's sake.

---

## BIBLIOGRAPHY

Goetz, Ronald. "The Suffering God: The Rise of a New Orthodoxy." *Christian Century*, April 16, 1986, 385–89.

# 10

# The Word of the Cross

*Oswald Bayer*

## UNDERSTANDING AND TRANSFORMATION

THE "WORD OF THE CROSS" (1 Cor 1:18) is so far from being self-evident that it allows of being understood only from within—albeit not without reference to the "wisdom of the world" (1 Cor 1:10).[1] Yet, just as water parts to either side of a bridge pier, so the Word of the Cross is foolishness to some, wisdom to others. It saves some and leaves others for lost; for some it means eternal life, for others eternal death (2 Cor 2:15–16)—for us it is enlightenment, for others a persisting delusion (2 Cor 4:3–4). From this perspective Paul assumes there can be no departure. Understanding and misunderstanding, faith and unbelief, can admit of no reference, say, to some third position, or be made intelligible therefrom.

In understanding, there occurs a transformation. Inextricably bound up with the God-given understanding of the Word of the Cross (1 Cor 2:6–16) is a conversion—like that of Paul. He who seeks his salvation in fulfillment of the law and would take his footing on his own just actions, and thus be his own man, is thrown to the ground (Acts 9; 22; 26) and broken (Phil 3:1–11). His demand for identity, which he endeavors to satisfy in a moral and metaphysical fashion, is thoroughly contradicted,

---

1. Baur, "Weisheit und Kreuz," 33–52.

and his striving for wholeness is resisted.[2] He is unable to establish any continuity across this divide, and in virtue of his experience, hitherto, of both world and self, he is not even able to recognize one. Rather, he is created anew and has his identity permanently outside himself, in another, a stranger: in one who has replaced him in a wondrous change and exchange of human sin and divine justice (Gal 2:19–20; cf. 2 Cor 5:21). With this occurrence of the vicariously atoning death of Jesus Christ, a "canon" (Gal 6:16: referring directly to 6:14–15) of truth (Gal 2:5, 14; 5:7) is given, from whence theology can only be critically disposed toward any philosophy of substance and subject, since such a philosophy permits no thought of an eccentric being.

The Word from the Cross effects a breach that cannot be more sharply or more deeply conceived.[3] It concerns not only pagan history, but also that of the Jews (Gal 3:13), and, with Jews and pagans, the history of all mankind (Rom 11:32; Gal 3:22). Insofar as the history of the world is a struggle for mutual recognition in the will to self-justification, it meets with its definitive end in the crucifixion of Jesus (Rom 10:4; cf. Amos 8:2)—though admittedly what can only be acknowledged in contradiction to historical experience. Jesus's crucifixion has to do not only with world history, for with the sun's darkening (Mark 15:33; cf. Amos 8:9) it affects at the same time the entire range of creation; by means of it creation is—first and already—completed (John 19:30; cf. Gen 2:1–2).

Only through such an end and judgment of all flesh, that would "glory" (Gal 6:13) and "covet" (Rom 7:7) to justify itself, does a "new creation" come about (2 Cor 5:17). In it, a person perceives life as undeservedly (Gal 6:15) granted and, in face of such *creatio ex nihilo* (cf. Rom 4:5, 17), marvels at self and world, and praises Creator and Judge: Romans 11:33–36.

## COMMUNICABILITY?

The Word of the Cross is no more convincing than it is self-evident. More precisely, it has its own power to convince. It does not convince by employ-

---

2. See Elert, *Das christliche Ethos*, 419–31; Elert, *The Christian Ethos*, 321–30.

3. Nietzsche had a feeling for this: "Modern men, obtuse to all Christian nomenclature, no longer feel the gruesome superlative that struck a classical taste in the paradoxical formula 'God on the cross.' Never yet and nowhere has there been an equal boldness in inversion, anything as horrible, questioning, and questionable as this formula: it promised a revaluation of all the values of antiquity" (Nietzsche, *Beyond Good and Evil* §46, 250).

ing the category of a general consensus, but by conveying to men their contravention of the truth imparted in it. Were it to be a wisdom of words, convincing in any other way (1 Cor 2:4; cf., 1:17), it would make the cross of the Christ of no effect (1 Cor 1:17). For a word can only convince when the speaker and the hearer have a common relation to truth. But if the one spoken to turns away and departs from the truth, the eternal Word, light, and life (John 1) by glorying not in the Lord (1 Cor 1:31) but in self and being mired in the *concupiscentia iustificationis sui,* then truth can be imparted only in a rebirth through the death of the "old man" (John 3; cf. 1:13)—through baptism (Rom 6) and a "journey through the hell of self-knowledge."[4] Truth, faith, is not communicable like merchandise; it resists being imparted in any such general and total fashion as is impressively and effectively advocated in Hegel's philosophy of religion.

It is not for general consumption, in the manner of conceptual mediation, that the Word of the Cross has its "truth in the inward parts" (Ps 51:6), albeit as external and bodily word, which meets us in foundational and authoritative fashion in baptism and the Lord's Supper. There, and in those words, all *mysteria mortis et resurrectionis5* are imparted. It is from thence that theology has to determine its commerce with both mythos and logos and thereby to work out the problem of the relationship between metaphysics and history.

## METAPHYSICS AND HISTORY

An irremovable component of the Word of the Cross is the brute historical fact of the crucifixion of Jesus of Nazareth *sub Pontio Pilato*.[6] It can neither be grasped in a speculative way, as Hegel attempted, nor be dealt with on practical lines, by systematic type, in the manner of Kant's resolution of the antinomy of practical reason.[7]

---

4. See Hamann, "Chimärische Einfälle," 2:164.17f.; Bayer, "Kommunikabilität des Glaubens," 108–16.

5. *WA* 9:660–61 [660.32–33]. Cf. Bayer, "Tod Gottes und Herrenmahl," 346–63; also reprinted in Bayer, *Leibliches Wort: Reformation und Neuzeit im Konflikt*, 289–305.

6. See Hengel, "Mors turpissima crucis," 125–184; Hengel, *Crucifixion in the Ancient World and the Folly of the Message of the Cross.*

7. Such a practically minded claim is given by D. Wiederkehr, s.v. "Kreuz/Leid," 3:354–63.

In opposition to this stands the attitude of Reimarus, whose reason will allow of no reconciliation with history. "Man is not made for a religion that is founded on facts, and particularly such as are said to have happened in one corner of the earth."[8] That which "all men can be justified in believing,"[9] cannot follow from the contingent fact of the crucifixion of Jesus. Between time and eternity, necessary truths of reason and contingent truths of history, there is a yawning gap.[10]

What Lessing and Kant paved the way for and Hegel carries out, against Reimarus and the whole pre-Hegelian world, by a sublimation of the historical into a speculative Good Friday,[11] cannot be overestimated in its significance, not only for philosophy, but above all for theology and the church. Treatment of the problem of natural theology hereby takes a radical turn. Having already been made plausible to the early church as a cosmic symbol—in reference to Ephesians 3:18—the cross now for the first time becomes "rational" and with it likewise the resurrection as a *negatio negationis*.[12] "A theology of the cross here serves not for the destruction of a metaphysically based ontology, but for its reinstatement."[13] Since Hegel, the gospel of the church has been threatened by a *theologia cruets naturalis*.

Against such a natural theology of the cross, we must listen to Kierkegaard, who insists that the cross—as well as sin, albeit differently—is not universally intelligible. What is universally intelligible, is the urge to justify oneself by works or deeds. The denial of that, however, is a "stumbling-block" and an "offence": "scandal" (Rom 9:32–33; 1 Cor 1:23; Gal 5:11). But when he makes a principle of the inability to derive or explain it and assigns it to the category of paradox, Kierkegaard misrepresents the fact and the process of believing in the Word of the Cross.

Even Barth's attempt in the *Church Dogmatics* to understand the Word of the Cross as a self-corresponding of God (*Selbstentsprechung*)—

---

8. Reimarus, *Apologie oder Schutzschrtftfur die vernunftigen Verehrer Gottes*, 1:171.

9. Lessing, "Ein Mehreres aus den Papieren des Ungenannten," 7:344.

10. See von Lüpke, "Hamann und die Krise der Theologie im Fragmentenstreit," 345–83.

11. Hegel, *Glauben und Wissen*, 123–24; Hegel, *Faith and Knowledge*, 189–91.

12. Hegel, *Vorlesungen über die Philosophie der Religion*, 2.166–67; Hegel, *Lectures on the Philosophy of Religion*, 3:219–20 and 323–24.

13. Thaidigsmann, *Identttätsverlangen und Widerspruch Kreuzestheologie bei Luther, Hegel und Barth*, 62.

and hence through the notion of analogy—takes the sting from the offence that the cross of Jesus continually gives, even to those who perceive it as both judgment and grace. The facticity of both the event *sub Pontio Pilato,* and the self-imparting of that occurrence in baptism and the Lord's Supper, runs the risk of dissolution through an analogical mode of thought. Insofar as what happens in time corresponds to the eternal election, history stands—contrary to Barth's intention[14]—in danger of again becoming metaphysics.[15]

## FACTUM AND TEXT

The universal validity of what once happened in history is guaranteed only by the prophetic Word (cf. 2 Pet 1:19) and its established letter. The unique story of the risen crucified, as the cry that was heard (Heb 5:7), is articulated, above all, in the diction of Psalm 22. It is by means of it that Matthew and Mark relate the Passion of Jesus Christ; and from hence that the Lord's Supper can best be understood.[16] It is at the same time the passage whereby we concretely experience in outstanding fashion, the interlacing of Jesus's death and God's life, of God's death and Jesus's life, and consequently Jesus Christ as the one person in two natures. It establishes the new insuperable communion between God and humankind, which permeates and encompasses together with the bread and the wine all the fruits of earth and human labor. It is determined by that hope in the salvation of all things natural and cultural throughout death and judgment that comes with the Holy Spirit, the presence of the crucified Lord, and thus also by the future of the crucified, toward whom we extend our petition, "*maranatha!*" (1 Cor 16:22; Rev 22:10). At the same time this communion and new covenant gives room to love. For such love the believer is made free, in that, in commerce with his fellows, he no longer has to seek for identity and self-justification, and thus—crucified to the world (Gal 6:14) and therewith dead to self-concern (Gal

14. See Jüngel, *Gottes Sein ist im Werden Verantwortliche Rede vom Sein Gottes bei Karl Barth: Eine Paraphrase,* esp. part 3; Jüngel, *The Doctrine of the Trinity,* esp. part 3.

15. Barth's theology can altogether be understood as the impressive endeavor—in utter contradiction to Plato's second τύπος περί θεόλιας (*Republic* 380d–83c)—to agree with the first (*Republic* 379b–80c).

16. See Gese, "Psalm 22 und das Neue Testament," 180–201. Also see Bayer, "Tod Gottes und Herrenmahl"; and Bayer, "Erhörte Klage," 259–72; also reprinted in Bayer, *Leibliches Wort,* 334–49.

2:19; 5:24)—can live outside himself in his neighbor. For in faith he lives outside himself in him, who has forever linked his eternal life with the temporal death of Jesus on the cross and has swallowed up death in victory (1 Cor 15:54–57).[17]

## JESUS'S DEATH AND GOD'S LIFE

Jesus's death is swallowed up by God's life; hence there is no life of God without Jesus's death. In the resurrection of the crucified something more happened than the fulfillment of an expectation of apocalyptic Judaism, which hoped of Yahweh that he would resurrect the dead and which praised him in appropriate terms. In it there is more taking place than that human suffering was merely brought into connection with God. Already by Old Testament witness God has concerned himself with suffering— and even death, by delivering those who lie under the bane thereof: from injustice (*Rechtlosigkeit*), sickness, and the affliction of enemies. But with the deliverance of Jesus from death in its ultimate extremity, God has taken up death into himself, assimilated it, because he raised precisely the one who had claimed to speak and act in his place and was put to death for it. God implicated himself, his own honor, his right, and his life in the dishonor, loss of right, and eventual death of Jesus. The depths of God's death thus accord with the magnitude of Jesus's claim. When God entered into the death of Jesus, he entered *entirely* into Jesus. For this reason the *modus loquendi* of "incarnation," "preexistence," "mediator of creation," and so forth, is necessary in order to guard the resurrection related to Jesus's death from an adoptionist interpretation and thus from misunderstanding.

If the resurrection is isolated, it degenerates into a miracle. Therefore, in order to prevent such a misunderstanding, it is said of the crucified in parallel to "God raised him from the dead": "God gave him glory" (1 Pet 1:21) and "he was vindicated" (1 Tim 3:16). This can only refer to the *entirety* of his words and deeds. Only this glorious vindication makes the relation of God to the death of Jesus—as established by the resurrection— what it in fact is. Through crucifixion and resurrection the Son became what he is from all eternity. So what it definitely calls for is strict attention to that which in dogmatic language is called the *communicatio idomatum*

---

17. Cf. the concluding thesis of Luther's treatise "On the Freedom of a Christian," *WA* 7:38.6–10; *LW* 31:371.

of the divine and human nature of Jesus Christ within the *unio personalis*. In this mutual giving and taking of parts, this reciprocal relation, lies the germinating point not only of Christology, but also of the doctrine of the Trinity.

With the resurrection of the crucified took place the divine recognition of him that was despised and rejected of men, the justification of one who, in men's eyes, was cursed even by God (Gal 3:13)—a rehabilitation, which does not just refer to the ignominious death of Jesus as an isolated event, but includes everything that the crucified said and did in his earthly life. God vindicated and justified the one who had claimed to act in his name. In so doing he tied down and established himself—as the "Father" of this "Son": "This is my beloved Son . . ." (Mark 9:7).[18]

The Son of God is our Lord. Whoever calls the crucified "Lord"—addresses him, in other words, with the divine name[19]—acknowledges the intimate relationship between the death of Jesus on the cross and God's life. In the Gospels—which unfold testimony to Jesus as Lord, as the risen crucified, and are both historically and factually "passion narratives with extended introductions"[20]—this intimate relationship is richly expressed; in the Christological hymns it is sung (Phil 2:6–11; Col 1:15–20; Heb 1:1–4; etc.); and in the early church's Trinitarian and Christological dogma it is clarified in the confrontation with misinterpretations.

## DOGMA BETWEEN METAPHYSICS AND MYTHOLOGY: GOD'S BEING AND COMING

The formation of trinitarian and Christological dogma took place in an atmosphere of both intimate relation to and severest conflict with Greek metaphysics and its criticism of mythology. The Christian theology determined by the Word of the Cross articulates itself in a manner critical of mythology as well as metaphysics, presenting itself thereto in the form of an unheard-of *skandalon* with its central thesis: "The eternally existing God *comes* in a contingent, unique, and therefore finite historical event."[21]

---

18. Cf. Mark 1:11 as well as 15:39 and before that even 1:2: concerning the speech of the Father to the pre–existent Son.

19. Rose, s.v. "Jahwe," 16:438.

20. Kähler, *Der sogenannte historische Jesus und der geschichtliche biblische Christus*, 59f., n. 1; or *The So-called Historical Jesus and the Historic Biblical Christ*, 80f., n. 11.

21. Elert, *Der Ausgang der altkirchlichen Christologie*, 70.

God's eternal being, in which he keeps faith with himself and his Word, and his temporal coming, whereby he enters into his sin-converted creation unto death on the cross, are together: "unmixed, unchanged, undivided, inseparable."[22] Even the eternal being of God is not left unaffected by Jesus's death on the cross. In trying to think this, Christian theology broke with the apathy axiom of Greek metaphysics—according to which God is incapable of suffering.[23]

On the other hand—in criticism of mythology—the idea of a metamorphosis is rejected: as if "divinity were transformed into humanity"[24] and God, in his death on the cross, had ceased to be God. The narrative of the crucified God is at the same time critical of mythology in this, that it does not give fantasy the free reign it usually enjoys in myth. Rather, it rivets attention to the historical fact of the crucifixion of Jesus of Nazareth in its temporal and spacial determination and does not allow itself to be pried loose from the texts in which it was originally recorded; a "symbolism of the death of Jesus" must keep these texts in mind.[25] The history of the risen crucified remains bindingly written in these texts and, having once and for all been done, permits no further elaboration—without being robbed of its eschatological character.

22. Deninger and Schömmetzer, *Enchiridion Symbolorum*, Nr. 302.

23. Elert, *Der Ausgang der altkirchlichen Christologie*, esp. 71–132; Elert, "Die Theopaschitische Formel," 195–206.

24. Cf. Symbolum Athanasii, 35: "Unus autem non conversione divinitatis in *carnem* [carne]" (Denzinger and Schönmetzer, *Enchiridion Symbolorum*, Nr. 302 §76; or BC/T 20).

25. See Bader, *Symbolik des Todes Jesu*.

# BIBLIOGRAPHY

Bader, Günter. *Symbolik des Todes Jesu*. Hermeneutische Untersuchungen zur Theologie. Tübingen: Mohr/Siebeck, 1988.

Baur, Jórg. "Weisheit und Kreuz." In *Zugang zur Theologie: Fundamentaltheologische Beiträge. Festschrift für Wilfried Joest zum 65. Geb.*, edited by Friedrich Mildenberger and Joachim Track, 33–52. Göttingen: Vandenhoeck & Ruprecht, 1979

———. "Weisheit und Kreuz." *Neue Zeitschrift für Systematische Theologie* 22 (1980) 33–44.

Bayer, Oswlad. "Erhörte Klage." *Neue Zeitschrift für Systematische Theologie* 25 (1983) 259–72. Reprinted in *Leibliches Wort: Reformation and Neuzeit im Konflikt*, 334–49. Tübingen: Mohr/Siebeck, 1992.

———. "Kommunikabilität des Glaubens," also in *Autorität und Kritik: Zu Hermeeutik und Wissenschaftstheorie*, 108–16. Tübingen: Mohr/Siebeck, 1991.

———. "Tod Gottes und Herrenmahl." *Zeitschrift für Theologie und Kirche* 70 (1973) 346–63. Reprinted in *Leibliches Wort Reformation und Neuzeit im Konflikt*, 289–305. Tübingen: Mohr/Siebeck, 1992.

Elert, Werner. *Der Ausgang der altkirchlichen Christologie: Eine Untersuchung über Theodor von Pharan und seine Zeit ab Einführung in die alte Dogmengeschichte.* Edited by Wilhelm Maurer and Elisabeth Bergsträsser. Berlin: Lutherisches, 1957

———. *Das christliche Ethos: Grundlinien der lutherischen Ethik.* Edited by E. Kinder,. Hamburg: Furche, 1961. Translated by C. J. Schindler as *The Christian Ethos.* 1957. Reprinted, Eugene, OR: Wipf & Stock, 2004.

———. "Die Theopaschitische Formel." *Theologische Literaturzeitung* 75 (1950) 195–206.

Denzinger, Henricus, and Adolphus Schönmetzer, editors. *Enchiridion Symbolorum.* Symbolum Chalcedonense 302. 34th ed. Freiburg: Herder 1967.

Gese, Hartmut. "Psalm 22 und das Neue Testament: Der älteste Bericht vom Tode Jesu und die Entstehung des Herrenmahles." In *Vom Sinai zum Zion*, 180–201. 2nd ed. Munich: Kaiser, 1974.

Hamann, J. G. "Chimärische Einfälle." In *Sämtliche Werke* 2:164, lines 17–18. Edited by J. Nadler. Historical-critical ed. 6 vols. Vienna: Herder, 1949–1957.

Hegel, G. W. F. *Faith and Knowledge.* Translated by Walter Cerf and H. S. Harris. Albany: State University of New York Press, 1977.

———. *Glauben und Wissen.* Edited by G. Lasson. Philosophische Bibliothek 62B. Hamburg: Meiner, 1962.

———. *Lectures on the Philosophy of Religion.* Vol. 3, *The Consummate Religion.* Edited by Peter C. Hodgson. Translated by R. F. Brown et al. Berkeley: University of California Press, 1985.

———. *Vorlesungen über die Philosophie der Religion.* Vol. 2, *Die absolute Religion.* Edited by G. Lasson. Philosophische Bibliothek 63. Hamburg: Meiner, 1974.

Hengel, Martin. *Crucifixion in the Ancient World and the Folly of the Message of the Cross.* Translated by John Bowden. Philadelphia: Fortress, 1977.

———. "Mors turpissima crucis: Die Kreuzigung in der antiken Welt und die 'Torheit' des 'Wortes vom Kreuz.'" In *Rechtfertigung: Festschrift für Ernst Käsemann zum 70 Geburstag*, edited by Johannnes Friedrich et al., 125–84. Tübingen: Mohr/Siebeck, 1976.

Jüngel, Eberhard. *Gottes Sein ist im Werden Verantwortliche Rede vom Sein Gottes bei Karl Barth Eine Paraphrase.* 4th ed. Tübingen: Mohr/Siebeck, 1986. Translated by Horton Harris as *The Doctrine of the Trinity: God's Being Is in Becoming.* Monograph Supplements of the Scottish Journal of Theology. Edinburgh: Scottish Academic, 1976.

Kähler, Martin. *Der sogenannte historische Jesus und der geschichtliche biblische Christus,* 1892, edited by E. Wolf. 4th ed. Munich: Kaiser, 1969. Translated, edited, and with an introduction by Carl E. Braaten as *The So-Called Historical Jesus and the Historic Biblical Christ.* Foreword by Paul Tillich. Philadelphia: Fortress, 1988.

Knaake, J. F. K. et al., editors. *WA.* Vol. 9. Weimar: Böhlau, 1883ff.

Lessing, G. E. "Ein Mehreres aus den Papieren des Ungenannten, die Offenbarung betreffend: Zweites Fragment." In *Werke*, 7:887–909. Edited by H. G. Gopfert. Munich: Hanser, 1976.

Luther, Martin. "On the Freedom of a Christian." In *LW* 31.

———. "On the Freedom of a Christian." In *WA* 40.

Nietzsche, Friedrich. *Beyond Good and Evil*. In *Basic Writings of Nietzsche*, edited and translated by Walter Kaufmann, 179–436. New York: The Modern Library, 1968.

Plato. *The Republic*. Edited by Eric H. Warmington and Philip G. Rouse. New York: New American Library of World Literature, 1956.

Reimarus, H. S. *Apologie oder Schutzschrtft fur die vernunftigen Verehrer Gottes*, edited by Gerhard Alexander. Frankfurt: Insel, 1972.

Rose, Martin. "Jahwe." In *Theologische Realenzyklopädie*, 16:438–41. Berlin: de Gruyter, 1987.

Thaidigsmann, Edgar. *Identitätsverlangen und Widerspruch Kreuzestheologie bei Luther, Hegel und Barth*. Gesellschaft und Theologie. Fundamentaltheologische Studien. Munich: Kaiser, 1983.

Lüpke, Johannes von. "Hamann und die Krise der Theologie im Fragmentenstreit." In *Johann Georg Hamann und die Krise der Aufklärung Acta des 5 Internationalen Hamann-Kolloquiums* 1988, edited by. Bernhard Gajek and Albert Meier. Frankfurt: Lang, 1990.

Wiederkehr, D. "Kreuz/Leid." In *Neues Handbuch Theologischer Grundbegriffe*, 3: ad loc. 4 vols. Edited by Peter Eicher. Munich: Kösel, 1984.

# 11

# Preaching the Word

*Oswald Bayer*

## CREATION THEOLOGY: ITS DEPTH AND BREADTH

HUMANS ARE PRIMARILY PERCEIVING, "aesthetic" beings. We are determined first and foremost by a host of motifs and images that, consciously or unconsciously, drive our actions, which in turn can fix or alter the direction of our will. Clearly, the crucial thing here is the nature of this stratum of motifs and its linguistic makeup. Likewise, the crucial thing about this storehouse of images is the power and general direction of its affects and passions, in brief, its pathos. The first question then that needs to be asked is: What do I experience? What is given to me? For our being and our actions do not begin with ourselves but they have their existence in a prior gift of freedom.

How is this freedom given? Is it given to us by nature? Can it be empirically established and described? Can it be grasped theoretically, or only postulated practically? It has its origin in a particular word: the word of the Creator. The freedom we have to perceive the world and to act is a response to the Creator's word. His word is creative and efficacious; it does what it says (Isa 55:10, 11). By his word he created the heavens and the earth (Gen 1:1). By this same powerful word he sustains all things (Heb 1:3), forgives sins, and thus creates life and salvation. Therefore, we have no need to worry about our existence, either in the past or in the future.

Hannah Arendt sees in promise and forgiveness the only possibility humans have of escaping the dilemmas caused by the irrevocability and the unforeseeability of their actions.[1] If the only effective way of dealing with the past is a justification of the ungodly, and if the only effective way of dealing with the future is a resurrection from the dead, and if both can only be a creation out of nothing, then the word that does all this is not a "natural"—immanent—possibility within human beings and their world, but must come from outside. This word is the Logos, God himself. It is the power of communication in itself and it empowers us to communicate with him and others. His word is of this kind: Let there be light and there *was* light (Gen 1:3). Be healed! (Mark 5:34) and she *was* healed. *Talitha koum!* (I say to you, get up) and immediately the girl *stood* up (Mark 5:41). *Ephphatha* (Be opened!)—and the man's ears *were* opened (Mark 7:34). Your sins are forgiven! (Mark 2:5) and they *are* forgiven. The most precise and pregnant term to designate this creative word is promise: *promissio*. According to the New Testament, Jesus Christ, the word become flesh (John 1:14), is the bodily form and history through which God in the Holy Spirit mediates his promise, or more precisely, mediates himself as promise—"I am the Lord, your God!" (Exod 20:2)—as *true* promise. His promise is *certain*; he delivers what he promises. "For the Son of God, Jesus Christ, who was preached among you by us, by me and Silas and Timothy," writes Paul, "was not 'Yes' and 'No', but in him it has always been 'Yes.' For all God's promises are 'Yes' in him" (2 Cor 1:19, 20). The promise is bound up with the *name* by, in, and with which we can call on God: I am the one, the one who goes with you in freedom (Exod 3:14; defined more precisely in Exod 34:6). God lets us hear his name and allows us to pass it on to others. He puts it in our mouths and on our lips, so that we can answer in faith by praising and confessing him. This is the highest dignity that we humans have as linguistic beings. It means the church is entrusted, "handed over" (*manum dare*) to us; it is a "mandate." Other mandates include the economy, marriage and family, as well as the state. All of them are God's gift; all are constituted[2] by his promise and so involve language and communication. They are handed over and entrusted, in good faith, to our reason which also has a linguistic character (*Sprachvernunft*), for it comes from God who gave us the gift of language

1. Arendt, *Vita Activa oder Vom tätigen Leben*, §§ 33–34.

2. Melanchthon too operates with a broader definition of *sacrament*, BC 220.11–17; BSLK 293.42—294.49 ("Apology to AC 13").

when he called us into existence by breathing into us the breath of life. Yet we humans are responsible for how we manage these mandates and we must give account at the final judgment not only for every deed, but also for every empty word we have uttered; in fact, for every evil thought.

God's promise, his *promissio*, extends far beyond these mandates. It creates, works, speaks, writes, rules and governs the entire world. Without the word, there would be no world. The reach and character of this efficacious word is clear from Luther's translation of Psalm 33:4b: what the Creator "promises, he surely does." Where the Hebrew text of this creation psalm uses a noun clause to say that God's 'work' is 'reliable,' Luther's bold translation says that God's work as Creator is indeed a work, but a work that speaks. God's work actually speaks, and because it is self-interpreting it makes itself understood. It is an effective word of address, a work that bespeaks God's faithfulness: a promise. If the world is a promised world, it mediates a promise to me, and I am addressed by God in, with and under that promise. I am "placed" in a God-given context, provided with a space to live, with its God-given rhythm of day and night, summer and winter, youth and old age. "And the Lord God took the man and placed him in the Garden of Eden to work it and take care of it" (Gen 2:15; see Gen 2:8).

Why did we need to consider the depth and breadth of the *promissio* and its basis in creation theology? So that the preaching of the word is not discussed positivistically and in isolation! The sermon must rather be seen in the context of an aesthetics that applies not only to a part of reality, such as the religious sphere, but rather to the whole of reality and to the world as such. It is a perception of the world in a comprehensive and communicative sense. The entire world and the whole of reality is a word that is given to me to hear along with all creatures, a word that I may answer. But because I am a sinner, I turn a deaf ear to it and put myself at odds with it. The decisive structural elements of this transcendental aesthetic that takes account of the linguistic space of human beings and their world can be inferred from the five meanings of the Greek word akoh/ These meanings are: 1) the organ of hearing, the ear; the capacity to hear; theologically, the capacity to hear receptively for which I am empowered; 2) the act of hearing: that I hear; 3) the mode of hearing: how I hear; 4) the thing heard, what I receive; and 5) what is spoken, what is to be heard. These five elements define the linguistic as well as the affective space of human beings and their world as a space for hearing. The visual field, the space for seeing and reading, is structured in a similar way.

## DISTINCTION AND CORRELATION OF GENERAL AND SPECIAL DIVINE (WORSHIP) SERVICE

If we regard the sermon as a particular part especially of the Christian divine (worship) service, then we must never lose sight of the breadth and depth of this creation theology. This means above all giving attention to the distinction and the correlation between general and special divine service[3] where the special, Christian divine service restores the church's order of creation. This order of creation is the realm where the creator calls his creatures to life so they can respond to him in praise and live in the knowledge that they owe their life to God. The creatures respond by receiving—hearing, taking, and eating (Gen 2:16)—the superabundance of God's gifts with wonder and delight, and sharing them generously with others. As Paul (Rom 1:18–3:20) points out, the Creator has done all he can to see that this happens.

Mysteriously, however, humans misunderstand, pervert and corrupt this creation understood as address. They cannot stand upright before God, but are curved in on themselves. "There is no one who seeks God. All have turned away, they have together gone wrong" (Rom 3:11–12). They have dragged the rest of creation into corruption with them (Rom 8:19–22). This "perverse world," "which is drowned in its blindness,"[4] has been restored and set right, so that it can again listen and speak to its Creator. It has been restored and reoriented through a miracle of healing, the miracle of the new creation (Mark 7:31–37; 2 Cor 5:17). This happens—through Jesus, the Christ—once again by means of the promise understood as gift.[5] Thus the universal significance of the proclaimed word is evident from the fact that it overcomes the corruption of the church as an order of *creation*. The Christian church is not some minority group, but the renewed humanity, "a new creation" (2 Cor 5:17). The

---

3. For more details on what follows, see Bayer, *Theology the Lutheran Way*, 86–93.

4. Luther, "Large Catechism" *BC* 433:21; *BSLK* 649.26–28.

5. In the "Proceedings at Augsburg" (*Acta Augustana*), the documentation of his hearing before Cardinal Cajetan at Augsburg in October 1518, Luther makes a very plausible appeal to the miracle stories of the New Testament and to the efficacious word of Christ, which in each case forms their heart and center: "According to your faith let it be done to you" (Matt 9:29), "You are set free from your infirmity" (Luke 13:12), "Go, your son will live" (John 4:50), and others. This interest in the miracle stories is bound up with Luther's new understanding of *promissio* that grows out of the impact that the reformational insights have on his life and theology. *WA* 2:13.6—16.3; esp. 14.14–29. See below nn. 29 and 30.

promise given to mankind in paradise—you are free to take and eat from any tree in the garden (see Gen 2:16)—the promise that was lost and corrupted by humanity's ingratitude and failure to appreciate the gift, is now finally promised and given to humankind in the new covenant "by my blood": Take and eat! Take and drink! (see 1 Cor 11:24, 25).

Jesus Christ, whose word is clear and certain and makes certain, not only promises the forgiveness of sins (Matt 26:28), but also enables us to endure the *Anfechtung* caused by the hidden God, when I do not know how I stand with God. God's terrible hiddenness, experienced as uncertainty and ambiguity, lies in the fact that he creates evil *and* good (Lam 3:38), life *and* death, light *and* darkness (Isa 45:7), prosperity *and* disaster (Amos 3:6). Beauty and cruelty in nature and history are for us inextricably woven together. This side of the grave, we experience God's omnipotence in all sorts of ambiguous ways. Because of this, we can only call on God as a good and merciful Father (as we do in the Lord's Prayer) in light of the certainty of Romans 8:31–39 that since Christ has overcome the world, nothing can now separate us from the love of God in Christ Jesus our Lord. This empowerment and confidence to call on God in prayer arises likewise from the proclaimed gospel in the form of the *promissio*, where the promise creates faith. This promise however is different from the word of the God who is active in the world as Creator and ruler. This God is also present in the word, but present in a thoroughly ambiguous way, so much so that none of us, not just sinners, knows how he or she stands before God.[6]

Therefore, the double focus, essential for the special proclamation of the gospel, is 1) the church, understood as a corrupted order of creation, and 2) God's terrible hiddenness. This double focus makes the universal scope and meaning of the gospel clear. It is the new creation, understood as the forgiveness of sins, which gives us the strength to endure the *Anfechtung* that we experience in the face of God's terrible hiddenness. And we can endure it because God invites us to bring our complaint to him in the confidence that he will hear and answer us.

## SERMON AS PARTICULAR PART OF THE CHRISTIAN DIVINE SERVICE?

If the divine service is nothing else than the fact "that our dear Lord himself speaks to us through his holy word and that we respond to him

---

6. For more on this distinction, see Bayer, *Schöpfung als Anrede*, 30–32.

through prayer and praise,"[7] if it is God's service to us through his word and our service in response, then the *entire* divine service is a "sermon" (and prayer): address and promise. It is part of God's downward movement and humble self-communication to us—especially in the form of the Lord's Supper and its gift-giving words of institution, which are a brief summary of the whole gospel.[8] The sermon as a particular part of the Christian divine service, a special type of speech, needs to be in harmony with this criterion and essence of the entire divine service.

The insight that the entire divine service is really a "sermon" that preaches the word relieves the sermon proper of the inflated claims and expectations that some people have of it. It is not as if the sermon is the only way of proclaiming God's word to his people and that it has to accomplish this all by itself, for the Bible readings themselves are also a form of God's word where he addresses us and where the word can create faith where and when it pleases God (CA 5).

## SERMON AS CATEGORICAL GIFT AND PROMISE

If the sermon proper has its matrix in the gift-giving word of the Lord's Supper, and if its purpose is nothing more than to unfold and highlight that word, then we can avoid three mistakes: the way of theorization, moralization and psychologization. In other words, the proclaimed word is not primarily statement, appeal, or expression. This cannot be emphasized too strongly. For the word and faith are closely connected: as the word, so faith. If the proclaimed word is statement and demonstration,

---

7. "Sermon at the Dedication of the Castle Church in Torgau, 1544," *LW* 51:333; *WA* 49:588.17 –18. See "A Prelude on the Babylonian Captivity of the Church, 1520," *LW* 36:42 (trans. altered); *WA* 6:516.30–32: "God does not deal with humans, nor has he ever dealt with them in any other way than through the word of promise. We in turn cannot deal with God in any other way than through faith in the word of his promise."

8. "A Prelude on the Babylonian Captivity of the Church, 1520," *LW* 36:56; *WA* 6:525.36: The Lord's Supper as the "sum and substance of the gospel." Thaidigsmann, "Die Gabe des Wortes und die Frage der Gerechtigkeit," 39, is afraid that if we assent to this thesis we might push "into the background the sacrament of penance with its understanding of *promissio* as the acquittal of the sinner who has failed"—and along with it "the experience of the law's demand for righteousness, the acknowledgment of a failed life, repentance and a new beginning for the sinner who is justified." Yet the word of absolution and the gift-giving word in the Lord's Supper, each of which is a promise, are actually identical, and distinguished only by the fact that the gesture of the gift in the Lord's Supper is more noticeable and hence clearer.

then faith is insight and knowledge. If however the word is appeal, then faith is actually its enactment in the deed, its realization in the form of a theory or an idea. Again, if the proclaimed word is expression, then faith is a fundamental part or experience of human life as such. Only if the word is promise and gift, is faith really faith.

## MAIN ELEMENTS OF THE SERMON AS SPEECH ACT

The evangelical understanding of the word of the sermon preserves Luther's great hermeneutical discovery, which, strictly speaking, is his Reformation discovery. Namely, *that the linguistic sign itself is the thing; it does not represent a thing that is absent but it presents a thing that is present.*[9] Luther made this discovery in 1518 as he thought again about the sacrament of penance in view of the indulgence controversy. If the sign itself is the thing, as in the absolution, this means that the statement: "I absolve you of your sins, in the name of the Father and of the Son and of the Holy Spirit," is not simply a judgment that states, describes and expresses what is already the case and therefore presupposes an inner, divine, or proper absolution. In fact, it is neither a statement, nor a description, nor an expression. It is rather a *promissio* in the form of a speech act that creates a relationship—between the person in whose name it is spoken and the person to whom it is spoken, who believes or does not believe the promise. If we consider the unconditional word of absolution as the basic word, model and matrix of an evangelical sermon, then there are four decisive features that make this sermon stand out. These features have to do with grammar and pragmatics. 1) The sermon is not a discourse in the third person about something but an address in the second person, where an "I" addresses a "you." 2) The verb is formulated in the present tense or in the present perfect.[10] 3) The performative verb used in the present or present perfect is semantically and pragmatically that of "promise"—a valid promise with immediate effect; it creates community. 4) The "I" of the preacher who speaks legitimates itself, implicitly or explicitly, as authorized to make this promise—like the prophet with the message formula, "thus says the Lord: . . ." The preacher is an autho-

9. "A sign in philosophy is the mark of a thing that is absent, but a sign in theology is the mark of a thing that is present" (Table Talk, 1540. *WA TR* 4:666 [No. 5106]).

10. The relation between the present and present perfect corresponds to the correlation between what was "won" and what is "distributed"; see below n. 14.

rized representative who stands in the place of his Lord and is authorized and empowered to speak on his behalf. The divine service is begun and continued in the name of the triune God. Baptism, absolution, and the Lord's Supper are celebrated in this name. The sermon is delivered in this name. And the preacher hears and takes to heart the trinitarian blessing promised by the words that many pastors use to greet the congregation before the sermon: "The grace of our Lord Jesus Christ, the love of God, and the communion of the Holy Spirit be with you all" (2 Cor 13:13).

## THE TEXT AND SITUATION OF THE LISTENERS; THE PREACHER

This apostolic blessing prefacing the sermon, the words of absolution, and the words of institution of the Lord's Supper are examples of key fundamental *scriptural passages* that are essential to the Christian divine service and are liturgically enacted in the service to give them prominence.[11] Yet this is the very way Scripture itself wants them to be used. Scripture, of course, is also cited in the sermon—assuming that even a thematic sermon is textual. But the sermon has a special place in the divine service. Apart from the fact that the sermon, like other elements of the divine service, both distinguishes and correlates God's word and our human response, it is unique in that no other part of the service affords and demands such freedom of discretion[12] as the sermon. Because the message of the sermon is not a dead relic from a bygone age but a word that is made alive by the Spirit's presence, preachers have an exceptionally challenging task. They must pass on to others the word that they himself have received, and they must do this responsibly, but in a way that bears the stamp of their own biography. This means two things. First, preachers need to receive the word themselves and allow it to address them. But secondly, they must dare to interpret, update and apply that word to the present situation so that it speaks to the hearts of their listeners as God's word for them today. The one gospel is an unconditional promise and a categorical gift. It must always be spoken anew without ever saying anything new, in the sense of different, for the *only* thing we can say new

11. See Lash, "Performing the Scriptures," 37–46.

12. A constitutive part of this freedom to shape the sermon is the insight and recognition that I am the work of the sermon text (see Eph 2:10) before the sermon becomes my human work. See Wannenwetsch, "Die Ökonomie des Gottesdienstes," 37–55.

is what will never again become old, like the new, final covenant. The gospel, therefore, must always be interpreted anew, but in such a way that it does not lose its definitive character. Preachers have the task of delivering to their contemporaries the salvation won by Christ. They live with them, they rejoice and suffer with them, and at the same time they minister to them in God's name—the God who promises himself to us. And so they often find themselves wedged between the text and the situation of the listeners, which is akin to being pulverized between the upper and lower millstone, as they try to repeat the sermon text in each different situation without losing the dynamic of its language.[13] All their powers and talents are harnessed in the service of letting the biblical text speak to the situation today. But at the same time, if the sermon touches the heart, if it speaks to people in their life situation, if it promises them courage for life, if it brings life to the dead and gives hope to those who are in despair—if it does any of this, the preachers cannot take the credit for that themselves. For they cannot do their hard work—the backbreaking work of preparing and delivering the sermon—without praying for the Holy Spirit. The prayer for the Spirit, however, means the end of any notion that the sermon is the preacher's own achievement. It makes clear that the sermon is not simply the work of a human individual but ultimately the work of the empowering Spirit.

## THE UNDERSTANDING OF "HISTORY": *PROMISSIO* AND *NARRATIO*

The gospel is always "distributed" anew, but it was only "won" once, under Pontius Pilate:[14] "And you are blessed [saved] forever!"[15] Therefore, it cannot be separated from the historical fact of the crucifixion of Jesus of

---

13. This picture must not be understood to imply that in every new time and situation the old text, conceived "purely empirically," is predefined in a way that is fixed and final. Rather, the text has the capability of already determining how the situation will be perceived, or at least it will play a part in that. But still that does not eliminate the anguish felt by preachers in their location between the text and the situation of the listeners.

14. For more on the illuminating distinction and correlation between the salvation "won" once for all and its "distribution" or delivery again and again, from the beginning to the end of the world, see "Against the Heavenly Prophets, 1525," *LW* 40:213–14; "Confession Concerning Christ's Supper, 1528," *LW* 37:193; *BSLK* 713.10–15; "Large Catechism," *BC* 469.31.

15. Luther, "Dear Christians, One and All Rejoice," *LBW*, hymn # 299, verse 8.

Nazareth and its temporal and spatial specificity, nor can it be separated from the original texts that testify to its meaning. These texts contain its authoritative formulation that cannot be extrapolated without losing its definitive, eschatological character as a once-for-all event. God's presence in the Spirit does not surpass what happened under Pontius Pilate, but "reminds" us of it (see John 14:26), recalls it, brings it into present, distributes it, and promises it.

The distinction and correlation between the salvation won once under Pontius Pilate and its ever-new distribution and application gives preachers a hint of how they can avoid two extreme positions. The one is a moribund traditionalism that does not communicate and is heard as lacking in compassion and solidarity. The other is a breathless actualism that is empty and blind. Preachers will not surrender to the "moment" in actualistic—not even mystical—immediacy but, placed in a center,[16] they will concentrate on the *kairos* of today ("Today, if you hear his voice . . . " Heb 3:7–4:13) in the middle of a field of vision stretching from the beginning to the end of the world. An isolated moment would only be a "dead torso, without head or feet"[17] that has, so to speak, neither hand nor foot. This means they would not consciously align themselves with the modern schemata of a *Heilsgeschichte* ("salvation history"),[18] but would instead work with the notion of remembrance that comes from the tradition of

---

16. See Bayer, *Zugesagte Gegenwart*, 101, 230.

17. Hamann, "Biblical Reflections," 131 (on 1 Chr 12:32). For more details, see Bayer, *Zeitgenosse im Widerspruch*, 220 and 227 (in the context of 214 –29).

18. See the cogent article "Heilsgeschichte" by Friedrich Mildenberger, 1584–86, esp 1586: The conceptions are so different—yet all of them "operate with a concept of actuality and temporal continuity, foreign to the biblical way of speaking, that is used to interrogate the biblical narratives in the search for a connection between the facts lying behind them. It is this constructed factual connection, understood as *Heilsgeschichte*, that is then supposed to be the objective basis of faith rather than the biblical language in historical narrative and doxology. The modern construction of history takes the place of biblical speech." Certainly, we cannot give up the concept of "Heilsgeschichte." It is best used in the sense of Luther's "story of stories" in the framework of his catechetical systematics (on that: Bayer, *Theology the Lutheran Way*, 67–74. "The symbol, the confession of our holy Christian faith, is a story of stories [*historia historiarum*], a story that beats all stories, the greatest of all stories. This story presents us with a recital of the stupendous feats of the divine majesty from the beginning to the end: how we and all creatures are created, how we are redeemed by the Son of God by means of his incarnation, suffering, death, and his resurrection, how we are also renewed and sanctified by the Holy Spirit and become a new creature, and how all of us, gathered together into one people of God, have forgiveness of sins and are saved eternally" (*WA TR* 5:581.36–43; No. 6288).

the Lord's Supper (1 Cor 11:24–25: "*anamnesis*"; see Ps 11:4) and that is constitutive for the Jewish and Christian understanding of history.[19] This remembrance always includes moments of history that cry out to be narrated. But faith that looks to the promise, that remembers the promise, is not founded on history; at any rate, it is more than mere "historical" faith (*fides historica*).[20]

As we consider the meaning of "history" for the proclamation of the Christian faith, we see that Luther's concept of *promissio* has the power to orient our thinking. But it does not mean "promise" in the sense of the modern schemata of a *Heilsgeschichte* (salvation history). It is not a philosophical category of *Heilsgeschichte* that allows us to think of revelation as (universal) history, but it is the essence of proclamation—namely, "the death of the Lord" (1 Cor 11:26)—and as such is a binding and valid promise with immediate effect. This gives us a quite definite understanding of God and history and in particular a quite definite view of the Old Testament. We cannot infer God's unity by observing history in its openness and totality. At the very most, we can anticipate it hypothetically. But we can know it for certain from God's promise.

The *promissio* however needs to be situated in and by the *narratio*. The stories that make up the main part of the biblical texts narrate varied life situations with the full range of emotions and all within a world that has a beginning and an end, like our own life. In view of these stories, J. G. Hamann speaks of the "historical truths, not only of those of past times but also of times to come."[21] They prove their truth by the fact that they are read, preached and heard *typologically*. Narratives offer possibilities of identification. Suddenly, I see myself in these stories and hear them as my own story. "Change but the name, and the story tells about you."[22] The inspired reader discovers himself in the text, recognizes himself as interpreted and addressed by it—even if in the preached story the transition from the third person of the narrative to the second person of the address

---

19. See Stuhlmacher, "Anamnese. Eine unterschätzte hermeneutische Kategorie."

20. Philip Melanchthon defines "*fides Historica*, that is, an opinion, such as, I believe Livy and Sallust and other trustworthy historians. Thus, the ungodly also believe that the world is created, that Christ is risen and many other things that even faith does not justify. But *faith that is related exclusively to the promise* is justifying faith," Capita 1520; *CR* 21:35–36).

21. Hamann, "Golgotha and Sheblimini," 182.

22. "Mutato nomine de te fabula narrator" (Horace, *Satires* I/1, 69, 70).

is not explicitly made by the preacher. In fact, the self-identification, freely made, with Abraham, Jacob, and David, with the Syrophoenician woman, with Peter who denied the Lord, with the centurion under the cross, or with unbelieving Thomas is the more effective.

It would be worthwhile to consider more thoroughly this transition from the third person to the second person and therefore the relation between the concept of narrative and that of promise. At any rate, biblical narratives that do not already have their center in the promise, like the miracle stories of the New Testament,[23] need it to make clear their connection with the listener and reader. We see this in the second creation account, where the narrated world is revealed paradigmatically to human kind as a gift: you are free to take and eat from everything (see Gen 2:16)! The *promissio* has criteriological significance. A sermon—not only on biblical stories but on any genre of biblical text—is only a sermon if it repeats and emphasizes the original promise identical with God's name, the original charter of Israel and the church: "I am the Lord, your God!" (Exod 20:2; see Exod 3:14 and Exod 34:6 for a more precise definition).

## GOD'S WORD AS HUMAN WORD

Every sermon, if it is a true sermon, takes up this name and hands it on as a "proclaimable mystery" (according to Luther's translation of 1 Tim 3:16). This is not a mystery to be kept secret but one to be "proclaimed," to be preached. It is a public mystery, an open secret. By proclaiming God's name, the sermon is, by God's will, his presence itself. Preachers *deliver* a message and are not the message themselves. But insofar as they speak "in the name of God the Father and of the Son and of the Holy Spirit," their human words are identical with the divine word, indeed, "they are one and the same."[24] For "whoever listens to you listens to me" (Luke 10:16; see 2 Cor 5:20). If in the name of God human beings preach God's name, if they publicly, audibly, clearly, and intelligibly offer God's promise of salvation to other people, then such a sermon, although it is a human

---

23. See above, n. 5.

24. "Therefore beware of making any distinction in baptism by ascribing the outward part to man and the inward part to God. Ascribe both to God alone" (Luther, "The Babylonian Captivity of the Church, 1520," *LW* 36:62; *WA* 6:530.27–28). "The Doer and the minister are different persons, but the work of both is the same work" (*LW* 36:63; *WA* 6:530.35–36). For more details, see Bayer, *Promissio*, 264–65. See below, n. 27.

word, is not only a *pointer* to God's own word (like the extra long index finger of John the Baptist in Grünewaldt's picture of the crucifixion on the Isenheim altar),[25] but it *is* God's own word itself. It is astonishing and highly offensive to a spiritualistic doctrine of God that God gives and forgives through human mouths and other creaturely means, such as the water of baptism. The almighty God in heaven is represented definitively on earth by a creaturely word: "Whatever you loose on earth will be loosed in heaven" (Matt 18:18). With the promise of the forgiveness of sins enacted in God's name, God binds himself in a specific way: he commits himself to this promise, surrenders himself to it in order to give us certainty. But there is a paradox here, for it is precisely by relinquishing his power and emptying himself in the oral, earthly word that he fills that word totally with his power, by means of a communication of attributes (*communicatio idiomatum*). In this way, God entrusts his word to humans, he puts it in their mouths and on their lips. Luther, in his sermon on Maundy Thursday 1523, says "that you must hear the absolution with true faith and not doubt that the words spoken by your confessor are indeed spoken by God himself. For God has so humbled himself and condescended that he places his holy, divine word in human mouths so that we have no reason to doubt that it is God himself that speaks it."[26] "So then, there should be no separation or distinction here between God and his word"[27]—between God and his earthly, creaturely word in human mouths.

25. See Marquard, *Karl Barth und der Isenheimer Altar*.

26. *WA* 12:493.3–7 (second version).

27. "Sermons on the Gospel of St John, Chapters 14–16, 1538," *LW* 24:66–67; *WA* 45:522.3–4, on John 14:10 in the context of 24:65; 45:521.24––522.4. "[Likewise, St. Paul and the other apostles and preachers affirm:] 'It is not we who are speaking; it is Christ and God himself. Therefore, when you hear this sermon, you are hearing God himself. On the other hand, if you despise this sermon, you are despising, not us but God himself.' For it is all from God, who condescends to enter the mouth of each Christian or preacher and says: 'If you want to see me or my work, look to Christ; if you want to hear me, listen to this word.' Christ transmits this command to the apostles; they pass it on to their successors, bishops and preachers; these, in turn, deliver it to the whole world. Thus, the apostles and pastors are nothing but channels through which Christ leads and transmits his gospel from the Father to us. Therefore, where you hear the gospel properly taught or see a person baptized; where you see someone administer or receive the sacrament; or where you witness the absolution, there you may say without hesitation: 'Today, I saw God's word and work. Yes, I saw and heard God himself preaching and baptizing.' To be sure, the tongue, the voice, the hands, etc. are those of a human being; but the word and the ministry are really those of the divine majesty himself. Therefore, it must be seen and believed as though God's own voice were resounding from heaven and as though we were

## SERVANT AND WITNESS

The precise definition of the preacher as a "minister of the divine word" (*minister verbi divini*) coming out of the Reformation is irreplaceable. The servant of God's word serves this word by ministering to his contemporaries with the promise. In this risky venture of translation and communication, he finds that being caught between the text and the situation is like being caught between that upper and lower millstone. As we have emphasized before, the preacher, the proclaimer, is not the message itself (2 Cor 4:5). This identity is given only in the person and work of Jesus Christ. Nevertheless, the minister is still important because he delivers the message, he announces the promise. But, as is made unmistakably clear in the recitation of the words of institution, which stress that the Lord's Supper is pure gift, it is really Christ himself who is speaking as these words are recited by the minister. Therefore, in performing this speech act, the minister is standing in the place of Christ (2 Cor 5:20) and hence also in the place of the triune God himself. The Small Catechism puts it clearly and simply when it says: "we receive the absolution, that is, forgiveness, from the confessor as from God himself, and by no means doubt but firmly believe that our sins are thereby forgiven before God in heaven."[28]

This mirrors the formula of confession suggested by Luther. The minister of the Word (*minister verbi*) asks those who come to him: "Do you also believe that my forgiveness is God's forgiveness?" "Yes, dear pastor." To which he says: "Let it be done for you according to your faith. [[29]] By the command [*ex mandato*] of our LORD Jesus Christ, I forgive you your sin in the name of the Father and of the Son and of the Holy Spirit. Amen. Go in peace."[30] Luther concludes his formula of confession with the remark: "A confessor, by using additional passages of Scripture, will in fact be able to comfort and encourage to faith those whose consciences are heavily

---

seeing him administering baptism or the sacrament with his own hands. Thus, here we do not separate, or differentiate between, God and his word." See above n. 24 and Luther's critical turn against the "metaphysical distinction" between the word of God and the word of human beings: Table Talk, 1538. *WA TR* 3:669–74 (No 3868).

28. *BSLK* 517.13–17; *BC* 360.

29. In using the words of Matt 8:13, Luther is taking up the promise of a miracle story. See above, n. 5.

30. *BSLK* 519.16–27; *BC* 361. See Mark 5:34; Luke 7:50; 8:48: The peaceful dismissal with its implied promise again comes from the New Testament miracle stories.

burdened or who are distressed or under attack."[31] This further embeds the Christian faith's standard language of promise in the situation of everyday life which, according to the formula, is expressed concretely in the confession of sins.[32] The promise cannot be isolated or reduced to a mere formula but, from the outset, is related to the listeners and their situation and life history. It is essentially address.

That an address can really strike a chord with the listeners in their concrete situation, that it can convict them, shock them and comfort them is without doubt the work of God himself: the Holy Spirit. This however does not happen apart from the "external word"[33]—not without the word of the preacher who ministers with the promise. But by serving in this way, the preacher is also always a witness, a witness to the truth. This is not meant in a Donatist sense. As if the authenticity and credibility of the preacher could prove the truth of the gospel! Rather, the truth and efficacy of the gospel is as little dependent on the dignity of the servant as it is on the dignity of those addressed who receive the promise and gift: "*nec pendere exdignitate ministri aut sumentis.*"[34] However, this clear, sharp anti-Donatist thrust, which in its own way is immensely comforting, does not mean that the preacher has no involvement at all in communicating the message, or that the preacher's own life history can be completely unaffected by the message. For, as Luther says, he ministers with the promise in solidarity as one who is always also a sinner, living in contradiction to God, a "false witness, betrayer, and liar."[35] So he always preaches the truth of the forgiveness of sins in the face of his own life testimony[36]—but his anti-Donatism is marked by humility rather than cynicism.

## AUTHORIZATION

In the usual ordination liturgies, the context of the ministry of the word is clarified by appealing to 1 Peter 2:9 (see Rev 1:6; 5:10; 20:6). It is defined

31. *BSLK* 519.28–32; *BC* 362. See the variant forms of the absolution in the sermon Luther preached at his first Mass, which is discussed in *WA* 4:655–59 (on the dating, see Bayer, *Promissio*, 166, n. 19).

32. *BSLK* 518.31–41; *BC* 361.

33. "Augsburg Confession," 5 (*BSLK* 58.12–13; *BC* 40–41).

34. *BSLK* 65.37–38 (note to *AC* 10): "The Wittenberg Concord, 1536."

35. "Sermon on Exod 20:16, 1524–27" *WA* 16:521.24–16.

36. See, paradigmatically, Hamann, "Gedanken über meinen Lebenslauf" and on that: Bayer, "Wer bin ich?" 437–56.

first and foremost by the priestly office that every Christian has by virtue of their baptism. This office is grounded in the office of apostle, which is unique and cannot be handed on to another. In other words, the priestly office of every Christian is grounded in the office of reconciliation, instituted and given by God himself (2 Cor 5:18–20). According to 1 Peter 2:9 every baptized person has the *ability* to teach; they are authorized, empowered and obligated to proclaim God's liberating act in Jesus Christ, the gospel, according to their own charisma and calling. The word does not depend on the office, but the office depends on the word with its power to call, just as all offices in the church depend on the word that calls people into the office. There is a distinction between the foundational and general office of the word that Augsburg Confession (*CA*) 5 speaks of, and the office connected with ordination that *CA* 14 speaks of. Luther makes a clear and sharp distinction here by his use of the two terms *sacerdos* and *minister* (priest and minister).[37] "It is true that all Christians are priests, but all are not pastors. For to be a pastor one must not only be a Christian and a priest but must have an office,"[38] the special office of the word of the ordained pastor. This does not require any special spiritual dignity beyond baptism, but it does demand a special professional competence. The task of acquiring and developing this has nothing to do with the gospel but belongs to the realm of the law in its worldly use. Part of the preparation for the pastoral office (where preparation also comes under the first use of the law) is the necessary requirement of a professional education and development, usually through a university, where the student becomes well grounded in academic theology.

When we speak of the public ministry, it is this notion of "public" that is tied up with the professional competence that we have been speaking about. Furthermore, according to *CA* 14, it is the public character of the pastoral office that distinguishes it from the priesthood of all believers. The *rite vocatus* (being regularly called) is really only of secondary importance in comparison with the public character of the office, for it has to do with the proper way in which professional competence is established and the candidate for ordination is called and placed into the office

37. See, for example, "De instituendis ministris Ecclesiae (1523)," *WA* 12:178.9 – 10: "*Sacerdotem non esse quod presbyterum vel ministrum, illum nasci, hunc fieri.*" ("A priest is not identical to a presbyter or minister—for one is born to be a priest but one is made a minister.") ("Concerning the Ministry [1523]" *LW* 40:18, translation altered).

38. "Psalm 82, 1530." *WA* 31:211.17–19; *LW* 13:65.

through a liturgical rite. Ordination is the performative act, the speech act, in, with, and under which the *right* to teach is authoritatively and legally conferred. Through this unrepeatable act, the person who is called to the ministry of the divine word is placed into that special office—not only *pro tempore* but *pro ecclesia*. It also remains valid even if the ordained resigns from the pastoral ministry and pursues a secular calling.

The distinctive thing about the office and ordination is that, according to *CA* 14, it is the task of the public ministry to ensure that the teaching and preaching (*doctrina*) together with the administration of the sacraments takes place "publicly" (*publice*). What exactly is meant by the "public nature" of these church practices? We can only answer that question theologically by referring to the modern concept of public[39] that arose in the eighteenth century. Yet we must do this in a critical way, by giving due attention to the key biblical texts and confessional documents.[40]

## THE PUBLIC DIMENSION

According to the biblical texts, the "public nature" of teaching is to be understood first and foremost eschatologically and apocalyptically. God has spoken decisively through the cross and resurrection of Jesus Christ. According to the so-called revelation scheme,[41] he has broken his silence and now reveals what was decreed from eternity. His secret is to be publicly announced: "Proclaim it from the roofs" (Matt 10:26–27). The gospel is for all: "Go into all the world and preach the gospel to all creation" (Mark 16:15). Luther insisted, against Erasmus, on the public and external clarity of Holy Scripture, which is tied to the ministry of the word (*in verbi ministerioposita*).[42]

Matters of the highest majesty and the profoundest mysteries are no longer hidden away, but have been brought out and are openly displayed before the very doors.[43] What still sublimer thing can remain hidden in the Scriptures, now that the seals have been broken, the stone rolled from the

---

39. See especially Habermas, *The Structural Transformation of the Public Sphere.*

40. Johann Georg Hamann's work is exemplary for its responsible yet critical engagement with the modern concept of "public" and its reality. On that, see Baur, *Johann Georg Hamann als Publizist.*

41. See Rom 16:25, 26; Eph 3:4, 5; Col 1:26; Titus 1:2, 3; 1 Pet 1:20; and others.

42. *BW WA* 18:609.5; *LW* 33:28.

43. *WA* 18:607.2–4; *LW* 33:26–27.

door of the sepulchre, and the supreme mystery brought to light, namely, that Christ the Son of God has been made man, that God is three and one, that Christ has suffered for us and is to reign eternally? Are not these things known and sung about even by children at school?[44] The testament that was inaugurated by the crucified Lord Jesus is opened and publicly, orally proclaimed by his resurrection[45]—like a cry of victory over Goliath: over hell, death and the devil, as Luther makes crystal clear in his Preface to the New Testament (1522) where he explains what the "gospel" is.[46] This gospel is meant to be made public, to be preached freely and openly, without fear or shame—in *parrhesia*[47]—and to stir up the whole world.[48]

The need to safeguard the seal of the confession is not in conflict with this public emphasis. The publicly proclaimed word creates faith, where and when God wills; it is a matter of the heart. Those who pour out their heart are highly vulnerable and must be protected from the public. It is not the publicly proclaimed word that they need to be protected from—for the word guards and protects our inmost being—but from every other public.

The phrase "publicly teach," which is clearly decisive for the definition of the office of the ministry in *CA* 14, refers not only to preaching *in* public, but most importantly to preaching *for* the public. Loudmouths can also hold forth *in* public but their words are empty. They cannot think *for* the public and speak *to* the public intelligibly. If then the gospel is not to be betrayed, it is vital that the outside perspective be brought into critical engagement with the inside perspective and that theology is appreciated as a discipline characterized by conflict, debate, and criticism. This means that the pastoral office, defined specifically by its responsibility for the "public teaching" of the church, has an apologetic task. This is not a second task in addition to the ministry of preaching, but is identical with it.

The *professional* competence empowers ministers to teach publicly and is exercised together with this teaching function in the office of the

44. *WA* 18:606.24–29; *LW* 33:25 (translation altered).

45. For more details, see Bayer, *Promissio*, 241–53, especially 248–50.

46. *WA DB* 6:2.23–25; 4.1–23; *LW* 35:358, 360, 361.

47. An essential part of *parresia* is the genuine freedom of preachers from all desires to deliberately manipulate their listeners, in which their pathos is tried and proven. For it is a mark of true pathos that preachers first of all experience and endure the text themselves before they communicate it and address it to others.

48. Luther, "Operationes in Psalmos, 1521"; on Ps 22:22 *WA* 5:657.37, 38. Psalm 22:22, 27, 28, 32 is the central psalm in the rite of ordination. *Evangelisches Gottesdienstbuch*, 444.

ministry that is committed to them in ordination.[49] The *spiritual* authorization and empowerment for this office is grounded in baptism. In the same way, the baptized are authorized and empowered to teach "privately." Although they are not ordained, they live out their Christian faith with their gifts and talents and bear witness to Christ in their secular, earthly "vocation."[50] In this way, especially in comforting and encouraging others[51] and in making intercession, they are priests in the same way as the ordained. For Luther drives home the point that "faith must do everything. Faith alone is the true priestly office. It permits nothing else to take its place. Therefore, all Christian men are pastors, all women are likewise pastors, whether they are young or old, employers or employees, wives or single women, learned or unlearned. Here there is no difference."[52] In this connection, we immediately think of Galatians 3:26–28.[53]

49. The ability to perceive the situation (see the section of this chapter titled "The Text and Situation of the Listeners," 203–4) as the *kairos* of the gospel is not a matter of having the power to interpret the signs of the times, nor is it a matter of professional competence, but essentially it depends on having the illumination of the Holy Spirit. Therefore, in the rite of ordination and in the responsibility of the ordained for the public teaching of the church, the prayer for the coming of the Holy Spirit and his promise, gift and impartation (John 20:22), bound up as it is with the laying on of hands, is a central element of ordination—if not the central element.

50. See the final strophe of the morning hymn by Georg Niege, "With All My Heart": "With joy I go my way, / My given tasks fulfilling / With ready hands and willing, / Thy grace and help my stay." *EG* 443.7. The immensely important cultural and historical connection that Lutheran theology makes between the spiritual calling of all Christians by God (the call to faith) that begins with baptism, and the worldly or earthly vocation and station in life goes back to 1 Cor 7:17–24.

51. See *BSLK* 449.12, 13; *BC* 319 ("The Smalcald Articles," 1537): "mutuum colloquium et consolatio . . . ratrum" ("the mutual conversation and consolation of the brethren").

52. "A Treatise on the New Testament, that is, the Holy Mass, 1520," *WA* 6:370.24–7; *LW* 35:101.

53. For a detailed account of the office of the ministry and ordination, see Bayer, "Amt und Ordination," 9–25.

# BIBLIOGRAPHY

Arendt, Hannah. *Vita Activa oder Vom tätigen Leben* [*The Human Condition*]. Stuttgart: Kohlhammer, 1960.

Baur, Wolfgang-Dieter. *Johann Georg Hamann als Publizist: Zum Verhältnis von Verkündigung und Öffentlichkeit.* Theologische Bibliothek Töpelmann 49. Berlin: de Gruyter, 1991.

Bayer, Oswald. "Amt und ordination." In *Ordinationsverständnis und Ordinationsliturgien. Ökumenische Einblicke,* 9–25. Beiträge zu Liturgie und Spiritualität 18. Leipzig: Evangelische Verlagsanstalt 2007.

———. *Promissio: Geschichte der reformatorator: Wende in Luthers Theologie.* 2nd ed. Forschungen zur Kirchen- und Dogmengeschichte 24. Darmstadt: Wissenschaftliche Buchgesellschaft, 1989.

———. *Schöpfung als Anrede: Zu einer Hermeneutik der Schöpfung.* 2nd ed. Tübingen: Mohr/Siebeck, 1990.

———. *Theology the Lutheran Way.* Grand Rapids: Eerdmans, 2007.

———. "Wer bin ich? Gott als Autor meiner Lebensgeschichte." In *Gott als Autor: Zu einer poietologischen Theologie.* Tübingen: Mohr/Siebeck, 1999. Originally published in 1980. Translated as "God as Author of My Life-History." *Lutheran Quarterly* 2 (1988) 437–56.

———. *Zeitgenosse im Widerspruch: Johann Georg Hamann als radikaler Aufklärer.* Serie Piper 918. Munich: Piper, 1988.

———. *Zugesagte Gegenwart.* Tübingen: Mohr/Siebeck, 2007.

Bretschneider, C. G., et al., editors. *Corpus Reformatorum.* 28 vols. Brunsvigae and Halis Saxorum: Schwetschke et Filium, 1834–1860.

*Die Bekenntnisschriften der evangelisch-lutherischen Kirche.* 11th ed. Gottingen: Vandenhoeck & Ruprecht, 1992.

*Evangelisches Gottesdienstbuch: Agende für die Evangelische Kirche der Union und für die Vereinigte Evangelisch-Lutherische Kirche Deutschlands.* Berlin: Evangelische Haupt-Bibelgesellschaft 1999.

Habermas, Jürgen. *The Structural Transformation of the Public Sphere: An Inquiry into a Category of Bourgeois Society.* Translated by Thomas Burger and Frederick Lawrence. Studies in Contemporary German Social Thought. Cambridge: MIT Press, 1991.

Hamann, Johann Georg. "Biblical Reflections." In *J. G. Hamann 1730–1788: A Study in Christian Existence with Selections from His Writings,* edited by Ronald Gregor Smith, 117–38. London Writings. London: Collins, 1960.

———. "Gedanken über meinen Lebenslauf, 1758." In *J. G. Hamann 1730–1788: A Study in Christian Existence with Selections from His Writings,* edited by Ronald Gregor Smith, 139–58. London Writings. London: Collins, 1960.

———. "Golgotha and Sheblimini, 1784." In *Writings on Philosophy and Language,* 164–204. Translated and edited by Kenneth Haynes. Cambridge Texts in the History of Philosophy. Cambridge: Cambridge University Press, 2007.

Horace, *Satires* I/1, 69, 70. Translated by H. Rushton Fairclough. Cambridge: Harvard University Press, 1966.

Knaake, J. F. K. et al., editors. *Luthers Werke, Kritische Gesamtausgabe*. Vol. 5. Weimar: Böhlau, 1883ff.

————. *Luthers Werke, Kritische Gesamtausgabe*. Vol. 12. Weimar: Böhlau, 1883ff.

Kolb, Robert and Timothy J. Wengert, editors. *The Book of Concord*. Minneapolis: Fortress, 2000.

Lash, Nicholas. "Performing the Scriptures." In *Theology on the Way to Emmaus*, 37–46. Eugene, OR: Wipf & Stock, 2005.

Luther, Martin. "Against the Heavenly Prophets . . . 1525." In *LW* 40.

————. "Bondage of the Will, 1525." In *LW* 33.

————. "Bondage of the Will, 1525." In *WA* 18.

————. "Confession Concerning Christ's Supper, 1528." In *LW* 37.

————. "Concerning the Ministry, 1523." In *LW* 40.

————. "Dear Christians, One and All Rejoice." In *Lutheran Book of Worship*. Minneapolis: Augsburg, 1978.

————. "De instituendis ministris Ecclesiae, 1523." In *WA* 12:.

————. "Large Catechism." In *BC*.

————. "Large Catechism." In *BSLK*.

————. "Operationes in Psalmos, 1521." In *WA* 5:

————. "Prelude on the Babylonian Captivity of the Church, 1520." In *LW* 36.

————. "Prelude on the Babylonian Captivity of the Church, 1520." In *WA* 6.

————. "Proceedings at Augsburg." In *WA* 2.

————. "Psalm 82, 1530." In *LW* 13:

————. "Psalm 82, 1530." In *LW* 31: .

————. "Sermon at the Dedication of the Castle Church in Torgau, 1544." In *LW* 51.

————. "Sermon at the Dedication of the Castle Church in Torgau, 1544." In *WA* 49:.

————. "Sermon on Exodus 20:16, 1524–27." In *WA* 16.

————. "Sermons on the Gospel of St John, Chapters 14–16, 1538" In *LW* 24.

————. "Sermons on the Gospel of St John, Chapters 14–16, 1538." In *WA* 45.

————. Table Talk (*WA TR* 4). In *WA* 6.

————. Table Talk (*WA TR* 3). In *WA* 6.

————. "A Treatise on the New Testament, that is, the Holy Mass, 1520." In *LW* 35.

————. "A Treatise on the New Testament, that is, the Holy Mass, 1520." In *WA* 6.

Marquard, Reiner. *Karl Barth und der Isenheimer Altar*. Stuttgart: Calwer, 1995.

Mildenberger, Friedrich. "Heilsgeschichte." In *Religion in Geschichte und Gegenwart*. 4th ed. 3:1584–1586. Tübingen: Mohr/Siebeck, 2000.

Pelikan, Jaroslav, and Helmut Lehman, editors. *Luther's Works*. Vol. 35. St. Louis: Concordia, 1955.

Stuhlmacher, Peter. "Anamnese: Eine unterschätzte hermeneutische Kategorie." In *Biblische Theologie und Evangelium: Gesammelte Aufsätze*. Wissenschaftliche Untersuchungen zum Neuen Testament. Tübingen: Mohr/Siebeck, 2002.

Thaidigsmann, Edgar. "Die Gabe des Wortes und die Frage der Gerechtigkeit." In *Wirksames Wort: Zum reformatorischen Wortverständnis und seiner Aufnahme in der Theologie Oswald Bayers*, edited by Johannes von Lüpke and Johannes Schwanke, 33–48. Wuppertal: Foedus, 2004.

Wannenwetsch, Bernd. "Die Ökonomie des Gottesdienstes: Eine Alternative zum Gestaltungsparadigma im liturgischen Handeln." In *Evangelisches Gottesdienstbuchund Kirchenrecht*, edited by Jörg Neijenhuis, 37–55. Beiträge zu Liturgie und Spiritualität 7. Leipzig: Evangelische, 2002.

# 12

# Lutheran Assertions Regarding Scripture

*Steven D. Paulson*

EDMUND SCHLINK ONCE REMARKED that the absence of a discrete article on Scripture in the Lutheran Confessions "amounts to a doctrinal declaration."[1] The heart and sum of that declaration is this: "since we receive the forgiveness of sins and reconciliation on account of Christ ['the Holy Spirit' in the *Quarto*] by faith alone, faith alone justifies."[2] That, in turn, means: "All Scripture should be divided into these two main topics: the law and the promises."[3] Any assertion regarding Scripture is then a footnote to this confession of faith alone, providing no recourse to praise of church structure, the age of Scripture, the holiness of its delivery system, theories of its origin, dissemination and miraculous preservation, or the psychological effects of its content or even its incomparable moral benefit. The world's favorite grounds for holding something "sacred" or "authoritative" are mercifully absent from the Lutheran Confessions. People expecting such religious arguments will mainly see *nothing* in our Confessions about Scripture's authority. Yet to the world's surprise, the church does not hallow the Word, but is hallowed by it. As the "Large Catechism" (Third Commandment) says, this Word of God is the only

---

1. Schlink, *Theology of the Lutheran Confessions*, 1, n.1, as opposed to the Reformed tradition's interest in extensive prolegomena on scriptural authority.

2. "Apology," 4:86, *BC* 135.

3. "Apology," 4:5, *BC* 121.

holy relic we actually have in life, and it is more than enough to deal with sin, death and the devil—it hallows sinners not the reverse, "[f]or this Word is not idle or dead, but effective and living."[4]

The most frequent mistake in the church regarding this "living Word" is to assume that a word "lives" only when a community or tradition has power to discard the letter in order to maintain something it considers "higher" called the "spirit" of this word. Any religion tied to an historical book (and what is worse, an historical savior) is thus doomed to become an anachronistic and bloody failure as time marches on. Such a word must live in the community or tradition, or else it ossifies, becomes brittle and must be discarded. Holy Spirit and charism must rescue Scripture by working within structures that are eternal, though often hidden, and preserve truth through the ravages of time.

The Lutheran Confessions consistently resist just this theological enthusiasm that seeks to make the function of letter and spirit nothing more than two malleable interpretations or "meanings." We especially resist when scrutiny of such meanings is handed over to authoritative church people who presumably serve as God's tools to adapt to history's surprising changes—changes that are regarded as nothing less than the absolute Spirit's means of ongoing revelation. Slogans such as "the church, reformed and ever reforming," or "the church, ongoing incarnation," or "behold, God is doing a new thing," are then thrown about as persuasions to be courageous and open to the future rather than stuck in the past with its dead letter. The main form of resistance to this siren song has been the assertion that Scripture is alone its own and final authority—not idle or dead, but effective and living. But how is it that a *writing* has such divine, original and final power? Let me propose a short detour.

---

4. *BC* 399.91ff. and 400.101. The location from which Scripture's authority is best considered in the Confessions is Luther's "Large Catechism" (or even the "Small"), Third Commandment. Shifting holiness from its legal definition in relation to places and times—a holy day that became "too narrowly and grossly" interpreted (397.81) ends with Luther's bombshell: "Therefore, according to its outward meaning, this commandment does not concern us Christians . . . from all of this we are now set free through Christ" (397.84). Keeping holy is not what you contribute to the day, but what the Word does to you, the exact reversal of the "turn to the subject" in modernity by God's sacramental Word: "This Word is not idle or dead, but effective and living" (400.101).

## SCRIPTURE, THE WRITING

The people of the Nambikwara tribe, observed Claude Lévi-Strauss (*The Savage Mind* and *Tristes Tropiques*), did not use proper names in public; they hid them. Until, that is, some children secretly began revealing names to the nosy foreigner in their midst in a violent game of obliteration of the other and of the tribe's own rules, rules from which otherwise there simply was no escape—and the children in the tribe knew it. They used the helpless anthropologist in their midst for their own violent purpose.

However, Derrida later corrected Lévi-Strauss's interpretation of this curious cultural rule. Withholding the proper name was not a case of original innocence (a tribe untouched by writing and the interrupting force of the entry of the West), but quite the opposite. It was an original violence in the tribe itself that first "classifies," then "conceals," and finally "reveals" one's naked vulnerability by a kind of manipulation of the name—abstracting the person into thought for purposes of humiliation. So, Derrida observed, the battle of proper names in the Nambikwara tribe occurred only after and because of the arrival of the anthropologist "who comes to disturb order and natural peace,"[5] not to record the way things are in the primitive state of innocence.

Derrida then concluded that there is no *exergue* (something outside the work, an addition, escape) when it comes to the law except death itself (St. Paul saw clearly that the only loophole in the law is death of the personal subject in Romans 7):

> The future can only be anticipated in the form of an absolute danger. It is that which breaks absolutely with constituted normality and can only be proclaimed, *presented,* as a sort of monstrosity. For that future world and for that within it which will have put into question the values of sign, word, and writing, for that which guides our future anterior, there is yet no exergue.[6]

According to Lutheran theology, however, we have experienced another sort of anthropologist in our midst who came to disturb order and natural peace permanently and deliberately—not to write down "what is the case." Jesus Christ put the question to both oral and written words as a law that "guides our future anterior," and in fact abolished such use

5. Derrida, *Of Grammatology*, 113.
6. Ibid., 5.

of Scripture. When you single out the law[7] and there do your theology without the distinction of law and gospel, oral proclamation must be the *original violence*. Writing (the letter of the law) would then be your only advance into abstract thought, but an advance with its future as an eternal monstrosity because it fears death as final judgment. Luther, unlike Derrida, found the only escape from original violence, "When I found this distinction of law and gospel, I *broke through*."[8] *Exergue*. The letter kills but the Spirit gives life (2 Corinthians 3). That is why Jesus, betrayed and killed, resurrected from the dead by his Father in the power of the Holy Spirit, called Mary by her proper name in the garden: "Mary." Thus, she was not only violently revealed as having exactly nothing left to do before God (killed), but had already arrived home and was given new life in that proclamation (the *viva vox evangelii* in Word and sacrament).

Mary became new, born from above, by a proclaimer who gives a future by passing *through* the monstrosity of death as the judgment of the law in order to defeat it. The proclaimed Word then translated her *to* the truly spiritual kingdom by the outrageous divine promise: "I am pleased with you, on account of Christ." Jesus said, "My sheep know my voice," thereby establishing a new relationship that "constitutes" who Mary "is" (or you now "are") having heard the living Word of the crucified and resurrected Jesus Christ as forgiveness of sins *for you*. This new situation in relation to Christ determines our reading of Scripture by making the proper distinction between a letter that kills and the Spirit who gives life. This eschatological distinction is made by hearing the Word (*fides ex auditu*)—we receive or suffer it, and so all things are made new—even our own selves in faith itself that clings to Christ's words like a drop of water clinging to a pitcher.

## FOUR CONFESSIONS

Lutherans argue, therefore, that the written and proclaimed Word of God culminates in two preaching offices: law and gospel.[9] Our shared Lutheran confession or theology contributes to the current ecumenical discussions of Scripture and authority by means of at least the following

7. As Melanchthon noted in "Apology" 4:7.

8. *LW* 54:442–43; *WA TR* 5:210.15–16 (r. 5518).

9. See Luther's "Answer to the Hyperchristian, Hyperspiritual, and Hyperlearned Book by Goat Emser in Leipzig of 1521," *LW* 39:105ff.

four confessions, each opposing a contrary tendency in the church (since the theology of the cross is always polemical theology). We assert first that Scripture alone is our authority (*sola scriptura*); second, that the simple meaning of Scripture is clear in the words themselves (*claritas scripturae*); third, that Scripture interprets itself (*sui ipsius interpres*); and fourth, that Scripture is all these things only when proclaimed according to the two offices of law and gospel, letter and spirit.

Presenting doctrine this way will no doubt sound elementary and "theoretical," I suppose. But our confessions actually begin with the assumption that the world is desperate for help that it cannot find. And here we sit with the story of the Father who gives us all in creation, the Son Jesus Christ who gives himself even as a curse, and the Holy Spirit who is busy giving all things to Christ apart from the law. When given truly, these two words comfort those who are terrorized, and terrorize those whose comfort is false because they trust things and persons who are not God.

Yet, I recognize that taken apart from the need to preach law and gospel each confession sounds insane. *Scripture alone,* we are told, is impossible. Scripture never claims such sole authority, and this "theory" is harmful to the church and its leaders, especially in a time like ours that despises public authority. So it is claimed that the church precedes Scripture, makes its canon, and alone is its proper community of interpretation through its liturgy, tradition and apostolic office. Or else we simply hear people prove their authority over and beyond Scripture by showing special charisms. There is a constant fear that the law and gospel preached are not enough, such that church usage and teaching or personal charisma must be added to them—a death-dealing exergue.[10]

That Scripture is *clear* seems downright foolish, as anyone who has taught introduction to religion can testify. Worse yet, Scripture *interprets itself is* patently false because there have always been and there always will be a myriad of interpretations—who are we to say we have the right one? Finally "law and gospel" is taken to be a tired old warhorse that just

10. Emser called such additions his "dagger and spear" to which Luther responded: "He may pretend that the Holy Spirit and Christ did not teach us enough, that Scripture is not enough, and that God's word must have an addition . . . and that all those who live with such words of God and such teaching and do not keep human teaching are condemned, cursed, and to be burned. Thus Christ and the Holy Spirit too must be guilty . . . since they produced and daily preserve such blasphemous, accursed, and condemned people through their word and teaching" (*LW* 39:198–99).

cannot pull the buggy anymore because people do not feel guilty and are not terrorized.

With these common-sense objections in mind, I maintain that each of these confessions regarding Scripture belong together and come to the same point: God is even now closing up all things of ours under sin by using the law so that Christ alone is all in all, the good news of a new future—*Die Mitte der Schrift*—our interrupting anthropologist with his new *exergue*: the worldly mediated, reliable promise of God from which the unfettered freedom of faith springs as certain comfort in the external Word. The underlying problem with grasping these Reformation confessions is that they are usually applied woodenly to written Scripture in the sense of an exegete working on a text, but they open up in quite a different way when the matter concerns the living Word of proclamation.

## SCRIPTURE ALONE

"Scripture alone" as a confession does not originate in the Reformation; it has a long tradition that is truly catholic, except for the Council of Trent. It means that God is going public with the choice of his people Israel through whom comes the incarnation of his Son, Jesus Christ for the sake of all sinners. That is what Scripture is "about" (its content) and what it is "for" (its purpose or function). Scripture reveals the office of Moses as God's magnification of sin (as Luther saw in Psalm 90). Scripture then reveals Christ as a Word of promise in the church's proclamation from the very point of its entrance with Adam and Eve, carried through Abraham and handed down by the Apostles to the present. Anything added to Scripture would be an attempt to add something to Christ, and thereby would bury him.

Any theologian or church tradition that says something different about Scripture's sole authority would be wrong, whether it was Luther, Peter, Moses, a church council or a local preacher—because, as Paul put it to the Galatians, preaching another gospel, as if there is another gospel, *anathema sit*. The criterion for gospel is clear: God is right in justifying the sinner apart from the law in Christ alone. The recent notions of the church as ongoing incarnation of Christ, or that the Holy Spirit reveals truths not in Scripture as time goes by, or that "tradition" interprets, completes, or extends Scripture by its ministry to a new day—are all notions ruled out by the Lutherans here. Scripture alone leads to preaching and the sacraments.[11]

Why do people resist this assertion: *sola scriptura?* Because God's authorship is in fact twofold in Scripture's proclamation: God authors our death by the law (a terror) and God authors our new life by the gospel (comfort). When we would rather find a way to improve as persons or churches according to the law, then out goes *sola scriptum* as an impediment to our dreams of getting better—especially our current dream of unity on earth in visible communion. Christ permanently interrupts such dreams.

## SCRIPTURE IS CLEAR

Scripture is God going public about salvation, announcing what God does with sinners and with his Son, Jesus Christ. Scripture does not hide things; it is the light in our darkness.[12] It is not in need of a group or individual office that explains Scripture by inheriting secret truths unavailable in this public document, perhaps passed from one apostle to his inheritors by some liturgical "action," or shown in other charismatic signs of power. Nor is Scripture split into two topics as Erasmus suggested: the majestic doctrines that no one can really understand and so are left for the church's theologians (Trinity, Two Natures, Free will—yes or no?) and the public policy (social) statements that can be applied to the unlearned masses in the form of rules of behavior.[13] Scripture is a problem to sinners because it is *too* clear for us when its double message is proclaimed rigidly, and so we actively choose to obfuscate by insisting upon reversing the direction of grace and thereby seek another clarity than that of the condemnation of what is ours and the reliable, external Word of promise.

Scripture condemns what is ours, wholly and completely, and gives everything to Christ—so we join the Byzantine churches in identifying

---

11. As Orthodox Lutherans used to say—it is *sufficient* and *perfect* for the task. Luther put this in close proximity to the main offender in Christian history, the liturgy and its growth into a sacrifice of the Mass: "It will not do to formulate articles of faith on the basis of the holy Fathers' works or words. Otherwise, their food, clothes, houses, etc., would also have to be articles of faith—as has been done with relics. That means that the Word of God—and no one else, not even an angel, should establish articles of faith" ("Smalcald Articles," II.2.15; *BC* 304).

12. As in "the clear writing of the Holy Spirit" ("Apology," preface, 9; *BC* 110).

13. So Melanchthon: "who taught these jackasses logic?" ("Apology," 12.123; *BC* 207).

John the Forerunner as chief among preachers thusly: "I must decrease that he increase." We cannot wish or want this for ourselves. It must be done unto us. Preaching something else is what the Solid Declaration is saying "no" to when it confesses: "Once again we wholeheartedly confess our adherence to this same Christian Augsburg Confession solidly based as it is in God's Word, and we remain faithful to its simple, clear, unequivocal meaning, which its words intend."[14] Scripture is clear and united as *one* (which is to say the same thing) in the "glorious light" of the distinction of law and gospel, and we do not like it—at first.[15]

Therefore, our Lutheran way of putting confession and Scripture together is not opposed to making a proper distinction between Scripture and tradition. As Cardinal Ratzinger once observed, "the real antithesis in the concept of church between Catholics and Protestants is not between Scripture and tradition but between Scripture and office. Protestants interpret Scripture without the Petrine Office, and therefore they are not *given* Scripture, but *take* it."[16]

I know that Lutherans do not make good "Protestants" in his sense. But Ratzinger is right in one respect; our difference is on the matter of *office*. We do not receive Scripture from that particular understanding of the Petrine office. Yet Ratzinger is wrong in thinking that this makes Lutherans individual subjectivists who *take* rather than *receive*. When law and gospel are distinguished in proclamation, tradition is no longer understood as the need to expand *law* into ever new situations, thus creating the necessity of a *magisterium* via the Petrine office.

That means there is no greater or final authority than that of preacher of the Word and sacraments in the midst of Christ's assembled sinners. Such preaching is the final and ultimate authority to bind and loose on earth as in heaven itself. For this reason the Lutheran Confessions are very forceful about the need to distinguish human tradition and divine institution, especially when it comes to such things as the office of the papacy, episcopacy, monasticism and liturgical rites. The history of the church cannot be a norm of doctrine as it stands by itself, nor can contemporary measures passed by any particular church.[17] Tradition is not extending the original meaning of Scripture into new conceptual frameworks, but is

14. *FC SD* 4; *BC* 524.

15. *FC SD* 5.1; *BC* 581.

16. Ratzinger, "Ein Versuch," 28.

17. See "Augsburg Confession," in *BSLK*, 28; "Apology," XII.66 and Tr. II.56.

rather "an account of what the community has heard."[18] Scripture cannot be understood as dogmatic content *about* God and humans, but as the Word from God. That reversal of direction assumes that Scripture is clear and is in no need of specially empowered interpreters, thus removing subjectivism in either its individual or collective forms.[19]

## SCRIPTURE INTERPRETS ITSELF

This confession clearly marks the reversal of direction between God and us in matters of salvation. Scripture is usually taken as *our* object, and we are *its* subjects. We can thus control it, or at least find our own meaning in it. God is then passive, at least for a time, waiting for us to discover divinity or apply divine law to new situations. Instead, we believe, teach, and confess that God is active, the divine Word is living, it accomplishes what it says, and therefore it turns the tables on us by making Scripture the interpreter of us.

In the Smalcald Articles (III.8 On Confession*)* original sin is identified as *enthusiasm*—"God-withinism." Enthusiasm substitutes its own word or form of worship that it prefers for Scripture's Word. Two basic forms of false authority recur in the church because of this enthusiasm— one is fanaticism that holds its inspired prophet as the Holy Spirit's *addition* to Christ and Scripture. The other form is the massive subjectivity of the Papacy (or even Councils) that holds its form of magisterial teaching as the certainty of true interpretation through time. As is often said, it is not enough to have a pure teaching, as the Lutherans do, one must be able to enforce it.

But Lutherans are left with nothing but persuasion and an apparently ineffective Holy Spirit. They are free to use various methods of

18. *Scripture and Tradition: Lutherans and Catholics in Dialogue IX*, 30. The first understands tradition only according to the law. The second according to the distinction of law and gospel.

19. At this point a person could fruitfully consider Luther's two kinds of clarity (external and internal) as he discusses them in Bondage of the Will. And one could also take up the Orthodox Lutherans who distinguished "obscurity in the object contemplated and that which lies in the subject contemplating it." As Quenstedt put it, "The words of the Testament are in themselves very perspicuous, but are variously interpreted; because many, neglecting the literal and proper sense, studiously seek a foreign one . . . because of the perverseness or imbecility of men. The obscurity which lies in the subject must not be transferred to the object[!]" Quoted in Schmid, *The Doctrinal Theology of the Evangelical Lutheran Church*, 73.

interpretation—*as long as they actually help true proclamation*. Historical critical method, for example, has played an important part in Scripture interpreting itself, even when it is used badly by sinners as a means for personal power. As Schweitzer showed, the first fruit of historical critical method is a revelation of the user. In trying to write the historical biography of Christ you succeed in showing the world what you alone believe, teach and confess. This is important, as sin must always be magnified. But it does not do all that Scripture wants. The second benefit of this critical method is that it did offer (temporarily?) the wild apocalyptic of the Jesus of history against the better judgment of many of its users. The problem with the method is the same as with previous methods: it cannot finally break out of interpretation as a solitary, inner monologue where one is thrown back on the self as the only true source of certainty.

But when we say "Scripture interprets itself," we are not describing how *you* use a method to unlock secrets from Scripture. Scripture interpreting itself is a truly *theological* claim about God. Scripture is used by the triune God in the process of interpreting us by putting us to death and raising us up anew. Scripture, this writing, provides the source and norm of words for the two preaching offices because it came from such preaching in the first place. It thus entangles you in its story as the one being addressed when Christ forgives sinners, neither as reader-response, nor as entrance into a covenant with God to respond to divine grace, but as perfectly passive sinners being made right by an alien righteousness who is Christ alone.

## LAW AND GOSPEL ARE THE TWO PREACHING OFFICES

How will you hear without a preacher (Rom 10)? It has always been dismaying to people that the comfort of the conscience comes down to a local "forgiveness person." But there is the Holy Spirit using weak people with little words to accomplish what nothing else does: the end of trusting idols and the beginning of faith in Christ. Law and gospel is thus not a *method* of preaching or interpretation, but the way that God authors you as unmistakable sinner in yourself; then outside yourself, in Christ, God authors you as pure saint. The preacher must learn the proper application of the pronoun: "you are the one" (as Nathan said to David) and "given for you for the forgiveness of sins" (as Jesus said to his betrayers).

The breakthrough by distinguishing law and gospel does not happen in the realm of doctrine or ideas or theology, it happens only when these words are given by a preacher *to you* in faith itself. Thus, Scripture is united, clear and alone your author by interpreting you when it enters your conscience via the declaration of the absolution of sin. Scripture alone authorizes this Word from God to you, and in this way is the sole "source and norm" of the oral proclamation. God uses the two preaching offices to kill and make alive so that we have no other God than this man Jesus Christ, otherwise there is no way out, no *exergue.* But Scripture does in fact yield preaching from time to time that creates actual faith in Christ alone who forgives our sins *gratis,* and therefore it authorizes its own authority. When that happens we have reached the origin, fountain, source, goal, *telos,* end, nadir and zenith of authority in the original author who is the Holy Spirit, or to put it more accurately, we have *been* reached. "Formerly, when you did not know God, you were enslaved to beings that by nature are not gods. Now, however, that you have come to know God, or rather *to be known by God,* how can you turn back again to the weak and beggarly elemental spirits" (Gal 4:8–9)? When the preacher's word, "for you," penetrates us we are finally freed from the demand to establish unity and reason in our imaginary world, thus opening the created world as the place and medium of Gods reliable address to the cloud of witnesses, the communion of saints as forgiven sinners who receive all as a daily gift—through the one holy relic we actually have, God's Word.

## CONCLUSION

Misused Scripture is a result of the loss of the true pastoral comfort given through God's reliable Word because the law was singled out. Certainty is lost when the Word is locked into a solitary monologue that knows only the one internal word we can manage to produce: "Do this!" (Of course, as Luther noted, it is never done.) Everything else is false comfort by pretending either that the law "in this particular case" does not apply (becoming antinomian), or else that the clear and certain gospel, who is Jesus Christ *himself* and *alone,* is not necessary for new life (becoming anti-Christ).

The present preoccupation with moral casuistry as a way of determining the Bible's authority, perhaps especially in the Evangelical Lutheran Church in America, namely, "What does the Bible demand or allow on this particular issue?," is a symptom of this sickness in the church, not the cause. One step beneath this symptom lies a deeper, "systemic" theological problem, the preoccupation with *method*, just as was once the case with the church's development of rules concerning proper allegorical method. Today, when we realize that the historical-critical method did not deliver an independent means of rising above denomination and private opinion, we occupy ourselves with fights between old critical and new cultural-linguistic versions of establishing some way of getting meaning or authority from Scripture.

But deeper still, the cause of the preoccupation with casuistry and method is the profound and demonic confusion of law and gospel. Is not the distinction between law and gospel precisely Scripture's one, clear, unique purpose—given to the ungodly? God desired a way to author our end and our new beginning through these two words. It is our only *exergue* (addition or escape) from the monstrous future of death under the eternal wrath of God. Otherwise, which of these basic assertions of faith will you finally attempt to remove in order to avoid death—*All have sinned and fallen short of the glory of God;* or that *we have no God but this particular man, Jesus Christ?* Scripture is one and alone, Scripture is clear, Scripture interprets itself, and all of this happens not in the realm of ideas, but *for you* in the living Word of proclamation with both offices: law and gospel. The proclamation of this written text of God's dealings with his people, proclaimed to actual sinners in the present so that, as Christ says to his preachers, "he who hears you hears me," is the way that a *writing* has such divine, original and final power. Then and there, Christ's voice alone sounds in the conscience with *your* proper name and *his* in a blessed exchange of greetings: "Mary"; "Rabbouni! . . . Lord!" Of course we are finally pleased to be so interpreted and authored, for where there is forgiveness of sins there is also life and salvation. That is a future beyond obsession with the grave and this monstrosity of original violence, a future given to us by Christ as pure, reliable gospel that makes us subject to none, servant to all.

---

## BIBLIOGRAPHY

Derrida, Jacques. *Of Grammatology Corrected Edition.* Translated by Gayatri Chakravorty Spivak. Baltimore: Johns Hopkins University Press, 1997.
"Formula of Concord, Solid Declaration." In *BC.*

Kolb, Robert, and Timothy J. Wengert, editors. *The Book of Concord.* Minneapolis: Fortress, 2000.

Luther, Martin. "Answer to the Hyperchristian, Hyperspiritual, and Hyperlearned Book by Goat Emser in Leipzig, 1521." In *LW* 39:175–203.

———. "Smalcald Articles." In *BC*.

Melanchthon, Philipp. "Apology." In *BC*.

Pelikan, Jaroslav, and Helmut Lehman, editors. *LW* 39. St. Louis: Concordia, 1955.

———. *Luther's Works.* Vol. 54. St. Louis: Concordia, 1955.

Ratzinger, Joseph. "Ein Versuch zur Frage des Traditionsbegiff." In *Offenbarung und Überlieferung* by Karl Rahner and Joseph Ratzinger, 25–69. Quaestiones disputatae 25. Freiburg: Herder, 1965.

Schlink, Edmund. *Theology of the Lutheran Confessions.* Translated by Paul E. Koehneke and Herbert J. A. Bouman. Philadelphia: Fortress, 1961.

Schmid, Heinrich. *The Doctrinal Theology of the Evangelical Lutheran Church.* Philadelphia: The United Lutheran Publication House, 1875.

Skillrud, Harold C. J. et al., editors. *Scripture and Tradition.* Lutherans and Catholics in Dialogue 9. Minneapolis: Augsburg, 1995.

# 13

# Preaching Repentance

*James Arne Nestingen*

## PREACHING REPENTANCE IS A PROBLEM

THEOLOGICALLY, THERE IS NO question about its priority. When the New Testament sums up the message of Jesus and the apostles, it identifies repentance with faith as the gospel's consequence: "The kingdom of God is at hand: repent, and believe in the gospel" (Mark 1:13). "And Peter said to them, 'Repent, and be baptized every one of you in the name of Jesus Christ for the forgiveness of your sins'" (Acts 2:38).

The Lutheran Confessions are equally adamant. Article twelve of the Augsburg Confession, in fact, speaks as though repentance were a condition for the forgiveness of sins. And when Luther in the "Small Catechism" addresses the significance of baptism, he describes a daily death by drowning in repentance that continues throughout the life of the faithful.

Yet even to name the theological priority of repentance is to come perilously close to undergoing it. For the preacher who is engaged by a text which calls for repentance immediately confronts a whole range of difficulties.

One difficulty is theological. The Lutheran witness to the gospel insists that it is an unconditional word of pardon and release in Christ. With much of the talk of repentance, there is the suggestion of a condition to be achieved. How can repentance be preached without giving the lie to the gospel?

Another difficulty is pastoral. The traditional language of repentance —sorrow over sin, contrition, desire to make amends—describes various dispositions of the heart. Such states are difficult to discern unambiguously. The problem is compounded when, in situations of pastoral authority, a person is called to assess repentance and make recommendations for action. Are there any signs of repentance which manifest its presence strongly enough to give those in authority sound footing?

Still another difficulty is perhaps even more basic: survival. There may have been good reason for the fact that the prophets generally lived out of town, not in parsonages, and not on housing allowances, either. Preaching repentance requires a willingness to stand against the hearer, to speak directly of matters that may call up conflict. How do you stand over and against people you are called to live in relation to? Is it possible to preach repentance without getting crucified for it?

Faced with such questions, one reasonable alternative would be to inquire of the Lutheran heritage to see what it might have to suggest. According to the church constitutions, model or otherwise, we are obligated to do just this. And there is the possibility, too, of finding something helpful.

It has to be acknowledged, however, that the generation of Lutheran theologians currently in its ascendancy has by and large worked by a different procedure. This has been to identify a problem such as repentance; to attribute the problem to some personal, psychological difficulty of Luther or to a failure of the larger tradition; and then to run a shopping trip through various metaphors, models, or ecumenical alternatives for attractive solutions.

The generation that came to its theological calling in the late 1950s and early 1960s, amidst bobby sox and the excitement of Kennedy's new frontier, has been around long enough now so that it should be possible to evaluate this procedure, to ask what it has produced. There has been some fine scholarship, especially concerning Barth and some other neo-orthodox theologians. There have been some outstanding exegetes. And in the corners, among those by and large excluded by their contemporaries, there has even been some fine Luther research.

But it is equally clear that pushing off from this heritage, this generation of theologians—with few but significant exceptions—has defined its calling by pushing off against the preaching of the church. Theology has been professionalized; it has become a guild unto itself. Turned in upon themselves, the theologians have kept the church at a safe distance, treating preaching as incidental instead of as the goal of theological reflection. And so the church, with rare exceptions, has passed over this generation of theologians when it has sought leadership, leaving the guild to its own standards and devices and telling the schools, with increasingly slim financing, to fend for themselves.

Given such results, more importantly, given the church's calling to serve the witness of the gospel, there is good reason for trying something different. And there is precedent. Karl Barth, Karl Rahner, Hans Joachim Iwand; so too Abraham Joshua Heschel or Emil Fackenheim, instead of rejecting their various traditions, went deep into them and built intelligently from what they had received to become the great theologians of the century. The best theologians in contemporary American Lutheranism have done the same.

In relation to repentance, there is especially good reason for proceeding to the heritage to see what it provides. The first of the Ninety-five Theses reads, "When our Lord Jesus Christ said, 'Repent,' he willed the entire life of the believer to be one of repentance," indicating how fundamental repentance is to Luther's thought.[1] In addition, a major source in his discussion of repentance is only recently being translated, so that it is now possible to get a deeper insight into Luther's understanding of the role of the gospel in repentance. And there is the deep sense, in Luther as well as in the confessional discussion, that repentance is not the end but the beginning of freedom, so that as the law breaks false alternatives, the gospel takes hold to break open the liberty of faith.

## REPENTANCE AND THE LAW

Some years ago, Gerhard Ebeling raised a question all the more critical for the infrequency of its asking: If the law is known by its uses, who is the user?[2] If this question is addressed to Luther and the Lutheran confessions, the answer is surprising. For the law is defined in a particularly concrete way that leaves the identity of the law's user an open question. Accordingly, repentance begins in the generic stuff of everyday life.

---

1. *LW* 31:25.
2. Ebeling, "*Triplex Usus Legis,*" 71.

The word "law" is one of the most complex in the Lutheran vocabulary, capable of any number of inflections. But for the purpose of analysis, it can be said that Luther uses the term in basically two ways: he speaks of law at the level of what it signifies or requires and he speaks of it in terms of what it does to its hearer.

The Catechisms, Small and Large, are some of the best examples of Luther's treatment of the requirements of the law. He explains the commandments in simple and direct language, identifying both what is enjoined and what is demanded. All the requirements of the law come down to two, the faith called for in the first table and the love of the neighbor set forth in the second.

Yet the very clarity of Luther's discussion masks the concrete way in which he moves at this level. On the First Commandment, for example, he does not begin with the Scripture, the Creed or the classical language of western theism—God's omnipotence, omniscience or omnipresence. Instead, Luther opens the discussion with a naked, seemingly naive inquiry: What is it to have a God? What do you have if you have one? How does it work?

> Answer: A god is that to which we look for all good and in which we find refuge in every time of need. To have a god is nothing else than to trust and believe him with our whole heart.[3]

The warrant of Luther's argument is that having a god is a fundamental requirement of life. To be human is to be a creature, to receive life from outside one's self rather than from within. Thus it is to be vulnerable, to be found in need, to have to look outside of the self for help, to suffer misfortune and distress that require some reliable form of assistance. The experience of life demands a god, insisting on it with such determination that everyone has one and, in fact, serves one.

That's the way a god works. God is whatever you depend upon for help. If your god doesn't provide for you in a time of trouble, you must provide for it and in the end, be consumed by the relationship. Thus there can only be one god per person—a god demands such a level of fear, love and trust as to exclude any other possibility.

Luther's explanations of the rest of the first table and all of the second to follow the same logic. Having a god, it is necessary to use the god's name for its proper purposes and to hear what the god has in mind. By

3. *BC* 365.

the same token, since having neighbors is a necessary feature of human life, there are some requirements involved in getting along with them: what happens with your original neighbors, your parents, has a way of playing itself out in the whole neighborhood. If there is going to be life in the neighborhood, killing must be kept under control; sexual disorder makes the neighbors nervous; a minimal level of property rights, the expectation of truth telling and an elastic public trust are constitutive of communal peace.

Set up this way, Luther's interpretation of what the law requires is analytical—a descriptive examination of the minimal conditions necessary for the determining relationships of life. The commandments hold not because God gave them to Moses, because they are found in Scripture, or because Torah is actually gift. They hold because they make explicit what is implicit in the ebb and flow of human interrelatedness, summarizing the nonnegotiables of creaturely life.[4]

Because the law is so embedded in daily relationships, it is ineradicable. Johan Agricola, Luther's old friend, who after a stint of teaching Latin in Eisleben came back to haunt him as the antinomian, argued that the law could be set aside in favor of the gospel. Luther answered in the Antinomian Disputations by sending Agricola back to school, this time in the declensions of the law. What the law signifies is eternal, Luther argues (2:40).[5] While the law is "emptied" or "quieted" in Christ for the believer,[6] it makes its requirements known wherever sin and death are at work (5:12). Thus "they are completely ignorant and deceivers of souls who endeavor to abolish the law from the church. For that is not only foolish and impious but completely impossible" (5:15–16). It is a theoretical and conceptual resolution of the law, "a play put on in an empty theater" (5:32), as Luther himself put it, a conceptual trick that equates absence with ignored presence.

The second level in Luther's discussion of law describes it in terms of its impact or function in the hearer. At this level, the law makes itself known by what it does. "Whatever shows sins, wrath or death, exercises

4. The best analysis of Luther's interpretation of the place of the commandments is Heinrich Bornkamm's *Luther and the Old Testament*.

5. *WA* 39/1:334–58.

6. *WA* 39/2:433. There are summary transcripts of the first three debates involving the Antinomian Disputations on pp. 359–584.

the office of the law . . . For to reveal sin is nothing else nor can be nothing else than law, or the most proper effect and power of the law" (2:18–19).

Significantly, the Formula of Concord—after a generation and a half of feuding over definitions of the law—returns to this level of the definition in its fifth article, citing the same passage from Luther's argument against Agricola.[7]

This second level is predicated on the first. Because the law is in the fabric of human relationships, it bears itself out in experience, particularly in relation to the First Commandment. The law is the accusing voice which sounds in the conscience. But the voice's speech may be inchoate —it may sound in a vague sense of dread, in being ill at ease, or in an apprehension of jeopardy. And the accusation itself may be difficult to formulate: in relation to the first commandment, it concerns faith and thus involves a sense of place, purpose, or belonging. But like the wolf in John 10, the law at this level doesn't announce its presence—the only sign of its work may be evidence that something is missing, a sense of loss that refuses reduction to specificity. The law may attack in this manner during some monumental point of passage: the death of a parent, irretrievable failure in something that has been life orienting or purpose giving, the death of a child, the end of a marriage, middle age's realization of mortality. Such an experience is a death in its own right, the real effect of the law, just because it cancels out what has been life shaping.

But this attack of the law doesn't necessarily always appear in such large proportions. It may arise from the bumps of a house settling at night in winter cold; from a spouse or child's unanticipated delay in returning home; from a minor slip at work or from reading about the most recent civic disturbances in the newspaper. However it happens, whether in something major or seemingly minor, in relation to the First Commandment the law's accusation is aimed at faith. Its result is despair.

Compared to the first table, the law's attack on matters of the second is exactly that, secondary. But just because the law's demands are inherent to life itself, moral disobedience also has its requital. The proportion is not necessarily one to one—Luther is as aware, as the psalmists, of the wicked, who seek financial consultants while the righteous suffer. But if the proportions vary, the rule generally holds. "Victimless crimes" are just

---

7. *BC* 561.

another illusion, a moral sleight of hand in which insensitivity empties the theater. The law doesn't turn away its eye.

So there is hardly a family that does not taste some deep levels of conflict, gaining firsthand experience of the way troubles play themselves out. The sense of hostility in communal life—whether in traffic or with competing neighbors—constricts it. The sexuality considered private and merely recreational has a way of implicating the public, and so on.

Again, this is a descriptive, indicative analysis. It is not that the law always should or must accuse. Rather, the law always approaches those in need, those who are troubled, those driven to the edge, as an accuser. In this age, under these conditions, law works this way. Its requirements, as good and just and right and true as they may be, are never neutral. They bear themselves out in attack that may vary in degree but proceeds nevertheless, relentlessly.

Because the law works this way, the question of its user is open ended. As Luther understood it, the law can become its own user—an aimless, purposeless power which simply makes demands or states conditions, continuing to expect fulfillment no matter what. This happens when as Luther put it in the great Galatians commentary, "the law ascends into the conscience and attempts to rule there." The law makes ultimate claims for itself, conditioning the most important relationships of life on obedience to its demands. When the law makes its ultimate claims, it becomes a torturer, ceaselessly grinding away at its demands and accusations.

If the law can be its own user, other powers may take hold of it as well. The devil can use the law, offering release on the basis of obedience to its conditions, only to disappoint and so confound the faith of anyone foolish enough to have accepted the original premise—that the law frees. There is a close relationship here. Allied with the devil, the law is also allied with sin and death. They are existential forces, powers of the age, that contend against the gospel and the Creator for the heart of the creature.

Placed in such a league, the preacher can only become a user of the law in a secondary sense. Since the law plays itself out anonymously, without stating its identity, it remains implicit in situations until it is stated. Much of its power is in its all pervasive hiddenness, its anonymity. Stating it, making it explicit, identifying the law as law is already an attack on its claim to ultimacy. Naming it brings the law out of its hiddenness, sets out the requirement in recognizable terms, and consequently gives the hearer standing, in relation to it.

This is the preacher's use of the law; this is why when Luther speaks of the commandment, *Gottes Gebot,* he does so in such positive terms. That which is unconditionally conditional in its relentless demand becomes in the speaking, in the naming, merely conditional. It is no longer high above you, but near to hand, as Moses and Paul have it (Deuteronomy 30; Romans 10). So the preacher uses the law neither to become the accuser nor to make the accusation—that's the law's work. Rather, the preacher speaks the unspoken word, bringing to expression what is unexpressed, identifying the point where the law stands against the hearer. One of the best examples is the story of Nathan and David. Nathan's quiet parable brought the law into focus for David so that he could hear through all the illusions and denials the conclusion the law required. Nathan merely stated in what must have been a very quiet and thoughtful way what was already clear but unexpressed, "You are the one" (2 Sam 12:7).

This is the beginning of repentance. The law comes first. Before any other word is spoken, it is at work in the conditions of human interrelatedness, making its requirements and bearing out its accusations. Such is generic human experience, the seemingly ceaseless round of encountering limits and living with the consequences—the crises, minor or major, of having to have a god and neighbors, of living in the callings of everyday. Here the law is being itself, doing what law does, grinding out despair and pride as though it feared a shortage.

Repentance starts in just such hiddenness, in the garden variety nuisances and pangs of the day. But if it is going to be anything but garden variety, if it is going to continue on as repentance, there must be a voice—a witness, a preacher who has the kindness to name the limit, to identify the accuser, to speak against the law by naming the law, showing the law its limits and its true master.

## THE GOSPEL AND REPENTANCE

The relationship of the gospel and repentance is disputed in Lutheranism. Philip Melanchthon floated some theological trial balloons on the matter in the later 1540s and 50s, raising a controversy as a result. The issue was settled in the fifth article of the Formula of Concord. Nowadays, mentioning the gospel in relation to repentance doesn't recall Melanchthon so much as it suggests, at least to some more careful Lutheran observers, *prima facie* evidence of Barthianism.

This is one of the unfortunate results of the Antinomian Disputations being left untranslated for so long. Apparently, the original translators— in German as well as English—took Luther's verdict on an early stage of the antinomian controversy as applicable to the whole of it. He dismissed that battle as a "war of words." His own Disputations, a set of six issued for public academic debate between 1536 and 1539, are far superior to such a verdict. For, in the theses which he prepared for the debates, he gave extended and careful attention to the contribution of the gospel to repentance.

Once again, the starting point is Ebeling's question—the true agency of the law, its ultimate user. So far, three possible users have been identified: the law itself, the devil, and in a smaller way, the preacher. The preacher's use of the law, however, already anticipates and is only possible in light of the fourth and only legitimate user: the Holy Spirit, working through the gospel.

There is a strange collection of passages in some of Luther's writings where, caught up in the argument and in what almost appears to be a kind of transport, he directly addresses the law as though it were another person. One of the best of these is contained in the transcript of one of his exchanges with Agricola:

> Although, moreover, we say that despair is useful, it is not so by virtue of the law, but of the Holy Spirit, who does not make a robber or devil of the law but a teacher. Thus whenever the law is dealt with, the nature and power and effect of the law is dealt with—that which it is able to do by itself. But when the law pretends that it follows or penetrates the gospel, "Hear, quiet down, O law, see lest you jump your fences. You ought to be a teacher, not a robber, you can terrify, but beware, you may not entirely crush, as you once did to Cain, Saul, Judas; remember that you are a teacher. Here is your office, not of a devil or robber but of a teacher." But these things are not by virtue of the law, but of the gospel and the Holy Spirit as interpreter of the law.[8]

Without the gospel, the law is indiscriminate. It merely drives, creating an appetite which in the realm of the legal itself is insatiable. So any port in the storm; when the trouble starts, any god will do. There is not one gospel, there are gospels by the thousands, all of them promising either to accommodate or possibly even to silence the voice of the law. "When in

8. WA 39:1.445.

doubt, buy an appliance"; smoke a Lucky or drink a Miller; or try a new hairspray; or find an ample bosom; or shop 'til you drop; or whatever it takes to give the lightness of being some weight of significance.

In fact, the law offers itself as gospel. It makes one promise after another—offering to restore order, to give a new ethical tone, to elicit genuine striving that will put apathy to flight—all on a condition of minimal obedience. But in the end, the masquerade is broken and along with it the last, desperate illusion—that somehow, the sinner can also become a user of the law. The law turns on its deluded manager with quiet ruthlessness, dealing out disappointments that turn to cynicism which culminates in despair. It is the foreplay of death. They are all the same in the dark.

The one and only gospel takes hold of the law in order to bring it to its true end, placing it under the power of Christ. The random hunting of the law, its aimless self-use, is brought to a point, its true point, its *telos* (Rom 10:4). Only when it has been brought to its end does the law become a teacher, driving to the gospel. This happens at both levels of the law, in relation to what it signifies or requires and in relation to its accusation.

At the level of requirement, Christ brings the law to its end by fulfilling it in the believer. As he kept the First Commandment himself, Christ fulfills it in the believer by bringing into being the faith required. This fulfillment or restoration, as Luther calls it, is the subject of an argument that extends through several theses in the "Antinomian Disputations."

> 4:35. But in truth, faith in Christ justifies, alone fulfills the law, alone does good works, without the law. 36. It alone accepts the remission of sin and spontaneously does good works through love. 37. Truly, it is after justification [that] good works follow spontaneously without the law, that is, without the help or coercion [of the law]. 38. In summary: The law is neither useful nor necessary to good works, much less for salvation. 39. But on the contrary, justification, good works, and wholeness are necessary to the fulfillment of the law. 40. For Christ comes to save that which was lost and to restore all things, as Peter says. 41. Therefore the law is not destroyed by Christ, but restored, so that Adam might be just as he was, and even better.

Faith is the turning point. Rather than taking God on at the level of requirement, as though the law were some list out of a job jar, in Christ faith meets God in the relationship signified by the First Commandment: as God. Related now, grounded in Christ, faith is free to go about its business in relation to both God and the neighbor. As Luther says at another point, "whoever believes this is brought back to the point from which Adam and Eve fell"—set free to live as a creature in relation to the Creator and the creation.

As Christ brings the requirement of the law to its end by fulfilling it, he brings its accusative function to its end by silencing it. This happens in the absolution, through the forgiveness of sins. Luther spells this out in another series of theses. "2:45. For the law as it was before Christ, certainly accusing us, under Christ is placated through the remission of sins and therefore is to be fulfilled in the Spirit. 46. Thus after Christ, in the future life will then be fulfilled even that new creature which [the law] in the meantime demanded. 47. Therefore the law in all eternity will never be abolished but will remain either to be fulfilled in the damned or already fulfilled in the blessed." Through the forgiveness of sin, the law loses its basis for accusation and consequently falls silent—it is "quieted," "placated," or "emptied." The silence of the law in Christ contributes directly to its fulfillment. When the law stops its nagging and denouncing, a person can finally begin to live with what it really signifies: faith, hope and love.

At the level of the law's requirement as well as at the level of its function, the end is an eschatological promise. The restoration begun is not yet complete. The "new creature" will only be himself or herself "what the law in the meantime demanded" when all things have been completely restored in the future life.

The meantime occurs under the sign of the *simul*. Brought under the power of Christ in faith, the believer begins to fulfill the law and, in eschatological earnest, experiences the silencing of the law's accusation—its mouth is stuffed. But until the final restoration, the law is always getting the gag off to shatter the silence once more. "5:40. Insofar as Christ is now raised in us, so far are we without the law, sin and death. 41. Insofar as he truly is not yet raised in us, so far are we under the law, sin and death. 42. Therefore the law (and likewise the gospel) is to be taught without distinction to the pious just as to the wicked." The *simul* itself will only finally be resolved at the last day. Then the law, sin and death will all have lost their power, and Christ will rule in the undisputed sovereignty of the gospel.

Preaching repentance in the meantime involves, as Luther points out, both law and gospel. By stating explicitly what is implicitly demanded in creaturely relationships, by identifying the point where God stands against us, the preacher is already placing the law under the gospel's control. But if the law is actually going to end in the gospel, if repentance is truly to find its end in faith, then the gospel itself must become even more explicit than the law.

This is a critical point in the dialectic, one often overlooked. If nature abhors a vacuum, the heart will not tolerate even the hint of one. To preach against the law and all the false gospels used to appease it without naming the name of the one who is the law's true end is merely to entrench false alternatives. If it takes good money to drive out bad, only the gospel can expose all of its counterfeits. So Jesus's own preaching of repentance begins not with the abstract demand or an attempt to convince people of their need for the kingdom of God, but with announcement of the dawn of the kingdom. Repentance and faith are the gift and consequence of the kingdom's presence, not prior conditions for its arrival.

This is risky business in traditional Lutheran discussions because here the gospel is entering into the law's realm, in effect, overlapping it. But Luther spoke of just this overlap, and as early as in the Commentary on Hebrews where he discussed God's alien and strange work.[9] By working this way, Luther argued, God takes the devil's weapons, that is, what Satan would use to drive to despair and unbelief, and uses them to drive to faith. So the Spirit through the gospel takes hold of the law and without intermixing them, joins them to make them both function in the very same words.

For Luther, the best example of this overlap is the First Commandment itself. It is both law and gospel, law in that it is aimed at unbelief, stating both requirement and accusation, and gospel in that it actually bestows what it demands: "I *am* the Lord, your God." The great "I am" sayings of John's gospel have the same character. When Jesus says, "I am the resurrection and the life," he simultaneously grants the gifts of which he speaks and excludes all other possibilities. Law and gospel function in the very same words.

When the unconditional character of the gospel is turned into an ideology, conceptualized as though it were just another theory about how God deals with us, this overlap is lost. Having lost its edge, the gospel turns to mush, to an unqualified endorsement or a universalism of unlimited tolerance. It doesn't have what in this age, under the *simul,* always remains its characteristic bite.

9. *LW* 29:135.

As well grounded in Luther's own theological reflection as they may be, such considerations may seem to put an impossible burden on the preacher. The law is in the web of things; the gospel is an alien word, sounded from without. If the law doesn't get through the ear, it will get its pound of flesh in another way. But if the gospel is to challenge all of its pretenders—the illusions and evasions, the false alternatives—it must be spoken. Finding a way to speak it so that it retains its bite can be extraordinarily difficult.

There is a formal way of speaking the gospel in which the church has historically expressed its confidence: absolution. In the direct and personal declaration of the forgiveness of sin in Christ, the gospel overlaps the law, both confirming its accusation and bringing the law to its end. Only sinners are forgiven; if you are forgiven, you must be the one. Yet it is the very act of the absolution, with the freedom it brings, that allows the conclusion of repentance, "I am a sinner," to be drawn. Precisely here, freedom dawns.

Though the rituals of absolution—private confession or the public confession which opens worship—have by and large passed from use in Lutheran congregations, there are still strategic points at which it must be spoken. One is in the pulpit. As in the Smalcald Articles, Luther equated preaching with the declaration of forgiveness.[10] Good preaching always moves toward such a directly personal word of assurance and, hope. Another such point is in person to person conversations, such as counseling or calling. It is reported that Karl Menninger said that some seventy or eighty percent of the people who want to talk to a counselor are looking for absolution. It is a matter of uttering it, of taking courage in hand and actually speaking the word of pardon in Christ's name. The *Lutheran Book of Worship* provides rites for the recovery of both private and public absolution.

But it is the genius of the Word that it is so preeminently capable of moving beyond what is formal or ritualized into more personal address. The gospel is never generic—it is always "for you." In direct contact, the gospel can be spoken in personal terms directly related to the situation of the hearer.

Far and away the example of such preaching is the story of Zacchaeus. When Jesus saw that little man dangling so far out on a limb, he didn't confront him with the abstractions of justice. Zacchaeus had undoubtedly

10. *BC* 310.

heard all of that before and simply redoubled his security. Instead, Jesus spoke a word that is both law and gospel at the same time, marking the overlap: "Zacchaeus, I am coming to your house today" (Luke 19:5). His presence at table was law. He broke through all the illusions and evasions that had allowed Zacchaeus to keep a safe distance from those he was exploiting. It was also gospel. Jesus at the same time broke through the opprobrium, the rejection, the condemnation that came with the distance. "And Zacchaeus stood and said to the Lord, 'Behold, Lord, the half of my goods I give to the poor; and if I have defrauded any one of anything, I restore it fourfold'" (Luke 19:8).

Under the power of the gospel, repentance can come to its true end: faith. Beginning in the generic stuff of daily life—in family struggles, the frustrations of work, the problems of the larger community or in some deeper crisis—repentance is set in motion as we are dislodged. This is the law's work, to demand that we find lodging and continually to dislodge us. When the gospel enters, it overlaps the law, confirming its requirement and accusation by bringing the law to its true end in Christ. The believer, then, experiences the peace which comes when the law's voice is silenced. The conscience comes to rest in Christ and so under the power of the gospel. The believer begins actually to fulfill the law.

Repentance and freedom are correlative. For, in the light of the utter self-giving of Christ, a person begins to see the web of self-preservation in himself or herself; to see through and so to loathe the self for its illusions, evasions and entanglements. And in the light of Christ, a person actually begins to know God for who he is—not a theistic projection attempting to catch up with his pretensions, but the one Mary mistook for the gardener, the one who after Simon Peter had been sifted like wheat, made a bishop of him. This is the freedom of the gospel—freedom from all that entangles, freedom for life as a creature in relation to God, the neighbor and the earth.

## REPENTANCE AND THE PREACHER

On the basis of this analysis, it is possible to address the three problems mentioned at the beginning: the condition implied in repentance, the question of the marks of repentance, and the situation of the preacher.

First, repentance is not a prerequisite for but a consequence of the gospel. In this sense, the gospel could conceivably be called conditional—

there is no faith without repentance. But anyone who wants to construe such a condition as though it were something to be achieved should not be allowed simply to talk about what good it would do the neighbors! Without the gospel, what is passed off as repentance will always go false in one way or another. It will degenerate into the cheap absolution of self-hatred, the perverse self-justification that thrives on its own putdowns. Or it will become a personal achievement that justifies the self's unyielding judgment of the others. If repentance is mere demand, the self will always lose itself one way or another, whether by drowning in its own mire or by claiming the ability to walk on it and then after brief delay drowning just the same.

True repentance happens along the lines of the prayer of St. Augustine that drove Pelagius crazy, "Give what you command, and command what you will." By providing the good money that drives out the bad, the gospel saves the self from becoming its own project. Then the law can rest, and happily, because its work is completed. And the joy of repentance is fulfilled in the easy laughter of faith.

Second, the problem of identifying repentance in progress is more difficult for it is not so much a theological as a political question. Theologically, the marks of repentance have traditionally been identified as sorrow over sin and a resolve to make amends, that is, to be restored to the relationship. According to Luther's analysis, these would be the appropriate marks to look for in a pastoral relationship, as persons are cared for in repentance.

But the question becomes considerably more complicated when it involves *the polis,* the larger community of the congregation, the church and possibly even state authorities. Then it becomes a political problem in the true sense of the term—that is, a problem of community order. The community may demand an evaluation of repentance to see if it is real or simply claimed. It may also be necessary to determine whether or not the person or people involved have come to terms with the situation sufficiently to be trusted once more.

Recognizing the problem as political is helpful in such situations because it allows a more limited burden of proof. Pastors undoubtedly have both the authority and the responsibility to speak God's word of judgment, addressing the person's relationship to God. But in such political situations, the question that complicates also helps to simplify the matter: it is the person's relationship with the community that is at stake.

This changes the evidence requirement—while the deeper question of the person's relationship to God is not to be neglected, in such circumstances what the community seeks is evidence of reliability in relation to itself.

In this context, there may still not be a hard and fast set of criteria. But there are some outward signs which do manifest a person's willingness to deal penitently with the people who have been offended. One sign is truth telling, the willingness to take responsibility for what has happened. The normal escapes—it was the other's fault, the circumstances were bad, I couldn't help it, and so forth—all indicate evasion. While it may take some time to straight forward acknowledgement of the offense and with it, acceptance of responsibility, indicate that the person is coming to terms with what has happened.

Another mark is to deal directly with those who have been offended. Denial requires a safe distance, just enough so that the offense may remain theoretical and the people offended mere abstractions. Facing the offense and the offended directly breaks the distance and gives external evidence of an internal willingness to deal responsibly with the matters. David did not give Nathan a lesson in the nature of sexual addiction or the risks of military engagement. Neither did Zacchaeus offer Jesus a chamber-of-commerce course in the free market economy.

Both marks require patience, however. Early denials may merely set the stage for later confessions; unwillingness to face those offended may recede as a person gains confidence of a future shaped by forgiveness. One of the arts of hearing confessions is timing—as urgent as the situation may be, the Word also has its due season. Sometimes the absolution can only be spoken after a thorough confession; at other times, there will be no confession without a prior absolution. Discerning the time, however, is more difficult in the abstract than it is in actual conversation. There is often a palpable sense of when further confession or immediate absolution is demanded.

Finally, the answer to Ebeling's question indicates the helpfulness of Luther's analysis for preachers. If it is assumed that the preacher is the user of the law in an unqualified way, then the preacher is put into an impossible situation. The preacher must literally be the Holy Spirit, calling, gathering, enlightening, sanctifying, keeping and thus bringing to repentance and faith every believer in every congregation that calls! Under such circumstances, it would make sense to break off the story of Jonah while he is in full flight, summing it up with an appeal to go and do likewise.

The fact that the Holy Spirit is the ultimate user of both law and gospel frees the preacher to preach, and to do so in the close pastoral relation to the congregation that characterizes effective ministry. If it is the work of the law to accuse and denounce, the preacher is called to a more limited responsibility: to destroy the law's anonymity by naming it, to identify what is beginning in the law so that the gospel, by overlapping it can bring repentance to its true end: faith in Christ. The preacher destroys the law's cover through the full-square declaration of the gospel, by declaring its end in Christ through the forgiveness of sin and then by going about the quiet business of nurturing the new life that comes forth with the Word.

There is still plenty of risk, here. To make explicit what is implicit is to be identified with what has become explicit in the law. To hit the overlap, to preach the gospel in such a way that it retains its bite, is to be held responsible for the tooth marks that follow.

The gospel is far more difficult to handle than the law. There is no resurrection without crucifixion. But in this connection, at least the crucifixion is for the right reason. And there's company in it, true companionship, the fellowship of his sufferings.

---

## BIBLIOGRAPHY

Ebeling, Gerhard. "On the Doctrine of the *Triplex Usus Legis* in the Theology of the Reformation." In *Word and Faith*, 62–78. Translated by James W. Leitch. London: SCM, 1963.

Bornkamm, Heinrich. *Luther and the Old Testament*. Translated by Eric W. Gritsch and Ruth C. Gritsch. Edited by Victor I. Gruhn. Philadelphia: Fortress, 1969.

Kolb, Robert, and Timothy J. Wengert, editors. *The Book of Concord*. Minneapolis: Fortress, 2000.

Knaake, J. F. K. et al., editors. *Luthers Werke, Kritische Gesamtausgabe*. Vol. 39. Weimar: Böhlau, 1883ff.

Pelikan, Jaroslav, and Helmut Lehman, editors. *Luther's Works*. Vol. 29. St. Louis: Concordia, 1955.

———, editors. *Luther's Works*. Vol. 31. St. Louis: Concordia, 1955.

# 14

# Preaching the Justification of Zacchaeus

*Virgil Thompson*

T HE FORMER POET LAUREATE Billy Collins has observed that fellow poet Frederick Seidel does "what every exciting poet must do: avoid writing what everyone thinks of as 'poetry.'" Collins's essay then sharpens the point by contrasting Seidel's poetry—alternately praised or loathed for its unabashed treatment of the coarser side of life—with contemporary poetry, so much of which dreamily imagines to escape the roughness of life.[1] Something of the same may be said for preaching. If the sermon is to be consequential for its hearers in relation to God, it must address the "roughness of life," the hard and intractable realities, whether they appear in life as it is or in the Bible as it is. From the standpoint of faith the most challenging matter which the sermon must face is the inescapable reality of God's terrible hiddenness, "experienced as uncertainty and ambiguity . . . in that God creates evil and good (Lam 3:38), life and death, light and darkness (Isa 45:7), prosperity and disaster (Amos 3:6)."[2] If the sermon has nothing decisively redemptive to say into such a theological predicament, then really it has nothing to say of consequence to faith. Sermons that merely counsel how to cope and be good, or worse, modestly speculate from below about what God may or ought to be up to, may

1. Mason, "Laureate of the Louche," 26.
2. Bayer, "Preaching the Word," 253.

seem at first to offer comfort and inspiration. However, like fiddling on the deck of the Titanic after that terrible bump in the night, in the end they do nothing to save the hearer from plunging into the cold sea of doubt and denial of God. Silence would be preferable to sermons which seek to "dreamily escape" or deny the obvious reality of God's terrible hiddenness, or which timidly stir around in ambiguity and uncertainty.

What if, however, the sermon was to speak a word which is otherwise not to be heard? What if the sermon were to face the ambiguity, uncertainty, and darkness of life squarely in the teeth and yet have a warrant to speak, like the music of Johann Sebastian Bach, the promise of God for us and not against us? Wouldn't it be our justification to worship God as God, to live down to earth, enjoying and caring for the creation for no reason but the joy and love of creation, justified to believe against everything to the contrary, that after all God keeps the promise which he washed over us in baptism, "I am the Lord your God, you shall have no others"? Wouldn't such a sermon be the fulfillment of the promise of Jesus, "I have come, as into the Wedding at Cana, to give life and give it abundantly?" Wouldn't the saying of it be the doing of it? If our sermons are to be heard in this way then we must learn to do what the "exciting" poets do: avoid preaching what everyone thinks sermons should sound like. In this essay I seek to explore on the basis of the Zacchaeus story in Luke 19 what it means to preach the justifying word of God's judgment to and for the ungodly.[3] My purpose, more specifically, is to make clear that preaching justification involves speaking the Word of God which, against everything to the contrary, justifies faith in the promise of God's redemption of sinners and in the same breath justifies living in the freedom of loving care for the creation and the neighbors with whom we have been given to share it.

When the justifying Word of God is spoken nakedly for what it is, it then does, when and where it pleases the Spirit of God to do it, exactly what Paul and the other apostles promised that it would: "the old sinful self, with all its evil deeds and desires,[4] is drowned through daily

---

3. While there are many variations on the "ungodly" life, in this essay, as it should become increasingly clear, our concern is to understand "ungodly" precisely in terms of the insistence on taking the conditional road to God and life against God's determination in Christ to extend his unconditional favor toward the creation, including, and especially to, the ungodly.

4. Among the evil deeds, in fact chief among them, is the desire to use life as the means to the end of justifying the self. According to Genesis 3, this is the original sin

repentance, that day after day a new self may arise to live with God in righteousness and purity forever." These beautiful words of Luther's Small Catechism are matched only by Paul's declaration regarding the new life of faith, "We have been buried with Christ by baptism into death, so that, just as Christ was raised from the dead by the glory of the Father, so we too might walk in newness of life" (Rom 6:4). All of which gives meaning to Luther's reflection on the whirlwind that was the Reformation: "While Philip and I drank our Wittenberg beer the Word did it all."[5]

The Word of Christ does not return empty but accomplishes that of which it speaks, the justification of the ungodly. That is the stake of preaching, no less today than in the sixteenth century. The preaching of the church is either animated by faith in God's unconditional promise to give life or it is animated by faith in the conditional way of life.[6] Apart from the continual preaching of the unconditional favor of God toward the ungodly there is no question but that we fall, willingly, captive to the conditional way which is finally a way that ends in death. The question is whether in our time as in times past there will be preachers to declare the promise of Christ, the Word by which God forgives sin, delivers from death and the devil, to the new life of faith in God as God and love in the other as neighbor. The question is whether the Word of the God who as Paul once put it to the Romans, "gives life to the dead and calls into being things that are not" (4:17) will today be given voice by preachers in the name of Christ.

---

which destroys the freedom and joy of life, which we receive by faith in God's providential promise as Creator to sustain life.

5. *LW* 51:77

6. In the ministry of the Word the fundamental art is to know where, when, and how to speak in God's name in conditional and unconditional terms. This essay addresses the art of preaching God's unconditional justification of the ungodly. To some extent the essay treats the relationship between the conditional and unconditional but only from the perspective of preaching justification. Space does not permit a fuller theological treatment of the place of God's conditional word in the life of creation. But the question has been addressed in ways helpful to ministers of the gospel by many theologians, especially Gerhard Forde, Oswald Bayer, Robert Kolb, Charles Arand, Timothy Wengert, Mark Mattes, and Stephen Paulson.

## THE ART OF PREACHING JUSTIFICATION

So then, how does one actually go about preaching the justifying Word of God? Although space does not permit full development here,[7] we should note that preparation for preaching justification involves the whole theological and spiritual formation of the minister. From an experiential point of view, the office of preaching involves doing to others what has been done to the preacher. However, the doing of it does not come automatically. When I was young I thought of the preacher as the vessel or the conduit of God's Word. Somewhere in the course of the last thirty-odd years of parish service, it became apparent that nothing could be further from the truth. The preacher is not the conduit of the Word. The preacher is a flesh-and-blood sinner, whom God, by forgiveness, has taken captive to his Word, the whole person, personality and all, no matter how peculiar. Oswald Bayer in an excellent article on preaching quotes Luther in this regard: the preacher, says Luther, "ministers with the promise in solidarity as one who is always also a sinner, living in contradiction to God, a 'false witness, betrayer, and liar.'" Bayer adds, "So he always preaches the truth of the forgiveness of sins in the face of his own life testimony . . . the servant of God's word serves this word by ministering to his contemporaries with the promise."[8] Effective preachers of justification by faith are then, simply, theologians of the cross,[9] for whom justification of the ungodly is the only gospel there is. For them justification is not just one theme among others, not just one strategy among others. It is what is to be done with every text, namely, to kill and make alive. As Gerhard Forde has pointed out, the law-gospel language of the Lutheran tradition reflects this concern to find a language that serves the central aim of preaching justification in such a way as to effect the justification of the believer, in such a way as to kill and make alive. The point to be emphasized is that preachers cannot be content merely to talk about justification, or merely to report what God has done. In this sense it is not the doctrine of justification that is so important in itself. Rather the important thing is to recognize that the doctrine drives to the actual preaching of justification, the doing of what the text authorizes the preacher to do in the present.

7. See my essay, "The Bible and Theological Formation."

8. Bayer, "Preaching the Word," 256. Also see this volume 196–216.

9. See Forde, *On Becoming a Theologian of the Cross*.

The doing of it is the church's reason for being.[10] So then, to the heart of our question: How does one go about it?

In the final chapter of his book *Justification by Faith: A Matter of Death and Life,* Forde focuses the aim of preaching God's justification of the ungodly.

> If justification by faith alone is death and resurrection, then it is the proclamation of that justification itself that does the deed we are looking for. It is the proclamation itself that puts to death and raises up—at one and the same time . . . It is the very unconditionality, 'the nothing to be done,' itself that administers the *coup de grâce,* because it kills and makes alive at once. The preacher, that is, leads from strength, announcing the unconditional word, knowing that in the first instance it is not going to be heard by the Old Being.[11]

This announcement is an attack on the conditional approach to God and life, an attack at the very heart of our reason for being, but just so, the beginning of the end so that the new may be brought to life. Consider the story of Zacchaeus in Luke 19. Because I am going to adopt the structure of the narrative as the structure of the sermon it is important to pay close attention to the way the incident is narrated. It is especially important to note the detail of the narrative, what the apostolic witness gives the preacher to work with, what is said by whom and what is not said. Because written narratives require in the oral recitation that the reader draw inferences, fill in gaps, and so forth, it is important to pay attention to exactly the way that is done, what the doing of it reveals about the faith of the interpreter or preacher.

According to the story Jesus is passing through Jericho. A man of the village, Zacchaeus, we are told, is curious to see Jesus. But being short in stature he is unable because of the crowd to get a look. So he runs ahead, climbs a tree, and waits for the entourage of Jesus to pass by. The only other information that the reader gets about Zacchaeus is that he is a chief tax collector and exceedingly wealthy. By this point in Luke's story of Jesus the rich have not made out especially well. In the Magnificat, Mary anticipates that in the encounter with Jesus the rich and the poor will experience a reversal of fortunes. The poor will be lifted up and the rich sent empty away (Luke 1:46–55). Later in the story Jesus himself tells of such

---

10. Forde, *Justification: A Matter of Death and Life,* 97.

11. Ibid., 93.

a case, where in the afterlife a poor man, Lazarus, dies and is escorted by the angels directly into the arms of Father Abraham, into heaven's lap of luxury. Meanwhile the rich man, who in the story is not even given a name, dies and goes straight to hell. When he protests his fate, Father Abraham explains that the judgment of God is just because it is God's judgment. In the earthly life Lazarus had nothing and the rich man had it all, now in the afterlife, as even the prophets and the law anticipated that they would be, fortunes are reversed (Luke 16:19–31). In another reported encounter with Jesus the wealth of a seeker proves an insurmountable obstacle to salvation, prompting Jesus to observe that "it is easier for a camel to go through the eye of a needle than for someone who is rich to enter the kingdom of God" (Luke 18:25). So the reader might imagine that Zacchaeus in the encounter with Jesus is not going to make out especially well. Not only is he exceedingly rich but a tax collector as well, a position which required complicity with Roman oppression of the Jewish people. For that reason one might well imagine that his Jewish neighbors looked down on the fellow Jew, Zacchaeus, with contempt.[12] In fact it is not impossible that the detail drawing attention to the physical stature of Zacchaeus functions metaphorically to describe public opinion regarding his moral stature: "He was trying to see who Jesus was, but on account of the crowd he could not, because he was short in stature" (v. 3). In any case, the narrative leaves no doubt as to public opinion in Jericho regarding Zacchaeus. He is regarded as a "sinner," undeserving of entertaining pious Israel. So, scandalizing public opinion, Jesus, when he comes to the place in the road beneath Zacchaeus's perch, stops the whole entourage, looks up in the tree and beckons Zacchaeus to come down, "for," as Jesus declares, "I must stay at your house today" (v. 5). Ordinarily the original Greek of the New Testament may not find its way into the sermon, but in this case it is worth pointing out that the Greek word (*dei*) which stands behind the "must" carries throughout Luke's story the sense of divine necessity. Jesus does not explain at this point why God necessitates that he stay at the home of Zacchaeus. Apparently at this point in the story it is not necessary to explain, at least not to Zacchaeus. Jesus's

---

12. In the view of their contemporaries the tax collectors were regarded as "an especially degraded and despised lot" inasmuch as they "had sold their services to the foreign oppressor . . . against their own people, and they were engaged in literal robbery. For they were helping principals to mulct the public, and no doubt part of what they collected stuck to their own fingers" (Bamberger, "Tax Collector," 4:522).

summons to Zacchaeus is itself heard by him as the proclamation of the good news of God's favor toward the ungodly. Zacchaeus seems to get the message of it straightaway! Upon the word of Jesus, Zacchaeus practically falls out of the tree with the promise of beginning anew. He no more hits the ground than he repents of his whole life. He vows on the spot that he will repay twice what is required by the law to anyone whom he has defrauded and further he vows to give half his wealth to the poor (v. 8). The people of the town for their part find the whole affair difficult to stomach. They waste no words, complaining about Jesus: "He has gone to be the guest of a sinner" (v.7). It is a complaint that Jesus has heard so many times in the course of his ministry, according to Luke's story, that the complaint constitutes a counter theme to Jesus's compassion for the lost and disenfranchised. The Zacchaeus episode concludes with Jesus explaining his actions, leaving nothing to the imagination, "Today," he declares, "salvation has come to this house." Why? "Because Zacchaeus too is a son of Abraham," and Jesus, as he himself goes on to explain, "has come to seek and save the lost" (vv. 9–10).

So then, while the story of Zacchaeus could be told from more than one theological point of view, our contention to this point is that telling it from the perspective of God's justification of the ungodly makes the best use of the narrative data that Luke has given the preacher to work with. From the perspective of God's justification of the ungodly, the plain literal sense of the story seems fairly straightforward. Jesus has done exactly what he has come into the world to do (Luke 2:11–12). In the promise of Jesus, the unconditional favor of God has succeeded in turning a life upside down, the end of the old Zacchaeus and the beginning of a new way of being. It all seems rather straightforward. As Jesus explains, after the tragic episode with the rich ruler, "What is impossible for mortals is possible for God" (Luke 18:27). More joy in heaven over one lost lamb restored to the flock than pebbles on the shore, as the parables of chapter 15 make the point. The story tells that in the sermon of Jesus the Word of God does not return empty but accomplishes that of which it has spoken.

The history of preaching and interpretation, however, tells another story. To illustrate: a quick review of commentaries and the popular online sermon source, "The Text this Week," reveals that readers and preachers of the story are very much divided on what to make of the Zacchaeus story. And in fact if we were to consider our reading of the story against the mainstream interpretation we would be forced to admit that our reading represents the minority opinion. The majority of preachers and interpreters, across the denominational spectrum, seem intent upon taking the story captive to the conditional approach to God. Some explain that what justifies Jesus's action toward Zacchaeus is Zacchaeus's vow to repay those whom he had defrauded and to give half his money to the poor. In other treatments the vow of Zacchaeus is treated as the evidence to prove that he was really saved. Others insist that it is not Zacchaeus's vow of repentance that saves him but his faith. As one contemporary preacher reasons: Zacchaeus "knew of Jesus, believed in Jesus, wanted to see him . . . In reaching out to Jesus, trusting Jesus for acceptance in the sight of God, he became an heir of the righteousness that comes by faith." Similarly in a sermon of Charles Spurgeon, Zacchaeus becomes an example of how to receive Jesus. In another treatment of the story, Zacchaeus becomes a model of repentance, the "condition for God to forgive the sin and eradicate illusion."[13] Even his physical stature is turned into a virtue. It is interesting to consider how frequently interpreters are inclined to construe the detail of the narrative about Zacchaeus's stature in such a way as to emphasize his willingness to risk ridicule in his desperation to "see" Jesus. It is as though interpreters are compelled to find some virtue in the character of Zacchaeus that justifies Jesus's interest in him.[14] In all of these treatments, the action of Zacchaeus constitutes the heart of the sermon. In one way or another Zacchaeus is pictured as a sincere seeker, meeting the condition of repentance, showing amendment of life, and thus rewarded by the company of Jesus. But if that were the case it would be difficult to see what the town's people had to complain about. In fact, it appears that such interpretative moves are taken precisely in the interest of removing the scandal of the story. But short of erasing the words from the page the scandal of God's justification of the ungodly remains the

---

13. "The Text This Week."

14. Consider a sampling of commentators in regard to seeing in the character of Zacchaeus some redeeming quality related to the notation regarding his physical stature: G. B. Caird writes, "No sightseeing curiosity would have induced such a man to risk either ridicule or violence . . . He must have been prompted by some powerful urge . . ." *Gospel of St. Luke*, 208. Fred Craddock writes, Zacchaeus's "intense desire to see Jesus, overcoming the risk of ridicule and embarrassment, is fundamental to the happy conclusion of the story" (*Luke*, 219). David Tiede writes, "Zacchaeus risked ridicule by climbing a tree to *see Jesus. That is the only reason his short stature is interesting.* What is most remarkable about him is not his height but his faith as displayed in this absurd position" (*Luke*, 320, italics added).

story of the gospel. As Jesus himself sums it up, "the Son of Man came to seek and save the lost" (v. 10). The only question is whether preachers today will dare to give voice to the glorious, redeeming scandal of Jesus.

## "ZACCHAEUS, COME DOWN"

Reading the story from the perspective of the justification of the ungodly Jesus appears as the divine seeker. What we could never have imagined nor have reason to hope apart from him, he comes to seek and save the lost sheep of the house of Israel. He comes to justify the ungodly. In the version of the story whereby interpretation makes Zacchaeus the seeker, no one—neither the people of Jericho nor the people of the contemporary congregation—has anything to complain about. According to that version Zacchaeus has decided to turn his life around and receives Jesus's approval for doing it. And of course from that version of the story it is only a short hop to the admonition: "That's all you need to do, as well, to justify yourself before others and before God: Respond to the invitation, believe in Jesus, live honestly, and don't forget the poor." The story according to the majority opinion is told in such a way as to integrate nicely into the conditional world as we know it. No free lunch and all that. The only trouble with the interpretation is that it does not make good use of the material that the apostolic witness has given the preacher to work with. The order of events in the Lukan story is not that Zacchaeus repents and then Jesus declares his intention to stay with him. Rather, first Jesus declares his intention—no ifs, maybes, or buts, no requirements to be met and no conditions to be kept, just—"Zacchaeus, come down, for the Lord your God requires that I stay at your house this day." In fact, you get the impression from the way in which the story is told that it was God's concern for Zacchaeus that necessitated Jesus's trip to Jericho in the first place. As Jesus explains, it was necessary to make this side trip because Zacchaeus too is a child of Abraham and God has sent Jesus to redeem the ungodly, the lost sheep of the house of Israel, the prodigal children, "for the Son of Man came to seek and save the lost" (Luke 19:10). The story in the plain sense is not about what Zacchaeus does to justify Jesus's action. It certainly is not about Zacchaeus inviting Jesus into his heart. It is about Jesus getting home to Zacchaeus with the truth of the gospel. The story in the plain sense of the words on the page is about what Jesus does to justify Zacchaeus. The story of Jesus's sermon to Zacchaeus sounds more like what happens in baptism than anything else. Jesus comes to announce, "I am the Lord your God, you shall have no others." Lucky for Zacchaeus! Lucky for contemporary hearers when the preacher's sermon hitches the hearer's name to the promise of Jesus. Why can't we leave it at that? Why are we compelled to rework the story, make it about something Zacchaeus has done, about something we are supposed to do? The answer is not difficult to discern.

But imagine what might happen if the sermon were to just launch into the biblical story, which is much preferred to the sermon which begins with a story from the experience of the pastor, or worse a story which sounds like it has come fresh from the Internet, a thousand and one stories to launch a sermon.com. But imagine if the sermon were just to jump into it. What if the sermon were just to tell of the action of Jesus that day in Jericho, beneath the perch of Zacchaeus? One must admit that the action of Jesus quickly got the attention of Zacchaeus and soon became the talk of the whole town. Imagine that contemporary preachers could preach sermons with such an effect.

"Zacchaeus, come down, for it is necessary that I stay at your house today." It is necessary because, as Jesus later explains, Zacchaeus, too, is a son of Abraham, and the Lord God has sent his own flesh and blood, the good shepherd, to seek and save the lost sheep of the house of Israel. And now that Zacchaeus has been found out by his Lord, he practically falls out of the tree, a new being, his life turned upside down. And it all transpires before the conditional theologians can get a conditional word out of their mouths. Before the promise of Jesus can be turned into one more condition to be met, the promise of Jesus has already spoken and has brought about that of which it has spoken. Zacchaeus comes tumbling out of the tree justified by the promise of Jesus: "Because I am the Lord your God and because I am determined not to lose you, but determined to be your God come hell or high water therefore I have been searching high and low for you, Zacchaeus. And now I have found you. Time to come in out of the cold, time to come home, Zacchaeus."

And down comes Zacchaeus by faith in the promise of God, after all, for him and not against him, nothing to prove but free to live by love in the neighbor—"to repay those whom I have defrauded fourfold and to give half my money to the poor." The conditional theologians do not need to worry about it. They have been silenced before ever they could get anything out. It is too late for conditions to be attached to the promise of

Jesus. Zacchaeus has heard the gospel, the voice of Jesus, finally the word of God's promise gets home to him, finds him out. In effect: "Where have you been all your life, Zacchaeus? What do you think you are doing with your life? You are a child of Abraham, for Pete's sake." Or better, "You are a child of God for Jesus's sake." The Word itself, the gospel of Jesus, is the deed which does it, turns Zacchaeus inside out toward the neighbor in love and toward God in trust in the promise of Jesus.

Of course all his life Zacchaeus has heard only the voice of the conditional theologians. He knows how to play their game. He knows all the loop holes. He knows how to justify himself. And if the self-justifying rationales sound all too familiar it is perhaps for good reason. We are self-justifying beings to the bone of the old sinful self. "I am only human, and to err is human." Conditional theologians, like us, are willing to admit that they are not perfect, but they are quick to add by self-justifying rationale that they have done the best they could in the circumstances, better than some, and therefore deserve a little consideration. Zacchaeus knows all the justifying rationalizations backward and forward. And where has it gotten him? Where has it gotten you? Zacchaeus is up a tree, nowhere to go, but down. Admittedly, there is nothing in the text about the way in which Zacchaeus has lived. But there does not need to be, because, as a friend of mine says, it takes one to know one. You can't kid a kidder. Sinners like us are known to each other. The story of the Bible tells the truth about us. It is our story. We know how Zacchaeus lived, because it is how we live. We have gotten quite good at justifying ourselves in conditional terms. We are so good at it as a matter of fact that we do not want to give it up. It is our conjured godliness that gets in the way of God being God for us. I know how Zacchaeus lived. I know how you think and live. I know the deadly project of self-justification inside and out. It is our self-justifying ways that make us so dangerous to the well being of the other. We easily, and without conscience, sacrifice the other, the creation, God, anything that gets in the way of our project in self-justification.

That's why Jesus came, to sacrifice himself for Zacchaeus, for our justification, that we, like Zacchaeus, might arise to life for the neighbor: "those I have defrauded I will repay fourfold and half my money I give to the poor" (v. 8). Jesus sacrificed himself to our demand for conditional justice, justice on our terms, justice which serves our advantage, always at the cost of the sacrifice or annihilation of the other.[15] But his sacrifice was to overcome the conditional way, to sacrifice his being to the final ultimate demand, to the final condition, death. But death did not hold him. He was raised for us, for the ungodly, we who refused God's unconditional promise, who sought to silence and finally to destroy it (Rom 4:25).

Zacchaeus has never before heard anything like what he hears from Jesus. It is no kidding, no maybes, and no doubt. Preach the sermon of it and this is exactly what the congregation will tell you, "Pastor, we have never heard it like that before." At last Zacchaeus has heard in the voice of Jesus what I am authorized to proclaim to you: "Where have you been? What have you been doing with your life? Playing hide and seek with the conditional theologians? Come down, for you see, Zacchaeus, this whole thing has been about you, those bound to the dead end of the law, nowhere to go, but down." But imagine his landing, restored to life and to God in one fell swoop, sins forgiven, freed from sin, death, and the power of the devil. And Zacchaeus knows exactly what to do with his new life, free to use his vocation to serve the need of his neighbor. Imagine it, even the tax collector belongs to Christ. This is what Jesus saves us from, from our deadly project of self-justification.

The story of Zacchaeus's justification may not be relevant in the sense that it advances the cause of self-justification, but it is relevant to the well being of the neighbor. The point of the story, the point of preaching God's justification is to save us from using the neighbor to justify the self, to save us for serving the neighbor in his or her need, to see life for what it is, as an end in itself. Not as the means to get to heaven, not as the means, no matter the cost, to nail down a secure future for ourselves, not as the means to face the image in the mirror with respect, but to free us to see life for what it is and to see ourselves for what we are—creatures of God, created to enjoy and care for the creation. Imagine a doctor, lawyer, father, mother, candlestick maker using life as a means to the end

---

15. One might add here, especially, for the reader who tends to see preaching justification only in personal terms, that the stake of justification is social and political every bit as much as it is personal. For example, this is the missionary danger of Christianity. It is not so much that we export the American way of life with it. That is admittedly a very mixed enterprise, bad enough perhaps. But what is still worse is that we export the deadly way of self-justification in the name of Christ. Then the culture of the other, the very life of the other, the being of the other becomes only a means to our ends, to elevate and justify the self. Apart from the gospel of justification we do not see deeply, clearly, into the full extent of our sin, which is so deadly toward the creation and the other.

of self-justification. Consider how much conflict we suffer as we seek to justify ourselves against the other. Imagine the oppression we impose in the course of using others to justify ourselves and our ways. Then imagine the freedom from the compulsion to justify ourselves, free to glorify God by serving the need of the neighbor. You begin to appreciate what is at stake in the preaching of God's justifying Word.

But now what of the conditional theologians? They have retreated; the story reports their murmuring, off in the corner: "all who saw it began to grumble and said, 'He has gone to be the guest of one who is a sinner'" (v. 7). The conditional theologians of the story have plenty of company in the rest of the Bible, as well as among interpreters of the Bible. In fact there is something of the conditional theologian in all of us. To me this is the remarkable thing about the story of the Bible. While we have been cautiously and carefully tiptoeing along the conditional way to God, the Lord comes thundering down the path to sweep us off our feet in the promise of his unconditional favor, like the father of the parable in chapter 15 of Luke's story, that father who "threw his arms around son and kissed him . . . feasted and celebrated . . . for this son of mine was dead but is alive, was lost but is found" (vv. 20–24). Of course the soberly responsible theologians of the conditional way, like the elder brother of the story, refuse to come in out of the cold, "It isn't fair; where's the justice? What if the prodigal should exploit the good will of the father?" Like deer in the headlights, the worried theologians stand frozen in unbelief, muttering but, but, but—like Nicodemus in the night, "How can such things be?" In the case of the Zacchaeus episode the murmuring of the conditional theologians sounds distinctly like the death rattle of a dying sinner about to give up the ghost of the conditional way of life. But the conditional theologians do not generally give up without a fight to the death. And that is the case here in Luke's story of God's justification of the ungodly. The conditional theologians will make one final assault on the Word of promise before Luke's story is finished. We hear the foreshadowing of what lies ahead for Jesus and for the preacher of justification: "He has gone to be the guest of a sinner." The conditional theologians could never have imagined. Not only does Jesus make himself the guest of a sinner, but he makes himself the God of the sinner, the God of the ungodly. While Zacchaeus was still an enemy, still weak, still hanging on to the conditional tree of life, that same tree which did in Adam and Eve, Jesus called to him: time to come home, Zacchaeus.

Of course the conditional theologians could never imagine. So they—we!—unable to bring ourselves to trust the promise, are compelled to silence the promise. Preachers of the conditional way don't dare speak the flat-out unconditional promise of Jesus "for you," because, "what if . . . ?" So the conditional theologians execute against Jesus the final condition, "Crucify him!" To which Jesus makes himself an ever bigger target. Read the story of his one and final trip to Jerusalem that way sometime and you see that he makes himself a target for our fear and unbelief, out of which we strike against him. But what are the odds against Almighty God? "I am the Lord your God, and in the end you will see that I am determined that you have no others." That's why he came back from the dead, to declare to you now: "Wake up! Smell the coffee! You are destined for the new life, by faith in the promise of God's justification and by love for the neighbor."

The Word itself provokes the crisis of faith, calls into being the new creation, silences the conditional voice of the law. What can it do now? The law has subjected Jesus to the final condition, death, in the way of his promise. If Jesus is dead the promise is silenced. He cannot be present in the promise of Word and sacrament to save us. But death did not hold him. God raised him up, beyond death, beyond every condition, to be "the living advocate of humans before the judgment throne of God," as Peter Stuhlmacher explains. But while the justification of the ungodly may be the soteriological climax of the event of justification it is not its goal. The "*telos*," as Stuhlmacher goes on to explain, "lies in the achievement of God's justice in heaven and on earth, that is, the reconciliation of the cosmos and the establishment of the *basileia tou theou* (cf. 1 Cor 15:28)."[16] This is the news that the preacher of the divine Word of justification is called to preach, the Final Judgment of God let out in favor of the ungodly. Nothing other and nothing less, for nothing else will do.

---

16. Stuhlmacher, *Revisiting Paul's Doctrine of Justification*, 52.

# BIBLIOGRAPHY

Bamberger, B. J. "Tax Collector." In *The Interpreters Dictionary of the Bible*, edited by George A. Buttrick, 4:522. Nashville: Abingdon, 1962.

Bayer, Oswald. "Preaching the Word." *Lutheran Quarterly* 23 (2009) 249–69.

Carid, G. B. *Gospel of St. Luke*. Pelican Gospel Commentaries. Harmondsworth, UK: Penguin, 1963.

Craddock, Fred. *Luke*. Interpretation: A Biblical Commentary for Teaching and Preaching. Louisville: John Knox, 1990.

Forde, Gerhard O. *On Becoming a Theologian of the Cross*. Grand Rapids: Eerdmans, 1997.

———. *Justification: A Matter of Death and Life*. Philadelphia: Fortress, 1982.

Mason, Wyatt. "Frederick Seidel, Laureate of the Louche." *The New York Times Magazine*, April 12, 2009. Online: http://www.nytimes.com/2009/04/12/magazine/12Seidel-t.html.

Stuhlmacher, Peter. *Revisiting Paul's Doctrine of Justification: A Challenge to the New Perspective*. Downers Grove, IL: InterVarsity, 2001.

Tiede, David. *Luke*. Augsburg Commentary of the New Testament. Minneapolis: Augsburg, 1988.

Woodard, Jenee, compiler. *The Text This Week*. Web site. "Luke 19:1–10." Proper 26. Online: http://www.textweek.com/mtlk/lk19a.htm/.

Thompson, Virgil F. "The Bible and Theological Formation: On Becoming a Theologian of the Cross." In *The Power to Comprehend with All the Saints: The Formation and Practice of a Pastor-Theologian*, edited by Wallace M. Alston Jr., and Cynthia A. Jarvis, 16–32. Grand Rapids: Eerdmans, 2009.